D STATES
ERICA

MAINE

VERMONT
NEW HAMPSHIRE

Boston

MASSACHUSETTS
RHODE ISLAND
CONNECTICUT

New York
Philadelphia

NEW JERSEY
DELAWARE
MARYLAND

Lake Superior

Lake Huron

Lake Ontario

MI CHIGAN

Lake Erie

Lake Michigan

WISCONSIN

OHIO

Chicago
Indianapolis

River

PENNSYLVANIA

WEST VIRGINIA

Washington DC

VIRGINIA

INDIANA

ILLINOIS

Ohio

St Louis

Mississippi

KENTUCKY

NORTH CAROLINA

MISSOURI

IOWA

TENNESSEE

APPALACHIAN

SOUTH CAROLINA

Charleston

ARKANSAS

River

MISSISSIPPI

ALABAMA

GEORGIA

OMA

LOUISIANA

FLORIDA

Dallas

New Orleans

Miami

nio

THE
ALL-AMERICAN
COOKBOOK

THE ALL-AMERICAN COOKBOOK

America's Favourite Dishes
for Non-American Cooks

Martha Lomask

BOOK CLUB ASSOCIATES · LONDON

For two much-loved Americans:
my son Miles Turner and in
memory of my cherished
daughter-in-law, Diana Turner

First published 1981 by Guild Publishing,
the Original Publications Department of
Book Club Associates

Designed by Richard Garratt

Artwork by Vanessa Luff

Photography by Paul Forrester

Endpapers by A.R. Garrett

Set in Lasercomp Melior

Printed and bound in Great Britain by
Morrison & Gibb Ltd, London and Edinburgh

Contents

Acknowledgments

I have most of all to thank my friend Harris Jackson, of Baton Rouge, Louisiana and New York, for his generous sharing of Southern recipes, for many airmail letters about American cooking, and for trusting me with his irreplaceable copy of 'How America Cooks', by the late Clementine Paddleford (Charles Scribner's Sons, New York, 1960). My second great debt is to my dear English friend Catherine Prowse, who lent me her encyclopedic collection of American recipes. And Madalynne Reuter, of New York, gave up a good part of a London holiday to organise the index for me – I thank her not only for her generosity but for her keen editor's eye.

My son Miles Turner, of Portland, Oregon, told me about Pacific Northwest cookery, and gave me Mexican-American recipes. Nina Lowry, of Portland, gave me recipes and lent me another priceless out-of-print book, 'Coast to Coast Cookery', edited by Marian Tracy (Grosset & Dunlap, New York, 1952).

I am most grateful to American friends on this side of the Atlantic, for their recipes and for helping me test my anglicised versions: Patricia Rich, Debby Turner, Mary Mackintosh, and Sonya Mackintosh in London, and Claire Lalor of County Cork, Republic of Ireland.

I have had the great pleasure of working with Susan Fleming, who not only copy-edited a manuscript that was a mass of crossings-out and rewritings, but gave much valuable editorial help. And Anne Siddall, of Book Club Associates, kept a cool head and perfect organisation through all the many stages of revision – as well as testing many of the recipes for me.

I have relied for reference on all the *New York Times* Cookbooks edited by Craig Claiborne, all of James Beard's noble works, books by Marian Tracy, and of course Irma Rombauer's 'The Joy of Cooking' (Bobbs-Merrill Company Inc, Indianapolis and New York, 1975 edition) – as delicious to read as it is easy to follow.

I am grateful to Precision Engineering Co Ltd of Reading, and to Terraillon (UK) Ltd, for making available their finely-calibrated scales, and to Tefal (UK) Ltd and Grosvenor Public Relations for lending me equipment for testing.

And as always, I have been sustained by my husband's kindness and enthusiasm – for shopping, errands, talk about food, and great willingness to eat the failures in civil silence as well as to praise the successes in my cooking.

Martha Lomask
London 1981

'From Sea to Shining Sea'

These words come from a lovely, almost hymn-like song, 'America The Beautiful', which in simpler days was sung by children in school. 'Oh beautiful for spacious skies, for amber waves of grain/For purple mountains' majesty above the fruited plain . . .', ending with '. . . and crown thy good with brotherhood, from sea to shining sea.'

Nothing could better express the great variety of American food, and American cooking, in the endless expanse of country from the sheer rocky cliffs of Maine to the parched cattle-country of the Southwest; from Hawaii, far out in the shining sea, up to the permafrost of Alaska. How does America eat? In many languages: American–Indian (succotash and hominy), French and Spanish (jambalaya, chili, café brulôt), German and Dutch (sauerkraut, bott boi), Italian (polenta and pizzas), Jewish (pastrami, latkes), Cornish pasties and English Sally Lunn; and in a tongue all its own – hoppin' john, perfection salad, chiffon pies, brownies, hot biscuits, red flannel hash, mulligan stew. It all sounds very exotic, and yet it's perfectly possible to make almost every classic American recipe from ingredients available in the United Kingdom.

There's no better place to begin than in New England, for that is where the English settlers landed nearly three hundred years ago. They came from the softness and lushness of Devon, and landed on the bleak rocks of Massachusetts in freezing December. They survived, some of them; they learned to catch codfish and open clams; they were taught by the Indians to boil up spruce bark into tea to cure scurvy; they discovered cranberries, corn (maize), pumpkins, maple trees. New England is a tiny region, only six small states, five of them with a foot in the sea. In midwinter, temperatures can dive to $-20°$ Fahrenheit. In high summer, hurricanes come screaming up from the southern Atlantic. The 'Fog Factory', where the warm Gulf Stream collides with the cold Labrador current, can produce solid banks of fog that stand towering and motionless for days. This harsh and unpredictable land has produced a people who coined the great New England phrases: 'make it do, make it over, make it last'. The classic New Englander is independent, inventive, and knows the value of every penny. New England cooking is hearty – as indeed it had to be, to sustain life in cold woods and stony-hearted fields – and thrifty – making the most of what's available, and combining some exceedingly odd ingredients into good rib-sticking food. New England hashes are famous, and who else would think of a slice of left-over apple pie for breakfast? Molasses was then – and often is now – a substitute for sugar, because Yankee ships from early days traded with the West Indian islands which spun off molasses when producing rum.

And the lovely China clippers, sailing gull-winged across the world, brought back ginger and cinnamon from India and Ceylon, lemons from the tropics, delicate China teas, curry, chocolate, and a certain taste for the exotic that lightens and enlivens the rather austere New England cuisine.

Looking south, one can draw an imaginary line below tiny Rhode Island, separating the Mid-Atlantic states (New York, Pennsylvania, New Jersey, Delaware et al., right down to the capital city of Washington, DC) from the rather more severe New Englanders. And New York City, of course, is a world within a world, the old cliché of the melting pot never more applicable than in its cooking. Its great waves of immigrants – often driven by the bitter wind of religious persecution from their European, Middle Eastern, and Asian homes

– brought *everything* with them: their cooking pots – iron 'soup kettles', Scandinavian waffle irons, Chinese woks, English teakettles – and their recipes – Italian tomato sauces and pasta; Jewish chopped liver and Hungarian salami; and 'pot cheese' from Holland. In New York city one can eat literally twenty-four hours a day, anything from chili dogs from a pushcart on a street corner for just pennies, onward and very much upward into skyscraper dining rooms with windows on the world, where just to look at the prices on the menu can bring on a heart attack. Small, smart French restaurants, English pubs with real ale from the wood, fast food that these days is apt to be Arab 'shawarma' on pita bread, Cuban-Chinese, elegant Japanese, Mrs Grimble's Pie Shop, and a place called simply The Front Porch. Is it America, or is it Europe? America, most definitely. And New York recipes, simply because they *are* so cosmopolitan, are quite easily translated and adapted for English cooks.

Philadelphia, the Quaker City, adores traditional food. Pepperpot soup, based on tripe, was first cooked as a desperation dish for George Washington's ragged troops, starving in the snow at Valley Forge. Philadelphia sticky buns, and pure Philadelphia ice cream which is nothing but triple-thick cream, sugar, and vanilla, are very American, and very easy to make. But Philadelphia, of course, is only part of Pennsylvania cooking.

To the west of the city lies the fertile country region called Pennsylvania Dutch, producing some wonders of American cookery. 'Dutch' here has nothing to do with Holland, it's a dialect corruption of 'Deutsch' meaning German. The 'plain people' of this land are descendants of Protestants who from the mid-eighteenth century fled to the sanctuary of William Penn's colony of brotherly love and religious tolerance. These solid, conservative people, superb farmers of their extraordinarily rich soil, still on the whole keep to their own ways of dressing,

travelling, and cooking. The 'Amish' (pronounced Ay-mish) wear clothes without ornament, without buttons, zippers, or hooks and eyes. The men are often bearded and in black suits and flat black hats, the women and young children in 'poke bonnets'. The true Amish will have nothing to do with automobiles, and cherish their horse-drawn carriages. The farmers' markets are a miracle of colour and flavour, with pickles, hams, sausages, and preserves. 'She sets a good table' is the ultimate praise. Penn-Dutch food is as robust as the people; great casseroles of home-made egg noodles, 'shoofly pie', and usually the traditional 'seven sweets and seven sours', such as bread-and-butter pickles, relishes, apple butters, and so on. Some of these traditional dishes are in this book, adapted for modern cooking.

Where does the South begin? Is it in Washington, the nation's capital, and where does it end – in Arkansas or Texas? Perhaps one should start in Maryland at the Chesapeake Bay, the 'Eastern Shore', with its aristocratic English heritage, and its abundance of oysters, crabs, wonderful game, and fruit. Then to the Old Dominion (Virginia), of smokehouse hams, Scuppernong grapes, pheasants, to the Carolinas where rice culture begins, and across Georgia into Tennessee, very much corn country.

In Mississippi and Louisiana, we pick up the first distinct French and Spanish accents that mean Creole cooking. There is a hint too of Africa in such words as gumbo, and something borrowed from the American Indians in filé (sassafras) powder. New Orleans cooking is especially sophisticated and ornately flavoured; for imaginative ways to deal with crayfish, oysters, and lobsters perhaps it has no equal in American cuisine. In the land-locked Southern states, one finds abundant river and lake fish, home-grown, home-cooked pork dishes, rice from Carolina swamps, and the ubiquitous chicken – fried, stewed, baked, barbecued, and dished up in

at least ten kinds of gravies and sauces. Where the South is pre-eminent, perhaps, is in its passionate love of sweet things. Pecan pie! If you can imagine a sublimated treacle tart, packed thickly with sweet-meated nuts, you can come near to pecan pie. Many Southern dishes look back to the appalling hardship of the War Between the States of 1860–5, and to the even greater trauma of Reconstruction which followed the peace, when living on the land meant exactly that. Turnip greens boiled with whatever part of the pig had not to be sold to raise money; peanut soup; quail shot with precious bullets; hominy grits made from home-grown grain; rice with everything. And always, the yearning for something luxurious, something special, something sweet. All these recipes, adapted for British ingredients, may give you an idea of the extreme variety of Southern cooking.

Florida in many ways isn't like a Southern state at all – settled, largely, by Northerners and Midwesterners looking for the sun – but it has its own lavishness of lemons, oranges, limes, seafood, and a seasoning of fascinating dishes brought by Greek sponge fishermen, and Cubans who came originally to make cigars in Tampa – picadillo and Cuban breads, luscious tropical fruits, guavas, avocados.

Going West, yet still in the South, we come to the Bluegrass Country of Kentucky, which in fact borders on the Midwest and partakes of some of its cookery. A very Kentucky dish is 'Burgoo', usually made in huge quantities for parties for the Kentucky Derby (pronoun-ced, in America, Durby) – and, of course, the perfect Mint Julep.

There's an immense category of what might be called All-American food, and indeed it rather merges with Midwest cookery. Some recipes – hot biscuits, waffles, brownies, apple pie, corn puddings, various salads, sweet corn, potato salad, hamburgers, steaks, fried chicken for Sunday dinner – appear across the country in almost identical form. Others, perhaps, can be more truly labelled as coming from the real Midwest – roughly from the Appalachian Mountains to the Rockies – call it the Cornbelt, the Great Plains, the Bible Belt as you like. Here are the states with the lovely Indian names: Illinois, Indiana, Ohio, Iowa, Nebraska, Kansas, the Dakotas, Wisconsin, and Michigan. And here one finds the perfection of strawberry shortcakes, the corn roasts, the baked tomatoes, home-made chili sauces, 'scalloped potatoes', great roasts of beef, steaks an inch thick.

Almost no lamb or veal is eaten in these great corn states – it's all beef and pork, based on the single greatest grain crop in the world, corn (in England, of course, called maize). Flying over the Midwest, you can look down and see wide, neatly fenced fields in geometric shapes. A 'quarter-section' is 320 acres, considered hardly more than a kitchen garden. Endlessly they roll out to the horizon, dense black earth in the ploughing season, golden with corn in growing time, with the occasional paler flicker of wheat bowing before the prairie wind. In the lake-patterned lands of Michigan and Wisconsin, wonderful freshwater trout and bass are caught, and sturgeon like small whales. But sadly, the Great Lakes, inland seas no man can see across, are dying of man's greed; the white-fish of my childhood are no more and even these ancient survivors, the turtles, are said to be almost gone.

The early settlers of the Midwest drove their cattle and pigs west alongside their ox-carts and covered wagons. They found wild turkeys, wild rice, doves, squirrels, raccoon, and opossum – and blueberry bushes, wild grapes, dandelions to make salads, 'poke-weed' to cook as a vegetable. Families were large, pioneer women often cooked chicken and stews in washtubs. Even now, a 'straw-berry social' in a small Illinois town will have bushel baskets of berries – sixty pounds (27 kg) or more – and the state fairs every autumn glow with huge jars of home-made pickles and preserves as though supermarkets hadn't been invented. Sunday dinner is still, most probably, fried chicken. The most traditional Midwest recipes can be made almost anywhere – even corn on the cob, fresh or frozen, is now in English markets. And English and Scotch beef roasted to perfection and served with a dish of scalloped tomatoes, or 'a mess of beans' from the garden – mighty good eating, as they say in the heartland of America.

Down in the Southwest, the immense spreads of cattle ranches are on an almost unimaginable scale – 10,000 acres is common-place. The cowboys of the nineteenth century cooked beef and lamb on camp fires, and they must have invented the fiery barbecue sauces first to preserve meat on the long trail rides, then to lend some interest to the monotony of beef, beans, and campfire bread. The Western plains states produce, as you can imagine, some superb barbecue recipes – although barbecues in Texas and Arizona now seem to be tremendously sophisticated affairs, with guests arriving in their own Learjet aircraft and Bell Ranger helicopters.

But Southwestern cooking is more than beef and lamb. It's a rich patchwork with contributions from the old South brought by the many dispossessed Virginians, Geor-gians, and Alabamians heading West after the Civil War. It has French, Spanish, Indian, and Mexican in its make-up. Everywhere, one finds a version of chili con carne – with beans, without beans, cooked with convenience foods in twenty minutes, or simmered half the

day. It is said that the first chili dishes were made by nuns in a convent in a part of Mexico which has now become Arizona or New Mexico – a way to feed their poor with the cheap, stringy local beef, long cooked to defeat its toughness, enlivened with red peppers, given bulk and sustenance with dried beans cooked until tender in the sauce.

Tortillas – originally made with lye-bleached cornmeal, but equally good made with wholewheat flour – are everywhere, tinned or packaged or homemade, used to wrap and scoop and make a base for any highly-spiced food. Mexican-American foods have quite suddenly become available in supermarkets all over the United Kingdom. And anywhere you find a Caribbean, Indian, or African community, you can find too the staples of Southwestern American cooking – garlic, fiery little chilis, a dozen kinds of dried beans and pulses, spices, and maize meal. Even tortillas can now be bought in the United Kingdom in tins, but they are easy enough to make at home from a New Mexico recipe.

Western cooking more or less begins at the Rocky Mountains, where the Midwest could be said to end. It is perhaps the most eclectic of all. Some of it could be called all-American, as Midwesterners and Easterners have gone out first to find fortune in gold and silver mines, then to find health in the unending sun, finally pursuing a special kind of relaxed, wide-open-spaces way of living. The Americans who transplanted themselves from Ohio, and Kansas, and New York State took along their best-loved 'receipts' for things like flapjacks (pancakes), mother's fried chicken, apple pies, and watermelon pickles. They found in the West native delights like deer and elk in Colorado, great Alaskan crabs a foot and a half wide (really!), salmon thick in the waters of Puget Sound in Washington State, wild berries in the hills, filbert trees flourishing in the soft North-western air.

The Western mountain states, Idaho, Utah, Colorado, and Wyoming, produce superb grass-fed beef and remarkable lamb. Many of the best local recipes came to them with Spanish-Basque shepherds (alas, now a vanishing breed, as sheep and cattle seem to be herded by helicopter). Idaho potatoes, scrubbed to bake in their jackets and split open to show a special glistening whiteness, are an American delight, shipped from one coast to the other. (Their nearest English equivalent, perhaps, is the Golden Wonder, if you can find it among all those boring all-purpose potatoes.) Marvellous barbecue sauces come out of the West, created for the game and fish that all but leap out of the spectacular landscapes.

The Pacific Northwest is salmon country, oyster country, and even now the tiny coppery-tasting Olympia oysters are cheap enough to be bought by the quart (about a kilo), fried in batter or even chopped up in pancakes! Oregon's apples of the lovely names – Gravenstein, Gascoyne's Scarlet, and those grown on English stocks, James Grieve and Egremont Russet – give the lie to the facile assumption that all American fruit is beautiful, big, and tasteless. They are a close second to Oregon pears, the rose-tinged golden Comice with the melting flavour, the little firm Seckels – so incredibly plentiful that they are sold by the peck and the bushel (sixteen pounds, about seven kilos; or sixty-four pounds, thirty kilos) – to be made into pies, preserved, or cooked down into rosy fruit 'butters'.

Washington State is peaches, apples, fish – and timber. Still very thinly settled, parts of it have never felt the touch of a human foot, never been mapped. Along its coast, early settlers were predominantly English, following the exploring sea captains. There still survives a tradition of steak and kidney pie, Christmas pudding, lemon curd for tea. Later came Finns, who grew great acres of cranberries, and Germans and Swedes who brought with them traditional ways of dealing with Washington halibut, salmon, lobsters, and crab.

California is a wonderful muddle of a state, with a coastline of nearly a thousand miles (in European terms, a stretch nearly from the South of Spain to the North Sea), and a little bit of everything from deserts and palm trees to vineyards, mountains, and fogged-in peninsulas. Its deserts of the south are so lavishly irrigated that they blossom with avocados, lemons, oranges, olives, almonds, lettuce. And here, near to Mexico, the Hispanic taste in foods goes back two centuries, with chili-hot recipes and refried beans and barbecues everywhere, even on the smallest patio or porch.

Further north, in the temperate zone that centres on San Francisco, is an extraordinary cultural mix: Italian and Portuguese fishermen; Chinese oystermen, who raise fat ducklings to end as Lacquered Duck in Chinatown; and even, I've been told, a group of Sikhs who harvest rice and artichokes. Everywhere, you'll find *cioppino*, a California-Italian fish stew, as well as crab, lobsters, and fresh tuna steaks. San Francisco cooking is worldly, and rather French, with splashes of Italian, Chinese, Spanish, Japanese, and Polynesian.

California's vineyards were first planted by friars in mission gardens in San Diego, and cultivated over the centuries by French, Italians, Germans, and Swiss. Today California wines range from 'jug wines' sold by the gallon for astonishingly low prices, to rare and precious bottles from very small personal vineyards. Today, they come to England, and indeed even to France, in increasing quantities (more about them on pages 247–8).

Los Angeles cooking, oddly enough, has many affinities with New York (perhaps *not* so surprising, since so many Angelenos seem to be transplanted Easterners), with corned beef, potato pancakes, and Lindy's cheesecake showing up alongside Japanese tempura and Mexican chili con queso. Always, everywhere in California north or south, are salads – fresh and lively mixes of locally-grown crisp cos lettuces, oranges, avocados, red Italian onions, California olive oil – often served as a starter for a meal. Then too there are the great wooden bowls of Caesar Salad and Chef's Salad, which have swept the country from one end to the other.

From California, miners going north for the next great gold-strike in the Yukon Territory – what is now the State of Alaska – took along sourdough bread 'starter' (how they stood the smell I can't think, unless it was lost in the ambiance of wet wool, wet dogs, and seal blubber). It is said that housewives there kept the 'starter' alive and used it for generations. Alaskan salmon and halibut go all over the world, canned and frozen. And up there in the endless summer days, Alaska produces astonishing quantities of berries.

Hawaii, out on the horizon, is all but synonymous with pineapple, thanks largely to the enterprise of a family that went out to the dangerous 'Sandwich Islands' as missionaries, and stayed on to grow, harvest, and market this remarkable fruit. In Hawaii, too, there is a strong Polynesian and Oriental flavour to the cooking, with spices, soy sauce, breadfruit, barbecuing of suckling pigs, and fish fresh from the sea.

Which brings us full circle, back to the Clipper ship captains of New England, homing from their two-year voyages with fruit-tree cuttings (which promptly died in the stark ground), and with the spices and aromatics to spark up stodgy puddings and stews. Their descendants, now, are apt to fly off casually for a week's holiday in Hawaii, bringing home yet another recipe for chicken-in-a-pineapple shell!

So vast, then, is America, so small now the world. Almost every ingredient of any American dish (except perhaps terrapin for Baltimore Turtle Stew, or Florida pompano) can be found in England today. Supermarkets are selling real chili seasoning from San Antonio, Texas, alongside lethally-hot red peppers from India, 'squash pumpkin' from France can be a surrogate for pattypan squash, and so on. Hibachis and charcoal grills are being sold in corner ironmongery shops. An eggplant is an aubergine, zucchini are courgettes, Indian pudding can be made with cornmeal from Pakistan, deep-dish pizzas are becoming as familiar in London and Bath as in Chicago.

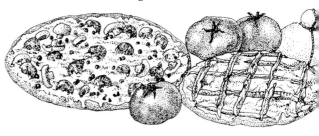

Many American recipes which came first from Europe, the Middle East, and the Orient, are identical in ingredients and methods to their originals, so I have not included them – lasagne in Los Angeles is made very much as it is in Rome, good homemade bread is the same in America as it is here, Sally Lunn and Cornish pasties are made in Michigan by great-grand-daughters of English immigrants from recipes handed down in the families. On the whole, 'receipts' that have a distinctively American twist despite their foreign origins have been included. All the recipes that follow have been adapted to English ingredients, methods, and measurements, and I can only hope they have lost nothing in translation! A brief note about the similarities and differences between English and American flours, sugars, and other ingredients, on page 20, may be of use – it doesn't do to be too pedantic, and I have found that in practice one's eye, taste, and the feel of an ingredient are more important than any hair-splitting rules.

Martha Lomask

London 1981

About Weights and Measures

Any conversion from one system of weighing or measuring to another can only be an approximation, not an exact equivalent. All the recipes in this book have been converted by me from their original American cup-and-spoon measurements, or ounces-and-American pints, to their actual equivalents in Imperial terms, and then to the nearest possible metric measurements.

As most scales available in Britain will not weigh in fractions of an ounce, nor less than 25 grams, I have based the metric figures on a unit of 25 grams (25 g), or 25 millilitres (25 ml). This is very slightly less than one ounce (which actually weighs 28·35 g). For convenience, I have rounded down, where practicable, all metric measurements to the nearest 25 gram or millilitre figure. This means that the metric version of any recipe will give you a result that is slightly less – about 8 per cent – than the Imperial version would yield.

It is vital to use either the metric figures, or the Imperial ones, but not a mixture of the two in any recipe.

If you want to work to completely precise measurements, you will need a balance scale like my favourite Waymaster, made by Precision Engineering of Reading, which weighs down to a $\frac{1}{4}$ ounce or about 7 grams. A beam scale from the French company Terraillon will weigh as little as one-sixteenth of an ounce, less than 2 grams, but you will need to be careful about the storage of their precision-milled brass weights.

In the table that follows, you will find a few apparently illogical jumps in measurements. For example 5 oz ($\frac{1}{4}$ pt) is calculated at 125 grams (125 ml), while 6 oz works out at 175 grams or millilitres. This can't be helped, and it's nothing to worry about. If one were weighing out gold, ambergris, or for that matter ground black pepper or some other precious substance in ounces and grams, much more attention would have to be paid to fractional measurements. But since we are here dealing with the everyday reality of flour, sugar, meat, water, and wine, the small differences are of no importance.

American cookbooks and cookery articles, to my mind, tend to be overprecise and finicky in small measurements. I have in front of me a recipe from a recent issue of an American food and wine magazine which calls for one-sixteenth of a teaspoon of ground black pepper. Another specifies '$\frac{1}{3}$ cup butter less 2 tbsp'. On the other hand, some English cookery books seem to me to be conceived on the wilder shores of romance. How much does 'a coffee cup' hold – is it a little after-dinner cup with about 3 ounces, or my morning coffee cup of at least 6 ounces? And what about 'a wine glass', are we talking about a ladylike 3 ounces, or one of my big Burgundy glasses that holds about 5 to 7 ounces? And when it comes to the recipe from a newspaper that specifies 'a mean saltspoonful' – first I look in the kitchen drawer for that mean little saltspoon, and then I tear up the article and do something else.

For anyone who has gone beyond baby-steps in cooking, minute measurements are not all that vital. Flours and sugars vary from manufacturer to manufacturer, or indeed from the various kinds of wheat from which they are milled or the cane or beet that is turned into sugar. Much depends on whether you are cooking on a dry day or a wet one, in a hot or cold kitchen, whether it is frozen or fresh crabmeat in front of you.

As my godmother, a soft-spoken but downright Quaker lady from Philadelphia, once said to me in another context,
'Use the brains God gave you, and get on with it.'

Weights and Measures

Solid Measures

Imperial	Metric
1 oz	25 g
2 oz	50 g
3 oz	75 g
4 oz	100 g
5 oz	125 g
6 oz	175 g
8 oz ($\frac{1}{2}$ lb)	225 g
10 oz	275 g
12 oz	350 g
15 oz	425 g
16 oz (1 lb)	450 g
20 oz ($1\frac{1}{4}$ lb)	550 g
24 oz ($1\frac{1}{2}$ lb)	675 g
32 oz (2 lb)	900 g
35 oz (approx.)	1 kilo (kg)
3 lb	1·35 kg
4 lb	1·8 kg
5 lb	2·25 kg

All metric measurements rounded down to nearest 25 g or 25 ml below actual equivalent

Fluid Measures

Imperial	Metric
1 fl oz	25 ml
2 fl oz	50 ml
3 fl oz	75 ml
4 fl oz	100 ml
5 fl oz	125 ml
6 fl oz	175 ml
8 fl oz	225 ml
10 fl oz ($\frac{1}{2}$ pt)	275 ml
12 fl oz	350 ml
15 fl oz ($\frac{3}{4}$ pt)	425 ml
16 fl oz	450 ml
20 fl oz (1 pt)	550 ml
24 fl oz	675 ml
32 fl oz	900 ml
35 fl oz (approx.)	1 litre (1 L)
40 fl oz (2 pts)	1·125 L
3 pts	1·70 L

All *spoon* measurements are level. They are based on the standard British measuring spoon sizes ($\frac{1}{4}$, $\frac{1}{2}$, and 1 teaspoon, and 1 tablespoon) which are approximately the same as the metric spoon sizes now available.

Solid butter and margarine measurements are expressed in ounces, since it is easier to cut off an appropriate-sized piece from a block of butter. *Melted* butter or margarine is set forth as spoon measurements.

In some places, you will find the phrase 'a generous 2 oz (50 g)' or similar; this is because I have tried to avoid odd measurements such as $2\frac{1}{2}$ oz or 60 g or ml. Weigh out a bit more of whatever substance is being discussed and your recipe will come out all right.

Oven Temperatures

Fahrenheit	Centigrade	Gas
225	110	$\frac{1}{4}$
250	130	$\frac{1}{2}$
275	140	1
300	150	2
325	165	3
350	180	4
375	190	5
400	200	6
425	220	7
450	230	8
475	240	9

Weights, Measures, and Equivalents

Food	American 1 cup (1 c)	Imperial scant 3 oz	Metric(approx) scant 75 g
Almonds, ground			
Apple, 1 medium, sliced	1 c	5 oz	125 g
Banana, 1 medium, sliced	1 c	6 oz	175 g
Barley, pearl (uncooked)	1 c	6 oz	175 g
Beetroot, 1 medium, sliced	1 c	5 oz	125 g
Beans, dry	1 c	8 oz	225 g
Breadcrumbs, soft fresh	1 c	2 oz	50 g
„ fine dry	1 c	4 oz	100 g
Butter	1 c	8 oz	225 g
„	1 stick	4 oz	100 g
Cabbage, raw shredded	1 c	generous 3 oz	75 g
Carrot, 1 medium, sliced	1 c	5 oz	125 g
Cheese – Cheddar, grated	1 c	4 oz	100 g
„ Parmesan, grated	1 c	3 oz	75 g
„ Cream, curd, cottage	1 c	8 oz	225 g
Chicken, raw or cooked, chopped	1 c	8 oz	225 g
Chocolate, plain dessert	1 square	1 oz	25 g
Cocoa powder	1 c	scant 4 oz	scant 100 g
Coconut, desiccated	1 c	generous 2 oz	50 g
Cornflour (US: cornstarch)	1 c	scant 4 oz	100 g
Cornmeal	1 c	4 oz	100 g
Courgettes, 1 medium, sliced	1½ c	5 oz	125 g
Crackers (US), crushed	1 c	3 oz	75 g
Cranberries, whole or chopped	1 c	generous 3 oz	generous 75 g
Cream, single, double, or whipping (1 c unwhipped = 2 c whipped)	1 c	8 oz	225 ml
Cucumber, 1 medium, sliced or chopped	1 c	5 oz	125 g
Currants	1 c	5 oz	125 g
Cut mixed peel (US: candied fruit)	1 c	5 oz	125 g
Dates, chopped or whole	1 c	7 oz	200 g
Graham crackers (UK: digestive)	1 c	generous 3 oz	generous 75 g
Eggs – whites, 8 to 10	1 c	8 oz	225 g
„ – yolks, 12 to 15	1 c	8 oz	225 g

Flour – plain, self-raising, or light			
„ – brown (85% wholewheat type)	1 c	4 oz	100 g
„ – 100% wholewheat (US: Graham)	1 c	5 oz	125 g
Gelatine, powdered	1 envelope	scant ¼ oz	scant 7 g
Herbs, fresh (parsley etc)	1 c	2 oz	50 g
Lemon, 1 medium	2 tbsp juice and 1 tsp grated rind		
Lemon juice	1 c	8 fl oz	225 ml
Lentils, uncooked	1 c	generous 5 oz	125 g
Liquids – milk, water, wine, vinegar	1 c	8 fl oz	225 ml
	1 pt	16 fl oz	450 ml
	1 qt	32 fl oz	900 ml
	1 gal	approx. 6 pts	3·75 litres
Macaroni, uncooked	1 c	generous 4 oz	generous 100 g
Mayonnaise	1 c	6 oz	175 g
Meat, raw or cooked, chopped	1 c	8 oz	225 g
„ thinly sliced	1½ c	8 oz	225 g
Mincemeat	1 c	10 oz	275 g
Mushrooms, raw, sliced	1 c	2–3 oz	50–75 g
Nuts, broken or coarsely chopped – walnuts, hazelnuts, almonds	1 c	4 oz	100 g
peanuts, pecans	1 c	5 oz	125 g
Oatmeal (UK: porridge oats)	1 c	3 oz	75 g
Oil	1 c	8 fl oz	225 ml
Onion, chopped	1 c	5 oz	125 g
Oysters, raw, shelled	1 pt	16 oz	450 g
Potatoes, 1 medium, raw, sliced or diced	1 c	6–7 oz	175–200 g
„ cooked, mashed	1 c	8 oz	225 g
Peanut butter	1 c	8 oz	225 g
Pepper, red or green, sliced	1 c	4–5 oz	100–125 g
„ chopped	1 c	5–6 oz	125–175 g
Pumpkin, tinned, cooked and mashed	1 c	6 oz	175g
Raisins	1 c	6 oz	175 g
Rice, uncooked (this quantity = 3–4 c cooked rice)	1 c	6 oz	175 g
Semolina	1 c	4 oz	100 g
Shallots, 6 medium	¼ c	1 oz	25 g

Suet, shredded	1 c	generous 4 oz	generous 100 g
Sugar, caster or granulated	1 c	7 oz	200 g
„ brown, 'Brownulated'	1 c	generous 5 oz	generous 125 g
„ icing (US: confectioner's)	1 c	scant 4 oz	scant 100 g
Sultanas	1 c	6 oz	175 g
Sweet potatoes, chopped	1 c	5 oz	125 g
Tomato, 1 medium, chopped	1 c	5–6 oz	125–175 g
Treacle, black (US: molasses)	1 c	12 oz	350 g
Yeast, fresh	1 pkg or cake	$\frac{1}{2}$ oz (see note)	15 g (see note)
„ dry	1 pkg	2 level tsps	scant 7 g

As most English scales will not weigh less than 1 oz or 25 g, the information above on yeast is perhaps academic, but may be useful if you have a finely calibrated scale.

Note. All metric weights have been rounded off to the nearest 25 g *below* the actual Imperial equivalent. If you are using the metric figures in any recipe, expect a result about 8 per cent smaller than if you had used the Imperial.

Very important: Use either metric *or* Imperial, do not mix the two in any recipe.

MISCELLANEOUS MEASUREMENTS

American standard measuring spoons. These give the same amounts as the metric spoons now widely available in Britain.

1 teaspoon (tsp)	= 5 ml spoon		
1 tablespoon (tbsp)	= 15 ml spoon		
2 tbsp liquid	= $\frac{1}{8}$ c American	= 1 fl oz	= approx. 25 ml
5 tbsp liquid	= $\frac{1}{3}$ c American	= $2\frac{1}{2}$ fl oz	= approx. 60 ml
8 tbsp liquid	= $\frac{1}{2}$ c American	= 4 fl oz	= approx. 100 ml
1 tsp	= $\frac{1}{3}$ tbsp		
1 tbsp	= 3 tsp		
1 jigger (for measuring alcoholic liquids)	= 3 tbsp	= $1\frac{1}{2}$ fl oz	= approx. 40 ml

Measures by volume. These measurements encountered in some American cookbooks always deal with solids, never liquids, and they are becoming obsolete. They usually refer to fruits, vegetables, corn on the cob, clams, or grain.

1 peck	= $\frac{1}{4}$ bushel	= 2 gallons	= 16 lb	= 7·25 kg
1 bushel	= 8 gallons	= 64 lb	= about 30 kg	

Liquids. If you have occasion to use American cookbooks often, this ready reckoner for quick conversion of American liquid-by-volume may be useful.

American	Imperial		Metric
1 pt (16 fl oz)	approx. $\frac{3}{4}$ pt		425 ml
2 pts, 1 qt (32 fl oz)	,,	$1\frac{1}{2}$ pts	850 ml
3 pts	,,	$2\frac{1}{2}$ pts	1·4 litres
4 pts	,,	$3\frac{1}{4}$ pts (scant)	1·925 litres
4 qts (1 gal)	,,	$6\frac{1}{2}$ pts	3·5 litres

Anglo-American Cooking Vocabulary

In many cases, there is no exact equivalent in Britain for certain American ingredients: for example, American bacon is not only cut differently to the English kind, it actually comes from a different kind of pig. American 'cake flour' is a silky, very white, fine flour which doesn't exist elsewhere. American 'corn syrup', best known under its brand name of Karo, can be bought in a very few shops in and around London – but failing that, there isn't a true equivalent among British products. However, this list of trans-atlantic semi-synonyms may help you, if you have occasion to use recipes from American books or magazines.

American	British
All-purpose flour	White (plain or self-raising)
American cheese, yellow cheese	Mild Cheddar
Bacon	Very thin-sliced streaky bacon
Bartlett pears	William pears
Beer	Lager
Bell peppers, sweet peppers	Red or green peppers (pimientos)
Biscuits (Hot, or Baking Powder)	Scones
Bok Choy, Chinese cabbage	Chinese leaves
Boiled dressing	Salad cream
Brown sugar, 'Brownulated'	Soft light-brown sugar

American	British
Canteloupe	Ogen or Charentais melon
Canadian bacon	Similar but not exact: Kassler Rippchen (Polish or German)
Candied fruit, chopped	Cut mixed peel
Celery knob, celery root	Celeriac
Chicory	Endive
Chili powder	Chili seasoning (Gebhardt's, McCormick's, Schwarz)
Coconut, dry	Desiccated coconut
Cookies	Sweet biscuits
Corn	Maize
Cornstarch	Cornflour

Corn syrup (Karo), light	No exact equivalent
,, dark	Golden syrup (for table use, not cooking)
Cream, heavy or whipping	Double cream
Cream, coffee or light	Single cream
Eggplant	Aubergine
Endive	Chicory
Farina	Semolina
French-fries, French-fried potatoes	Chips
Fresh ham	Leg of pork
Graham crackers	Nearest, but not exact: digestive biscuits
Graham flour	Wholewheat or wholemeal flour
Half-and-half	Half milk, half single cream
Hot dogs, wieners	Frankfurters
Jelly roll	Swiss roll
Jell-o, gelatine dessert	Jelly
Kasha	Buckwheat groats
Kettle	Saucepan
Ladyfingers	Sponge fingers
Molasses, blackstrap	Black treacle
Molasses, regular	No precise equivalent: but half golden syrup and half black treacle is acceptable alternative
Monterey Jack cheese	Mild Cheddar
Oatmeal	Porridge oats
Okra	Ladies' fingers, bamye
Oyster plant	Salsify
Rattrap cheese	Sharp aged Cheddar
Rock Cornish game hen	Nearest equivalent: squab pigeons
Romaine	Cos lettuce
Saltines	Salted cream crackers

Scallions	Spring onions, green onions
Shortening	Cooking fat (white fat, lard, margarine)
Skillet, spider	Frying pan
Store cheese	Cheddar
Stick of butter	4 oz (100 g) butter
Sugar:	Nearest equivalent:
White or granulated	caster sugar
Brown, 'Brownulated'	Light brown sugar
Dark brown	Muscovado, molasses sugar, soft dark brown
Confectioner's, Powdered, XXX or 10-X	Icing sugar
Sweet butter	Unsalted butter
Swiss cheese	Gruyère, Emmenthal
Tomato sauce, tinned	No exact equivalent: tinned meatless 'Napolitan' sauce comes closest
Vanilla extract	Vanilla essence
Wiener, Vienna sausage	Frankfurter
White raisins	Sultanas
Yeast, active dry (one package)	Dry yeast, 2 level tsp
Zucchini	Courgettes

Note on American Flour and Sugar

All-purpose flour, often mentioned in American cookery books, contains some hard wheat and therefore has a certain gluten content. It is for all practical purposes interchangeable with English plain white flour. It is not self-raising.

In some parts of the country, 'strong' un-bleached white flour is available for use in bread-making, but because it is not universally distri-buted, it is seldom specified in American recipes. Throughout this book, for making bread, I have used the 'strong' bread flour which is widely available in Britain. For pastries and cakes, I have used plain white flour.

'Instantized' flour is a fairly recent invention, a flour with a fine granular structure that does not lump when added to liquids, and is therefore ideal for sauces. In any American recipe which specifies this type of flour, plain white flour is a perfectly acceptable substitute. Cake flour is a very finely milled, highly bleached, low-gluten product which has no exact equivalent in Britain. In practice, any plain white flour available here will give almost exactly the same results, with perhaps a margin-ally less fine texture in the finished product. Sifting together 4 oz (100 g) of cornflour and 14 oz (400 g) of plain white flour will produce a fine, silky cake-flour very like the American product, but cakes made this way may have a slightly starchy taste. Potato flour used instead of wheat flour makes a very fine-grained, slightly dry, but delicious cake (as in the Idaho Sunbeam Cake, p. 231).

Wholewheat flour is called 'Graham flour' in the United States, and in many parts of the country is available only in healthfood shops. Flour sold in Britain as wholewheat or wholemeal can be used wherever an American recipe calls for Graham flour. The more refined '81%' or '85%' type has had some of the coarser bran extracted, and gives a lighter and finer result in bread-making, but can be substituted for 'Graham flour'.

'81%'–'85%' light brown flour: this reference in some of the recipes refers to the type of flour which has been milled so as to retain about eighty-one to eighty-five per cent of the wheatberry, with its nutrition intact. It is finer than wholewheat or wholemeal flour, makes superb bread, and I often use it in cakes, shortcrust pastry, and other recipes where plain white flour would otherwise be indicated. It gives a pleasant nutty flavour to pastry, and makes moist, long-keeping cakes. It can't be used, of course, in making angelfood or American sponge cakes, or wherever the delicacy of white flour is desirable. It furnishes a certain amount of essential roughage in the diet, although of course not as much as stone-ground pure wholewheat flour.

The word 'sugar' in American cookery always means white sugar: sometimes it is called granu-lated sugar. However, this is not to be confused with the British sugar of that name as it is not so coarse. In texture, it is somewhere between British granulated and British caster sugars. Caster sugar should always be used wherever plain sugar is called for in an American recipe.

American light and dark brown sugars are made almost entirely from cane, while many of the British and European brown sugars are based on sugar beets. It seems impossible to find out which brand is cane and which is beet, and I can only say that in this book I have done my best to make recipes using brown sugar foolproof, whatever its origin. The brands I have used with complete success are Sainsbury's Light and Dark Brown Sugar; Bejam Dark Brown, and Safeway's own brand of Light Brown.

Demerara and coffee sugars exist in America only as they are imported from England; the dark Muscovado type familiar to British cooks is available in certain parts of America, and is called 'dark moist brown sugar' or 'molasses sugar'.

Powdered sugar, confectioners sugar, XXX or 10X, are regional names for what in Britain is called icing sugar.

Starters

Potato Biscuits (savoury cocktail crackers)

Makes about 36

6 oz (175 g) potato, peeled and steamed or boiled

Half a medium onion, peeled

2 oz (50 g) soft butter or good margarine

4 oz (100 g) plain flour

1 oz (25 g) Cheddar or Parmesan cheese, grated

$\frac{1}{2}$ tsp baking powder

$\frac{1}{2}$ tbsp celery seeds

$\frac{1}{2}$ tsp celery salt

Sea salt, sesame seeds, or poppy seeds

Preheat oven to 375°F (190°C), Gas 5.

1. Shred the potato and onion finely, and mix with the butter or margarine. Add the flour, cheese, baking powder, celery seeds, and celery salt and mix well.

2. Pinch off pieces of the dough and roll them between your palms, until they are the size of small marbles. Flatten to about $\frac{1}{8}$ in. (0·5 cm) thick. Put them about 2 in. (5 cm) apart on a lightly oiled baking sheet. Sprinkle with sea salt, sesame seeds, or poppy seeds, or dust with more grated cheese if you prefer.

3. Bake for twenty to twenty-five minutes until the biscuits are brown and crisp. Slide them off the baking sheet at once and cool on a cake rack. Store in an air-tight tin.

Green Garden Pie

Serves 4

4 spring onions, chopped

1 oz (25 g) butter or margarine

2 oz (50 g) mushrooms, wiped and sliced

5 oz (125 g) frozen spinach, thawed and well drained

1 clove garlic, crushed

$\frac{1}{2}$ tsp dried tarragon

2 eggs, size 3

3 fl oz (75 ml) milk

Salt, freshly ground black pepper

1 oz (25 g) grated Parmesan cheese

Preheat oven to 375°F (190°C), Gas 5.

1. Sauté the onions in hot butter for about three minutes, stirring. Add the mushrooms and sauté for five minutes. Stir in the spinach, garlic, and tarragon, and simmer on a medium heat, stirring from time to time, until all the liquid has evaporated.

2. Whisk the eggs with the milk, salt, and pepper. Stir this mixture into the vegetables, then add the cheese and mix everything together lightly. Pour into a lightly-buttered 7 in. (18 cm) round tin.

3. Bake about forty minutes, until a thin knife blade put into the centre comes out clean. Let the pie cool for about ten minutes before cutting in wedges to serve.

Anchovy and Pimiento

9 oz (250 g) tin of good pimientos in oil
   (Spanish or Italian)

2 small tins anchovies, 1½ oz (35 g) each

Lemon wedges

Olive oil, red wine vinegar

This is a New York Italian (and San Francisco and Chicago too) 'appetiser'/first course, which I think is unknown in Italy. Sharp, lively, an encouragement to an appetite for pasta or veal parmigiana to follow. Lots of Italian bread for mopping up the sauce.

1. Drain the pimientos of most of their oil, cut in even-sized strips, and divide between four plates. Drain the anchovies well and pat them dry with kitchen paper. Cut into matchstick strips, and lay them in a lattice pattern across the pimientos.
2. At the last minute, mix olive oil and red wine vinegar. Use as much or as little as you like, but a rough guess for four would be 2 fl. oz (50 ml) oil and the same of vinegar. Pour it on. Don't salt or pepper them.

Devilled Chicken Liver Canapés

3 oz (75 g) butter

12 thin slices French bread

8 oz (225 g) chicken livers

2 tbsp parsley, finely chopped

Good pinch of dry mustard

2 fillets of anchovy

2 tbsp lemon juice

½ tsp salt

Freshly ground black pepper

1. Heat three tbsp of butter in a frying pan and quickly sauté the bread slices on both sides. Keep warm in a covered dish.
2. Wash and trim the chicken livers and chop finely. In the same frying pan, melt the remaining butter and sauté livers and parsley for three minutes, stirring constantly. Add all other ingredients and cook for two minutes more, stirring. Spread on the bread and serve at once.

Devilled Sardine Canapés

Four large slices thin toast, buttered

1 tin (6 oz – 175 g) good sardines in oil

2 tbsp Dijon mustard

Juice of one lemon

1 oz (25 g) fresh soft breadcrumbs,
   brown or white

Lemon wedges

1. Cut toast in strips the size of the sardines. Drain oil from the sardine tin and mix it with the mustard and lemon juice. Turn each sardine over in this mixture until it is evenly coated, then roll them in the breadcrumbs. Keep toast hot in covered hot dish.
2. Lay a big piece of aluminium foil in the grill pan, and heat the grill very hot. Lay the sardines on the foil, and cook them for two minutes, watching carefully. Turn them over with great care and grill for about one minute on the other side.
3. Put a sardine on each toast strip and serve at once with lemon wedges.

Brioche Loaf *and* Brioche and Onion Sandwiches

3 oz (75 g) butter

4 tsp caster sugar

½ tsp salt

2 tsp dried yeast

2 fl. oz (50 ml) hand-hot water

2 eggs, size 3

9 oz (250 g) plain flour (*not* strong bread flour)

1 egg yolk, any size, mixed with 1 tbsp milk

Sliced onions, mayonnaise

A most delicious new starter (or partner for drinks) suddenly appeared in New York a few years ago: almost transparent slices of mild onion on small thin rounds of finely-textured brioche. The brioche dough, instead of being baked in the usual small fluted tins, is done in a smallish bread tin. And with this recipe, the usual overnight resting process is greatly reduced.

1. Cream the butter, sugar, and salt together. Dissolve the yeast in warm water, stir in well, and let stand in a warm place until it is frothy. Pour this into a large bowl and stir in the butter and sugar. Beat in the eggs and flour, and with a hand or electric mixer beat it all very smooth. Cover the bowl with plastic film and let the dough rise in a warm place until double in bulk.
2. Stir down the dough and beat it well again. Preheat the oven to 400°F (200°C), Gas 6. Let the dough rest about ten minutes. Grease a small bread tin, shape the dough into a loaf and let it rise in the tin, covered with oiled plastic film, until it has risen above the top of the tin. Brush the top with the egg yolk and milk mixture. Bake about thirty to forty minutes, until well-browned. Remove from the tin and cool on a wire rack. Slice very thinly.
3. With a small plain cutter, about 1 in. (2·5 cm) diameter, cut out rounds. Choose small onions that will give you circles just smaller than the brioche rounds. Slice them as thinly as you can. Spread the brioche rounds with mayonnaise, and lay a slice of onion on half the rounds, then cover with another round of brioche.

Chopped Chicken Liver

Serves 4

12 oz (350 g) chicken livers

Scant 1 oz (25 g) butter or chicken fat

3 hard-boiled eggs, size 3

1 small onion, finely chopped

Salt, freshly ground black pepper

This is most emphatically not a chicken pâté or mousse. It's much less sophisticated, rather coarse, a great New York and Los Angeles dish as a first course – or part of a buffet that would probably include corned beef, potato salad, coleslaw, dark rye bread, pickled tomatoes, and a bowl of unsalted butter.

1. Wash and pick over the chicken livers carefully, removing any bitter yellow or green bits. Heat the butter or chicken fat in a heavy frying pan, and cook the livers gently until they are browned on the outside and still very slightly

pink on the inside when you prod them with a sharp knife. Turn them frequently as they cook. Strain the fat from the pan and reserve.

2. Cool the chicken livers and chop coarsely with a knife, not a blender or food processor. Chop the eggs fairly finely, mix with the livers and chopped onion, and stir in the reserved fat. Season well. (If you don't like raw onion, you may want to blanch it for about three minutes in boiling water, and drain well.)

Cheese Spreads and Blends

An all-American favourite – served on celery, with drinks, or as part of a salad lunch. They are useful, too, to have on hand to spread on savoury biscuits – they keep well in earthenware jars in the refrigerator – and these four are among the dozens that one finds from coast to coast. Cheese balls or logs are easy to make and pretty to look at, and can be made from any of these blends.

BLUE CHEESE SPREAD WITH CELERY

Makes a scant 1lb (450g)

2 bunches celery

6 oz (175 g) unsalted butter

8 oz (225 g) blue cheese

2 tbsp brandy

Dash of hot pepper sauce

½ tsp Worcestershire sauce

Freshly ground black or white pepper

Wash and trim the celery. Cream the butter and blend in the blue cheese until fluffy and light. Add all the other ingredients, mix well, and fill the hollows of the celery stalks. Chill well. Or pack the cheese into a decorative jar and surround it with little biscuits for spreading.

BEER CHEESE SPREAD

Makes a generous 20 oz (550g)

6 fl. oz (175 ml) lager

12 oz (350 g) sharp Cheddar cheese, grated

2 oz (50 g) blue cheese

½ tsp dry mustard

1 rounded tbsp softened butter (generous 1 oz (about 35 g))

Dash of hot pepper sauce

Chopped chives

This spread can be made in seconds in a blender or food processor, or beaten together with a hand whisk. Blend the lager with Cheddar until smooth, crumble in the blue cheese, mustard, butter, and hot pepper sauce, and blend again. Scrape into a bowl and lightly cover with chopped chives; fill celery stalks, or store in an earthenware jar, covered, in the refrigerator.

CHEESE-CARAWAY SPREAD

Makes about 10 oz (225g)

6 oz (175 g) cream or curd cheese

2 tbsp capers, drained

2 tbsp caraway seeds

4 tbsp plain natural yoghurt or soured cream

Small clove garlic, crushed

Salt to taste

Blend all together well and taste for seasoning.

GARLIC CHEESE SPREAD

Makes about 14 oz (400g)

3 oz (75 g) Parmesan cheese, grated

8 oz (225 g) butter, softened

2 garlic cloves, crushed

2 fl. oz (50 ml) olive oil

3 tbsp chives, chopped

1 tbsp parsley, chopped

$\frac{1}{2}$ tsp freshly ground black pepper

Optional: Worcestershire sauce

Blend all ingredients well, let stand for two hours at room temperature, then chill. A good spread for biscuits or toasted French bread.

Dips

These can be made firm or soft, depending on whether they're to be spread on crisp crackers (biscuits), or served as a dip with carrot spears, cucumber sticks, cauliflower florets, green pepper strips, celery stalks, or strips of fennel. They're quite nice, too, served with very thin crisp toast, unbuttered, as a first course. Dips and spreads are found everywhere in America, with certain regional variations in flavouring.

CHILI DIP

8 fl. oz (225 ml) soured cream

1 tbsp fresh basil or 1 tsp dried basil

1 tsp paprika

½ tsp chili seasoning

Salt to taste

Mix well and chill. Makes about 8 oz (225 g) of dip.

BLUE CHEESE DIP

8 oz (225 g) Danish or Irish blue cheese

8 oz (225 g) cream or curd cheese

4 fl. oz (100 ml) single cream or
 evaporated milk

3–4 tsp celery seed

Pinch of garlic salt, or more

Mix until fluffy and chill well. Makes about 1¼ lb (550 g) of dip.

WALNUT DIP

2 oz (50 g) broken walnut pieces

2 small cloves garlic, crushed

2 slices white bread, crusts removed

1½ tsp cider or white wine vinegar

1 tsp olive oil, or olive and groundnut
 oil mixed

Salt to taste

1. Pound the walnuts, or put them in a blender or food processor until finely chopped but not ground to powder. Add garlic and mix well. Soak the bread in cold water, squeeze it out, mix well with the garlic and nuts.
2. Slowly add the vinegar and oil, and season. Makes about 5–6 oz (125–50 g) of dip.

HERBED CREAM CHEESE DIP

Makes a scant 8 oz (225g)

1 clove garlic crushed

1 tsp onion, very finely chopped

¼ tsp salt, or more to taste

¼ tsp paprika

3 oz (75 g) cream cheese

2 oz (50 g) mayonnaise

1 tbsp lemon juice

¼ tsp dried thyme

Good dash of hot pepper sauce

1 tsp chives or parsley, finely chopped

This goes very well with Potato Biscuits (p. 22), or with a platter of raw vegetables as a starter.

1. In a mortar, blender, or food processor, blend the garlic, onion, salt, paprika, and cream cheese until very smooth. Add the mayonnaise and the lemon juice and taste for seasoning, you may need more salt.
2. Stir in the thyme and hot pepper sauce and fill a decorative bowl with the mixture. Cover with chives or parsley, pressed onto the cheese with a knife.

PHILLY DIP

8 oz (225 g) cream cheese

1–2 tbsp top of milk or single cream

Good pinch of sea salt

Freshly ground black pepper

1 tsp finely minced anchovy (about two anchovy fillets)

Very small clove of garlic, crushed

½ tsp paprika

The Philadelphia Cream Cheese made by Kraft is of a slightly firmer consistency than delicatessen cream cheese, and seems to lend itself well to this recipe – of course, you can use any cream or curd cheese you like. Thin it to a dipping or spreading texture to suit yourself.

Blend the cream cheese with the milk until it is smooth, adding more to your taste. Stir in the remaining ingredients and taste for seasoning. Makes about ¾ pt (425 g) of dip.

TUNA DIP

7½ oz (210 g) tin good firm tuna

3 oz (75 g) cream or curd cheese

2 fl. oz (50 ml) dry sherry

2 tbsp parsley, finely chopped or 1 tbsp chopped chives

¼ tsp dried tarragon

Salt to taste

Soured cream

Optional: hot pepper sauce, capers

One of the all-American recipes which can be very simple, or rather more special when dressed up with capers. For Potato Biscuits (p. 22), potato crisps, or any small savoury crackers.

1. Blend together all the ingredients except the soured cream, then add enough of that to make a smooth spreading or softer dipping texture.
2. Add a few drops of hot pepper sauce if you like it, and stir in some drained capers for a sharp lively taste. This is an agreeable sort of bastard pâté to serve with something crisp like Belgian chicory if you like rather than biscuits. Makes about 14 oz (400 g) of dip.

VEGETABLE DIP for savoury biscuits

1 lb (450 g) cottage cheese

2 fl. oz (50 ml) single cream

1 small carrot, finely grated

3 spring onions, thinly sliced

8 radishes, topped and very thinly sliced

½ tsp salt, or to taste

Freshly ground black pepper

Optional: garlic salt, paprika

Mix all the ingredients well, or for a smoother texture blend for fifteen seconds in a blender or food processor. Chill well. Makes about 1 pt (500 ml) of dip.

Devilled Ham Spread

8 oz (225 g) cooked ham, chopped (or boiled bacon or gammon)

1 small onion (about 3 oz, 75 g), finely chopped

2 tbsp Dijon mustard

3 tbsp mayonnaise

2 tbsp milk

¼ tsp cayenne

There's a marvellous, tinned devilled ham sold in America, spicy and salty and very concentrated. While this home-made version will never take its place, it's extremely good on French bread, or to stuff celery, or pile into a hollowed-out ripe tomato.

This is best made in a blender or food processor. Chop the ham very finely, not quite to a paste, and blend it with all the other ingredients. Taste and add salt if necessary – this depends on the ham. Makes about 10 oz (275 g).

Eggs à la Russe

Serves 4

6 hard-boiled eggs, size 2

About 6 rounded tbsp home-made mayonnaise

Good pinch of dried tarragon

2¼ oz (32 g) jar of Danish black lumpfish roe, *or* red sturgeon 'caviar'

This is probably the world's simplest starter, but because of the (inexpensive) caviar, it seems very special.

1. As soon as the eggs are cooked, plunge them into cold water, crack the shells all over with a knife handle, and peel them. Cool them until you are ready to serve. Cut eggs in halves and put three halves on each plate.
2. Flavour the mayonnaise with tarragon, and completely mask the eggs with this mixture. Scatter the 'caviar' evenly over the eggs.

Golden Gate Salad

Serves 8 as a first course

1 large soft lettuce

2 bunches of watercress, leaves only

1 small, very ripe avocado

2 fl. oz (50 ml) lemon juice

2 tbsp water

¼ pt (125 ml) salad oil (olive and groundnut oil mixed does well)

½ tsp sea salt

½ tsp caster sugar

2–3 medium seedless oranges

3 preserved kumquats, thinly sliced

Optional: about 1–2 oz (25–50 g) flaked almonds

In California, salad is almost always served at the beginning of the meal. This one makes the most of the golden bounty of fruits and vegetables that seem to spring out of the rich coastal plains. Don't be surprised at the idea of preserved kumquats in a salad – they're the gift of the large Chinese colony of San Francisco.

1. Wash the lettuce and watercress thoroughly, dry well, and chill in the refrigerator for several hours. Peel and chop the avocado and mash it with lemon juice, water, oil, salt, and sugar until very smooth. Chill well.
2. Line a large salad bowl with the best lettuce leaves, tear up the rest and mix with watercress. Peel and section the oranges and tuck the thin kumquat slices among the leaves, and pass the avocado dressing separately.

Guacamole

2 large ripe avocados

2–3 tbsp lemon or lime juice

1 tbsp chopped fresh coriander or about ½ tsp ground coriander

Hot pepper sauce to taste, or chopped tinned hot jalapeño chillis to taste (see Appendix)

Salt

Even someone who doesn't warm to avocado in any other guise is apt to become a guacamole fiend. Basically, it's mashed avocado seasoned with anything lively and bright-flavoured, and serve with something crisp like miniature tortilla chips, potato crisps, or thin biscuits. This is a recipe from Mexico.

1. Cut the avocados in half, and remove the stones, retaining the shells. Scoop out the flesh carefully with a sharp spoon and mash with lemon or lime juice. Add salt and other seasonings and pile back lightly into the avocado shells.
2. Brush avocados with lemon juice to preserve the colour, and serve as quickly as you can.

Variations: add one clove crushed garlic. Or finely chop a large ripe tomato and stir it in. Or season with chili seasoning to taste instead of hot pepper sauce.

Chinese Shrimp Toast

1 very thin slice peeled ginger root

6 oz (175 g) cooked shrimp or prawns

3 oz (75 g) tinned water chestnuts

1 spring onion, chopped

2 tsp cider or white wine

Good pinch of salt

½ tsp cornflour

1 egg, size 3 or 4, beaten

4 slices day-old good white bread, crusts removed

8 fl. oz (225 ml) groundnut oil for frying

1. Very finely chop the ginger root. With a very sharp knife, chop the shrimp, water chestnuts, and spring onion as finely as possible. Mix with cider or wine, salt, ginger root, cornflour, and enough beaten egg to make a stiffish mixture.
2. Cut the bread in quarters and spread the shrimp mixture on them. Chill about fifteen minutes in the refrigerator. Heat the oil in a deep-fryer or wok to 380°F (190°C).
3. Very carefully put in four pieces of bread, shrimp side down, and fry until top is golden. Turn bread over carefully and fry another fifteen seconds. Drain and keep warm in the oven until all the Shrimp Toasts are fried.

Tabbouleh

6 oz (175 g) boulgour wheat (sometimes called pourgouri, or fine cracked wheat)

4 fl. oz (100 ml) water

3 fl. oz (75 ml) olive oil, or olive and groundnut oil mixed

2 fl. oz (50 ml) lemon juice

Middle Eastern food has in the last twenty years swept across America, in a sort of pincer movement from the Armenian community of San Francisco to the Greek sponge-fishing colony of Tarpon Springs, Florida, joining up with Lebanese, Syrians, and Armenians in New York and Chicago. I found this recipe in a good little notebook-type cookbook produced by a Lebanese women's group in Detroit.

1½ tsp salt

1 tsp ground allspice (optional)

2 ripe tomatoes

1 bunch spring onions, green and white parts, chopped

2 oz (50 g) parsley

About 1 tsp fresh mint leaves, finely chopped

1. Bring water to the boil, add the boulgour, reduce the heat and simmer for five minutes. If liquid is absorbed before that time, add more water, and cook until the boulgour is still slightly crunchy and not soggy. Put it in a bowl and stir in the oil, lemon juice, salt, and allspice.
2. Dice the tomatoes, mix into the boulgour with the spring onions, parsley, and mint. Cover and chill for an hour.

Serve with leaves of cos lettuce or chicory, using them as scoops. Or hollow out ripe tomatoes, fill with tabbouleh – and provide forks and spoons.

Chopped Herring

Serves 4

2 salt herring

1 thick slice white bread

1 medium onion, peeled

1 large cooking apple, peeled

2 tsp caster sugar

2 eggs, size 3, hard-boiled

Freshly ground black pepper

This American-Jewish appetiser or starter must trace its ancestry to the Baltic countries. Serve it with thin crisp biscuits, matzos, or as a sandwich filling on dark rye bread spread with unsalted butter. Or surround it with cos lettuce leaves, sliced tomatoes, cucumbers, for a pleasant lunchtime salad.

1. Skin and fillet the herrings, and soak them in water overnight, or for at least twelve hours.
2. Soak the bread in a little cold water and squeeze it fairly dry. Finely chop the onion with the bread, apple, sugar, one of the eggs, and the white of the second egg. Finely chop the herring and stir it lightly into the onion mixture. Sieve the yolk of the second egg and scatter it over the chopped herring.

Herring in Soured Cream

Serves 4

5 salt herring

8 fl. oz (225 ml) soured cream

2 tbsp cider vinegar

1 tsp Worcestershire sauce

½ tsp dry mustard

2 medium onions, very thinly sliced

1 bayleaf

Pinch of cayenne

In New York, Chicago, California, and doubtless in other places, it is easy to buy this super delicatessen delicacy in glass jars. It is a bit fiddly to make at home, but so good to eat.

1. Clean the herring and remove heads and tails. Soak in cold water for twenty-four hours, changing the water three or four times. Skin and bone them, rinse well and drain, and cut into 1 in. (2·5 cm) pieces.
2. Mix the remaining ingredients, add the herring pieces and mix lightly, without breaking up the fish. Put it all in a glass or earthenware casserole and refrigerate, covered, for about twelve hours. Serve with thinly-sliced dark rye bread and unsalted butter.

Poor Man's Caviar (or Eggplant Caviar)

Serves 4 as an appetiser

1 large aubergine, about 1½ lb (675 g)

1 medium onion, very finely chopped

1 large clove garlic, crushed with 1 tsp salt

Juice of half a large lemon

4 fl. oz (100 ml) olive oil, or olive and groundnut oil mixed

Optional: 1 small green pepper, seeded and chopped

This isn't at all like caviar, but that's what a Russian friend in New York calls it. It's an American edition of a Middle Eastern dish often called Aubergine Salad or something like that. It seems to crop up in such diverse places as Michigan and California, where there are Greek and Armenian colonies. Wonderful with pita bread, and it can go further as a spread for savoury biscuits.

Preheat oven to 350°F (180°C), Gas 4.

1. Put the aubergine on a piece of foil and bake it until the aubergine collapses and the skin is brown. (Check it carefully as this can happen quite suddenly. It's a good dish to make when you have the oven going for other dishes.) Remove from the oven and cool until you can handle it. Peel, and cut the aubergine flesh in large pieces.
2. If you have a blender or food processor, put all the ingredients in together and blend, turning the motor on and off quickly several times, until it is coarsely chopped but not puréed. If by hand, chop the aubergine flesh finely and mix with the other ingredients. Chill well. Serve with slices of lemon if you like.

Shrimp Tempura

Serves 4–6 as a lavish starter

1½ lb (675 g) uncooked prawns, shelled

2 eggs, size 3, separated

¼ pt (125 ml) lager

1 tbsp groundnut oil

1 tbsp soy sauce

½ tsp dry mustard

4 oz (100 g) cornflour

Oil for deep frying

About 2 tbsp extra cornflour

One of the delicate and beautiful Japanese-American recipes, so popular on the West Coast and in New York.

1. For the batter, whisk egg yolks, than beat in the lager, the oil, mustard, and soy sauce. Sift the 4 oz (100 g) cornflour and blend with the egg yolk mixture. Whisk the egg whites stiff and gently cut and fold the two mixtures together.
2. Put the extra cornflour in a plastic bag and toss the shrimp in it until well-coated. Dip them in the batter just before frying.
3. Heat the oil in a deep-fryer to 380°F (190°C), and drop in the shrimp in small handfuls (use a frying basket if it's easier). Cook three minutes and drain them well on kitchen paper. Keep the temperature of the oil high.

Serve with a bowl of soy sauce, grated horseradish, or any highly-seasoned sauce you like.

Opposite Mexican and Italian influences on American cooking. Top Tostadas; Centre Tacos with Tex-Mex filling; Bottom Anchovy and Pimientoes for a starter
Overleaf From American oceans. Top Avocado Stuffed with Shrimp; Centre Mussel Chowder; Bottom Jambalaya

Soups

Instant Borsch

Serves 4

¾ pt (425 ml) soured cream

½ small lemon, peeled and without pips

¼ tsp salt

¼ tsp celery salt

8 oz (225 g) cooked beetroots, peeled and diced

1 tsp instant chopped onion

For this recipe you will need a blender or food processor. And it's done in about fifteen seconds.

1. Put ½ pt (275 ml) of the soured cream in the blender, add all the other ingredients and purée until smooth. Taste for seasoning, and add more salt if necessary.
2. Put into chilled soup cups with a blob of the remaining soured cream on top of each.

Hot Borsch

Serves 5–8

4 pts (2·5 litres) clear beef stock

5 small beetroots

4 medium potatoes, peeled

2 medium onions, very thinly sliced

1 small head firm white cabbage

4 fl. oz (100 ml) lemon juice

2 tbsp caster sugar

Salt, freshly ground black pepper

About ½ pt (275 ml) soured cream

Optional: about 4 oz (100 g) meat from stock, diced

This is the simplest of the Russian-immigrant borsch recipes that I know. There are others that must cook all day, and include almost every vegetable known except corn and okra.

1. Bring the stock to the boil. Peel and shred the beetroots and cook them in the hot stock for fifteen minutes. Dice the potatoes. Strip off the coarse outer leaves from the cabbage and shred. Add the potatoes, cabbage, and onion to the saucepan and cook until the cabbage is very soft.
2. Add lemon juice and sugar and taste for seasoning. It should have a sweet-and-sour flavour. Add the meat if used, and cook for another five minutes. Serve in heated bowls, and hand round a bowl of chilled soured cream separately.

Creamed Onion Soup

Serves 4

8–10 oz (225–275 g) onion, finely chopped

3 stalks celery, finely chopped

8 fl. oz (225 ml) chicken stock

2 oz (50 g) butter (*not* margarine)

Scant 3 tbsp flour

¾ pt (425 ml) milk

1 tsp sea salt

¼ tsp freshly ground black pepper

Good pinch of freshly grated nutmeg

2 oz (50 g) flaked toasted almonds

¼ pt (125 ml) double cream

1. Combine the vegetables and chicken stock in a large heavy saucepan. Bring them slowly to the boil, lower the heat, and simmer until the onions and celery are soft. Purée the mixture and set aside. This can be done in advance.
2. In a small heavy saucepan, mix the butter, flour, and milk all at once. Bring to the boil, stirring constantly, then lower the heat and cook, still stirring, for about two minutes. Add salt, pepper, and nutmeg. Thin the mixture with some of the soup, then stir everything together and reheat, stirring, until very hot.
3. Serve in heated bowls, with a float of unwhipped cream and some toasted almonds on each.

Mexican Black Bean Soup

1 lb (450 g) dried black beans

2½ pts (1·5 litres) water

1 tbsp good oil

1 lb (450 g) lean pork, cubed

2 medium onions, peeled

2 large tomatoes

1 green pepper, seeded

2 cloves garlic, crushed with 1 tsp salt

¼ tsp ground cumin

½ tsp chili seasoning

Freshly ground black pepper

Lemon or lime slices

This recipe (and its variations) is a country-wide favourite. It freezes well, so if this quantity isn't eaten up at one meal, put it in a tight-lidded freezer container. It will keep for up to two months.

1. Wash and pick over the beans. Put in a saucepan with just enough cold water to cover, and bring to the boil. Boil for two minutes, cover, and let stand for two hours. Drain the beans, add the 2½ pts (1·5 litres) of cold water, and bring slowly to the boil.
2. Heat the oil and fry the pork cubes on a high heat, stirring, until they are well browned. Add them to the beans. Chop the onions, tomatoes, and green pepper as finely as you can, and add them with the garlic and salt to the beans. Season with cumin, chili, and black pepper.
3. Bring the soup to the boil again, and simmer for about four hours until the beans are very soft. Purée in a blender, food processor, or a food mill such as the Mouli-légumes. Taste for seasoning, reheat, and serve with a thin slice of lemon or lime in each bowl.

Peanut Butter Soup

1 large stalk of celery, chopped

Half a medium onion, peeled and chopped

1 tbsp butter or margarine, melted

1 pt (550 ml) milk

2 chicken stock cubes

1 tinned pimiento, finely chopped

Pinch of freshly ground black pepper

2 oz (50 g) smooth peanut butter

Croûtons

I have read that peanut butter was invented in the late nineteenth century by a Midwestern doctor who wanted to give an easily-digested, high-protein, palatable food to some of his patients. Shelled, roasted, and ground peanuts flavoured with salt, and with a little peanut (groundnut) oil added, seemed to be the answer. It's hard to describe the flavour and texture of peanut butter – addicts will need no words, those who dislike it will have gone no further than the title of the recipe. Because of its high fat content, peanut butter is a concentrated source of energy. When cooking with it, any other fat should be reduced in quantity.

1. In the top part of a double boiler, on direct heat, sauté the celery and onion in hot butter for about three minutes until they are soft but not brown. Add the milk and bring to the simmering point, then put the pan over boiling water in the bottom of the double boiler. Add the chicken stock cubes, pimiento, and pepper and cook for fifteen minutes, covered.
2. Stir in the peanut butter and heat. Scatter croûtons on each serving.

Congressional Bean Soup

Serves 6 as a starter

12 oz (350 g) white haricot beans

1 large onion, peeled and stuck with
two cloves

8 oz (225 g) cooked ham, or a ham bone
with some good fragments of meat
still clinging to it

2 tbsp lard

1 lb (450 g) potatoes, diced

2 cloves garlic, crushed with 1 tsp sea
salt

1½ tsp paprika

Salt

The bean soup served in the Senate dining room in Washington is famous; this is one of the many recipes that claims to be 'the' authentic one. It's another hearty, satisfying soup – this quantity will serve four as a lunch or supper.

1. Wash and pick over the beans, put them in a saucepan with cold water to cover. Bring to the boil, boil for ten minutes, then remove from the heat and cover. Let them stand for two hours. Drain and cover with fresh cold water, add the ham and onion, bring to the boil again, and simmer for about an hour and forty-five minutes.
2. Heat the lard, and sauté the potatoes with the crushed garlic and salt until the potatoes just begin to brown. Drain them and add to the hot soup. Taste for seasoning, stir in the paprika, and cook for about fifteen minutes until the potatoes are tender.

Chicken Soup with Kreplach

Serves 4–6

For the soup

Boiling chicken, about 4 lb (2 kg)

2 carrots, scraped and roughly chopped

2 onions, peeled and diced

1 white turnip, scraped and diced

1 stalk celery, roughly cut up

6 black peppercorns

Salt

For the kreplach

8 oz (225 g) chicken livers

1 tsp chicken fat or margarine

1 small onion, very finely chopped

1 egg, size 3

1 tsp parsley, finely chopped

8 oz (225 g) plain flour

Pinch of salt

2 eggs, size 3

1 tbsp oil

No American cookery book could be complete without some of the masterpieces of Jewish cooking. Chicken soup is the subject of many jokes: it's what every good Jewish mother rushes to provide in time of trouble, whether it's someone down with a streaming cold or the family rescued from a burning house. Kreplach are delicious little stuffed dumplings, related in a remote way to Chinese won-ton and Italian ravioli.

1. Cut the chicken into serving pieces, cover with salted water, and bring to the boil, skimming off the scum from the surface as it rises. Add all the other soup ingredients, and simmer until the chicken is tender (about one hour).
2. Remove the chicken, and if you want to serve it as boiled chicken for the main course, keep it warm in a heated casserole in an oven set at 250°F (120°C), Gas 1. Strain the stock, taste for seasoning, cool it quickly, and skim off the fat.
3. Make the *kreplach*: sauté the chicken livers in the margarine or chicken fat until they are lightly browned, remove, and chop finely. Gently brown the onion in the same fat. Whisk the one egg, and mix the onion, parsley, and chicken livers with it. Cool.
4. Make the dumpling dough by sifting the flour and salt, whisking the two eggs with the oil, and mixing with the

flour. Work it well with your hands, and add just enough cold water to make a firm dough. Chill for fifteen minutes, wrapped in plastic film.

5. Roll out the dough very thinly and cut it in 3 in. (8 cm) squares. Put a blob of liver filling on one side of each square, brush the edges with water, fold the dough into a triangle, and pinch the edges well. Let them stand for half an hour. This quantity will make about thirty *kreplach*.

6. Bring a large saucepan of water to the boil, lower the heat to simmering point, cook the *kreplach* gently for about fifteen minutes. Drain and keep hot while you reheat the chicken soup, and put several *kreplach* in each bowl.

MATZO BALLS

Serves 4 in soup

3 eggs, size 3

3 fl oz (75 ml) water

2 oz (50 g) white fat or chicken fat, melted

$\frac{1}{2}$ tsp salt

Freshly ground black or white pepper

3 oz (75 g) matzo meal

This is another of the great Jewish recipes – served in chicken soup – and very filling and comforting.

1. Whisk the eggs with water, fat, salt, and pepper. Stir in the matzo meal and mix very well. Let it stand, covered, about twenty minutes in the refrigerator or cold larder.

2. Form into balls about $\frac{1}{2}$ in. (1·5 cm) in diameter, and drop into freshly made, boiling chicken soup (see above). Cook uncovered for about twenty minutes.

Canadian Bean and Bacon Soup

Serves 4–6

10 oz (275 g) dried white beans, or 2 14 oz (400 g) tins of beans

8 oz (225 g) cooked bacon or gammon

$2\frac{1}{2}$ pt (1·425 litres) cold water

2 tbsp lard or bacon drippings

3 medium potatoes, peeled and diced

1 large onion, coarsely chopped

1 clove garlic, crushed with $\frac{1}{2}$ tsp salt

1 rounded tsp paprika

This is a marvellous recipe from New England, thriftily using up the last scraps from boiled bacon or gammon. You can start with dried haricot beans or do a short-cut edition with tinned Italian cannelini (white haricots). A bowl of bean and bacon soup, with salad, is a very good winter lunch.

1. If using dried beans, wash and pick them over, cover with twice their weight in cold water in a saucepan, and bring to the boil for ten minutes. Remove from the heat and let them stand, covered, for two hours. Drain. Cut the bacon or gammon into smallish dice, and add to the beans with the cold water. Bring to the boil, then simmer for about an hour and a half until the beans are fairly tender. Taste for salt.

If you are using tinned beans, simmer them with the bacon and water for about an hour, then finish as in Step 2.

2. Heat the lard or drippings in a heavy frying pan, and sauté the onions, potatoes, and garlic until soft and slightly browned. Stir into the soup and simmer for another fifteen minutes. Add the paprika and stir well.

Cream of Corn Soup

Serves 6

5 ears of corn *or* two 7 oz (about 350 g) tins whole-kernel corn

3 tbsp butter or good margarine (generous 1 oz or 25 g)

2 medium onions, finely chopped

1 small green pepper, seeded and chopped

¾ pt (450 ml) milk

Salt, freshly ground black pepper

Flaked almonds

2 egg yolks, size 3

¼ pt (125 ml) single cream

This recipe came from a very sophisticated restaurant in Indianapolis, Indiana. Its ancestor is in a handwritten cookery book from a nineteenth-century local farm wife, and omits the almonds.

1. If using fresh corn, strip off all the silk and cut off the kernels. Drain tinned corn well. Heat the butter in a heavy saucepan and sauté the onions and green pepper until limp. Stir in the corn, add milk, and season. Simmer on a low heat for ten minutes. Toast the almonds lightly by spreading them on a sheet of aluminium foil and putting it in a very hot oven for five minutes, or under the grill for three to four minutes – but watch them carefully as they burn quickly.
2. Purée the corn mixture in a blender or food processor until smooth. Whisk the egg yolks, and beat in two tbsps of the hot mixture. Heat the cream almost to boiling and stir into the egg yolk mixture, then blend all this back into the soup. Reheat gently if necessary. Scatter the toasted almonds over each bowl of soup and serve at once.

Corn Chowder

Serves about 6

2 oz (50 g) salt belly of pork, diced

1 medium onion, coarsely chopped

3 medium potatoes, peeled

¾ pt (425 ml) hot water

10 oz (275 g) frozen corn, or tinned whole-kernel corn

Salt, freshly ground black pepper

1¼ pts (700 ml) milk

Optional: cream crackers

This chowder with Hot Biscuits (see p. 154) and a salad can be a whole meal. Dress it up with chopped chives or a scatter of paprika for colour if you like.

1. In a heavy saucepan, on a hot fire, fry the pork until the fat runs. Sauté the onion until limp and soft. Dice the potatoes and stir in, add hot water, and simmer on a low fire, covered, for about half an hour.
2. Stir in the corn, raise the heat, and cook three minutes more. Taste for salt and add more if needed. Add milk, and heat slowly but do not boil. Season liberally with black pepper, and to be completely traditional, break up cream crackers roughly and stir into each soup dish at serving time.

Pennsylvania Dutch Rivvel Soup

Serves 4

1½ pts (775 ml) chicken stock

4 oz (100 g) tinned or frozen whole-kernel corn

1 egg, size 3 or 4

2 oz (50 g) plain flour

¼ tsp salt

'Rivvel', in the Amish country of Pennsylvania from which this recipe comes, means something like 'lumps', and the little dumpling-like bits of dough and the corn give it its name.

1. Bring the chicken stock to the boil and add the corn. Whisk the egg well. Sift the flour and salt together, and stir into the egg to make a soft dough. Dip a teaspoon in cold water, spoon up some of the dough, and with a knife push half-teaspoon bits of the dough off into the boiling stock.
2. Cover, and simmer about fifteen minutes until the soup is a mass of fluffy miniature dumplings.

Cold Courgette Soup

Serves 4–6

12 oz (350 g) courgettes

¾ pt (425 ml) chicken stock

1 tbsp onion, very finely chopped

¾ pt (425 ml) plain natural yoghurt

1 tsp fresh or dried dillweed

1 tbsp chives, chopped

Salt, freshly ground black pepper

Optional: a little fresh dill

1. Trim, peel, and dice the courgettes. Cook in the hot stock with the onion until the courgettes are just tender. Season and mix in a blender or food processor until as smooth as you like it – some prefer it puréed, others like a bit of texture. Cool and mix with yoghurt, dillweed, and chives.
2. Chill, and taste for seasoning. Serve in chilled cups with a few sprigs of fresh dill if you can.

Cold Courgette Soup II

Serves 6–8

4 courgettes about 6 in. (15 cm) long

2 oz (50 g) butter

1 small green pepper, seeded and coarsely chopped

3 medium onions, thinly sliced

1 large clove garlic, crushed

Salt, freshly ground black pepper

2½ pts (1·5 litres) good chicken stock

8 fl. oz (225 ml) double cream

Chopped chives

Optional: 1 tbsp fresh thyme

This is a more luxurious version of the simple cold soup above.

1. Top and tail the courgettes and slice three of them. Heat half the butter in a heavy saucepan and sauté the courgettes, pepper, onions, and garlic on a low flame, stirring, until tender but not brown. Season, add the chicken stock, cover and cook for fifteen minutes.
2. Heat the remaining butter in a frying pan and slice the remaining courgette very thinly. Sauté until just tender but still slightly crisp. Remove and cool.
3. Cool the soup and mix in a blender or food processor. Taste for seasoning. Stir in the cream and courgette slices and chill very well. Sprinkle some freshly chopped chives on each serving, and some fresh thyme if you like it.

Cold Senegalese Soup

Serves 6

2 oz (50 g) butter or good margarine

1 medium onion, finely chopped

2 stalks celery, finely chopped

1 tbsp flour

½ tbsp curry powder (hot or mild, to taste)

1 dessert apple (crisp and firm – not Golden Delicious), peeled and chopped

6 oz (175 g) cooked chicken, finely diced

1½ pts (850 ml) chicken stock

6 tbsp single cream

How ever did a soup like this pick up the West African name of Senegal? Dione Lucas, a French-trained American cookery writer, speculated that it may have been called at one time 'Singhalese', implying that its first home was Sri Lanka (then called Ceylon). Whatever its provenance, it's a cool, rich, pungent golden soup, a delight on a sweltering day. It is very popular in New York, where a temperature of 100°F (38°C), with humidity of eighty per cent, is normal August weather.

1. Melt the butter in a heavy frying pan and sauté the onion and celery until soft but not browned. Stir in the flour and curry powder, and cook, stirring, on a very low heat for about three minutes.
2. Pour the mixture into a blender or food processor, add the diced apple, chicken, and about half a pint (275 ml) of the chicken stock and blend until it is smooth. Return the mixture to the saucepan, stir in the remaining stock, and bring to the boil. Taste, and add some salt if necessary.
3. Cool, then chill, and serve with a tablespoon of cream in each bowl.

Philadelphia Pepperpot Soup

Serves 10–12

1 lb (450 g) honeycomb tripe

3 oz (75 g) salt belly of pork

1 small onion, finely chopped

2 stalks celery, coarsely chopped

1 large carrot, scraped and coarsely chopped

2 cloves garlic, crushed with 1 tsp salt

5 lb (2·25 kg) shin of veal on the bone, cut up

1 bayleaf, broken up

1 tsp crushed red pepper flakes, *or* half a small dried red chili, seeded and finely chopped

½ tsp dried thyme

Freshly ground black pepper

1 potato, about 8 oz (225 g), peeled and diced

This soup, an old favourite from colonial days, reheats very well, so it seems sensible to make it in large quantities. It can be frozen, but thawing and reheating can alter the rich velvety texture. It is literally a meal in itself, made more so by the addition of fluffy dumplings (see p. 64).

1. Wash the tripe and drain it. Cut it in small thin shreds about 1 in. (2·5 cm) long. Dice the salt pork and fry it in a large saucepan or a heatproof casserole until the fat runs. Add the onion and stir until it is soft, but not brown. Add the tripe, celery, carrot, garlic, and salt and cook, stirring, for five minutes.
2. Add the veal shin pieces, bayleaf, red pepper flakes, thyme, and a good grinding of black pepper. Pour in water to cover generously, bring to the boil, cover, and simmer for three hours. Fish out the veal bones, leaving the meat in the soup.
3. Add the potato and cook gently for another hour, until the tripe is completely tender. Stir in the paprika. Make *beurre manié*, stirring the flour into the butter on a small plate, and blend it in pea-size pieces into the soup, stirring well. Cook

1 level tsp paprika

2 tsp flour

2 tsp butter or margarine

$\frac{1}{4}$ pt (125 ml) double cream

until the soup is thickened, and remove from the heat before adding the cream.

If you are having dumplings in the Pepperpot, drop the dough by spoonfuls into the boiling soup before the cream is added, cover tightly, cook for fifteen minutes, remove from the fire, and add the cream.

Szechuan Hot and Sour Soup

Serves 4

3 dried Chinese mushrooms

Half a chicken breast, boned and skinned

2 oz (50 g) bean curd (*tofu*)

1 spring onion (for garnish)

1$\frac{1}{2}$ pts (850 ml) chicken stock

2 oz (50 g) bamboo shoots, tinned

2 tsp soy sauce

$\frac{1}{2}$ tsp caster sugar

$\frac{1}{2}$ tsp salt

1 egg, size 2

1 tbsp cornflour

2 tbsp cold water

1$\frac{1}{2}$ tbsp wine vinegar (red or white)

1 tsp sesame or groundnut oil

Good grinding of black pepper

For many years, American-Chinese cooking was very largely Cantonese, as the first immigrants from China had come from that province. In the past twenty years, however, many other more exciting kinds of Chinese dishes have become very popular, beginning with the Chinatowns of San Francisco and New York, and spreading across the country. This lively soup is one of them.

1. Remove the stems from the dried mushrooms and discard. Soak the mushrooms in hot water to cover for fifteen minutes, then drain and slice. Cut the chicken in thin, small pieces, and cut the bean curd into half-inch cubes (1·5 cm). Slice the spring onion thinly, using both the white and green parts.
2. Heat the chicken stock in a large saucepan, add the mushrooms, chicken pieces, drained bamboo shoots, and bean curd. Bring the soup to the boil and simmer for fifteen minutes. Add soy sauce, sugar, and salt. Whisk the egg, mix the cornflour with the cold water and stir into the whisked egg. Pour in a few tablespoonfuls of the hot soup, mix well, then stir this back into the soup.
3. Remove the soup from the heat, add the vinegar, sesame or groundnut oil, and black pepper. Pour into a heated tureen and float the thin slices of spring onion over the top.

Pumpkin Soup

Serves 6

1$\frac{1}{4}$ pts (700 ml) milk

2 lb (900 g) cooked pumpkin, strained

1 tbsp butter

1 tbsp light brown sugar

Pinch of salt, freshly ground black pepper

3 oz (75 g) cooked lean ham

This is identical to a French recipe, and probably came to New England through Canada. The pumpkin can be steamed or boiled, or tinned.

1. Heat the milk to just below boiling point and stir in the pumpkin, butter, sugar, salt, and pepper. Cut the ham in small thin strips and stir in.
2. Do not let the soup boil, but serve it as soon as everything is heated through.

Creole Shrimp Soup

Serves 4

1 tbsp butter or margarine

½ tbsp flour

1 medium onion, finely chopped

1 lb (450 g) peeled cooked prawns

3 large ripe tomatoes, or 14 oz (400 g) tin of Italian peeled tomatoes

8 fl. oz (225 ml) water

1 small green pepper, seeded and diced

½ tsp dried thyme

1 tsp parsley, finely chopped

Small bayleaf

Good dash of hot pepper sauce or Tabasco

Salt, freshly ground black pepper

This is a very thick and luscious soup that could be the main dish of a meal, with steamed long-grain rice.

1. Melt the butter in a large heavy saucepan, stir in the flour, and cook until it is light brown. Add the onion and sauté on a medium heat until it is pale gold and soft. Stir in the prawns and remove the saucepan from the heat to let it cool slightly.
2. Add all the other ingredients, and bring to the boil, then turn down the heat and simmer for about ten minutes, stirring often to break up the tomatoes. You may need to add about ¼ pt (125 ml) more water at the beginning of Step 2, as tomatoes vary so much in their liquid content.

Boston Clam Chowder

Serves 4–6

Two 7½ oz (210 g) tins of clams

1 lb (450 g) potatoes, peeled and diced

3 thick slices of streaky bacon

1 medium onion, finely chopped

Salt, freshly ground black pepper

¾ pt (425 ml) single cream

Good pinch of dried thyme

½ tsp paprika

This is the veritable New England chowder. There, of course, it would be made with clams freshly dredged from the sea, here, it can be made quite satisfactorily with tinned clams which are now reasonably available. There's a perennial war between the Boston Clam Chowder-ites and the Manhattan Group: the latter dissidents add a few peeled, chopped tomatoes, two tablespoons of butter, and a few broken cream crackers stirred in at the last minute.

1. Drain the clams and chop them, reserving the liquid. Cook the diced potatoes in boiling salted water until they are just soft but not mushy, drain, and reserve the cooking water.
2. Coarsely chop the bacon and fry until crisp in a very hot frying pan, remove, and sauté the onion in the hot fat. In a large saucepan, combine the bacon bits, onion, potatoes, potato water, and the liquid drained from the clams. Bring it to the boil and simmer gently for ten minutes. Taste for seasoning, add the salt and pepper, stir in the cream and chopped clams.
3. Reheat but do not let it boil. At the last minute, put in the thyme, and serve in heated bowls with paprika scattered over each. Water biscuits are the traditional accompaniment.

Oyster Stew

Serves 4–6

16 fl. oz (450 ml) milk

12–16 oz (350–450 g) shelled oysters – the weight to include the liquid from the shells – this could be up to 100 medium oysters

2 oz (50 g) butter (*not* margarine)

Sea salt

4 fl. oz (100 ml) single cream

Freshly ground black pepper

Paprika

This extravagant and extravagantly good soup is as near as I can come to the famous one served in the Oyster Bar of Grand Central Station in New York. It is really only possible to make if you live near a coast where oysters are plentiful and cheap. The cooking time is very short, only until the oysters are heated through.

1. Put the milk, oysters, butter, salt, cream, and quite a lot of black pepper in the top of a large double boiler. Half-fill the bottom part with violently boiling water and put it on a moderate flame. Heat the oyster stew until the milk is really hot, and the oysters have curly edges.
2. Have ready heated deep soup bowls, ladle the soup into them, and dust each serving with a little paprika. Serve Oyster Stew with the best water biscuits you can find. American 'oyster crackers' are tiny, crunchy dry things that don't exist anywhere else, alas, but water biscuits are an excellent substitute.

Mussel Chowder

Serves 4

2½ lb (1·125 kg) mussels, weighed in shells

4 oz (100 g) unsmoked streaky bacon

1 medium onion, finely chopped

1 stalk celery, finely chopped

2 medium potatoes, peeled and diced

1 bayleaf

4 black peppercorns

1 tbsp butter or margarine

1 tbsp flour

1 pt (550 ml) milk

¼ pt (125 ml) single cream

Paprika

A New England recipe, a rather less rich version of Boston Clam Chowder.

1. Discard any mussels which are already open and scrub the rest well, steam in a little water until they open (discard any still closed). Remove from shells. Cut rinds from the bacon and fry them in a small heavy frying pan until the fat runs, then discard them. Dice the bacon and brown it in the fat, stirring so that it does not stick.
2. Sauté the onion and celery with the browned bacon. Put potatoes, onion, celery, bacon, bayleaf, and peppercorns in a small saucepan, cover with water, bring to the boil, and simmer until the potatoes are almost cooked.
3. In a large saucepan, put in the butter, flour, and milk all at once, and cook, stirring, until it comes to the boil and thickens. Turn down the heat and simmer for two minutes. Add the potato mixture with its liquid, and the mussels. Simmer five minutes, taste for seasoning, remove the bayleaf, stir in the cream, and pour into a heated tureen. Scatter paprika over the top of the chowder and serve at once. Add freshly-ground black pepper to taste.

Fish and Seafood

Codfish Balls

1 lb (450 g) salt cod, freshened as right

1 lb (450 g) freshly mashed potatoes

1 egg

1 small onion, finely chopped

Freshly ground black pepper

Oil for deep frying

Salted, dried codfish was a lifesaver for the early settlers in New England, who learned about it from the Indians. New England cod cakes, or codfish balls, are a Sunday-morning breakfast dish in Boston. In America, salt cod can be bought in packets. Here, it is often available as fillets from grocers who have a Spanish, Portuguese, or Caribbean trade. It should be thick and white, not yellow. Soak it in cold water for twenty-four hours, changing the water five or six times. Drain it, and remove the skin and bones.

1. Put the freshened cod in cold water in a saucepan and bring it to a rolling boil. Drain well and discard the water. Flake it and mix with all the other ingredients.
2. Heat the oil to 375°F (190°C) in a deep fryer. Drop the codfish mixture by tablespoonfuls into the oil, and cook until brown, crisp, and 'whiskery'. You will probably have to do this in batches. Drain on kitchen paper and keep warm until all the frying is done.

If you prefer, you can form the codfish mixture into flat cakes and shallow-fry it in about ½ in. (1·5 cm) of hot oil.

New England Codfish Hash

4 medium potatoes, cooked and peeled

1 small onion, finely chopped

1 lb (450 g) cold poached cod or halibut

4 oz (100 g) salt belly of pork, cubed

Salt, freshly ground black pepper, a
  good pinch of cayenne

A very New England dish, this, thriftily using up a few left-over cooked potatoes, some cold poached fish, and a few other things such as salt pork and onions which every Maine or Massachusetts housewife of the eighteenth or nineteenth century would always have had on hand. For modern tastes, freshly-boiled or steamed potatoes, and just-cooked cod or halibut makes a much tastier dish.

1. Chop the potatoes rather coarsely and mix with the chopped onion. Flake the fish or chop it not too finely, and lightly mix it with the potatoes. Heat a heavy frying pan very hot and fry the salt pork cubes until the fat runs. Pick out the crisp fried pork (eat them – to me they are one of the reasons for making this dish), scrape the fish mixture into the hot fat, and stir it lightly but thoroughly.
2. Cook the hash without stirring until the underside is brown – lift it cautiously with a palette knife to check. Fold one side over the other, like an omelette. Serve with Home Made Chili Sauce (see p. 144) if you can, or a good spicy ketchup. Well-drained pickled beetroots are a very 'New England' accompaniment to any plain hash like this.

Devilled Crab

Serves 4

2 oz (50 g) butter (*not* margarine), melted

3 oz (75 g) onion, finely chopped

Half small green pepper, seeded and chopped

2 tbsp parsley, finely chopped

¾ pt (400 ml) rich béchamel sauce (see below)

1 tsp dry mustard

Good pinch of cayenne

1 lb (500 g) cooked crabmeat, mixed white and brown

3 oz (75 g) fresh breadcrumbs, mixed with 1 tbsp melted butter

I've found seventeen recipes for devilled crab in my collection, but this is the one (loosely adapted from a recipe of the great James Beard) that seems to please everyone.

Preheat oven to 425°F (220°C), Gas 7.
1. Melt the butter in a heavy frying pan, sauté the onion and green pepper until soft but not brown. Mix with the parsley, béchamel, mustard, cayenne, then lightly fold in the crabmeat, taking care not to break it up.
2. Gently heap the mixture into shells or ramekins. Divide the buttered crumbs between them, and bake about twelve to fifteen minutes until golden and bubbling.

RICH BÉCHAMEL

Makes a scant pint (550g)

2 oz (50 g) butter or good margarine

4 tbsp flour

8 fl. oz (225 ml) milk

8 fl. oz (225 ml) double cream

Salt, freshly ground *white* pepper

Melt the butter, blend in the flour, and remove the pan from the heat. Slowly add the milk and cream, stirring until smooth. Return to a low heat, and cook, stirring with a wooden spoon and reaching all around the sides and bottom of the pan, until the sauce is smoothly thickened.

Chesapeake Crab Cakes

Serves 4

1 lb (450 g) crabmeat, fresh or a very good frozen kind

2 tbsp, more or less, of mayonnaise

1 tbsp Dijon mustard (or to your taste)

1 tsp parsley, very finely chopped

1 egg, size 3 (or for frozen crabmeat, about 1½ tbsp beaten egg)

Scant 1 tbsp butter, melted

½ tbsp very good vegetable oil

This is an adaptation of a very old recipe from the 'Eastern Shore' of Maryland. Backfin lump crabmeat from Maryland is perhaps the most delicately-flavoured, and desirable, of all the American varieties. On the West Coast, in Oregon and Washington, there are the great Dungeness crabs with legs so big that the meat from a single leg will make a crab salad for four people. In Florida, cracked stone crab is one of the local delicacies. However, for any recipe like crab cakes, the Maryland variety is the one of choice. The fresh crabmeat sold by good fishmongers in every part of Britain seems to me to be very much like the Maryland crab. This recipe is pure extravagance, I'm afraid, unless you live near the sea. It softens the blow a bit to use half-white and half-brown crabmeat. If you are using frozen crab, which is much 'wetter' in texture, I suggest that you cut down the amount of mayonnaise a bit, and perhaps use only half a beaten egg instead of a whole one – this is a matter of experimentation to obtain a mixture that is soft and workable for frying, but is in no way limp and damp.

1. Pick out all the membranes and stiff bits from the crabmeat, and with your fingers gently mix it with the mayonnaise, mustard, parsley, and well-beaten egg. Flour your hands well, and working quickly and lightly, make eight flattish balls from the mixture. On a floured surface, flatten each one out to a cake about $2\frac{1}{2}$ in. (6 cm) in diameter, and quite flat and thin. This size is purely arbitrary: if you find it more convenient make sixteen smaller cakes, or six, or nine. But I have found that a crab cake larger than about 3 in. (7·5 cm) is hard to fry.

2. Heat the oil and butter together in a heavy, large frying pan until it sizzles, but do not let it brown. Quickly sauté the cakes on each side, drain them on kitchen paper, and keep them warm until all the crab cakes are made. Please – only lemon wedges or slices to go with this delicate dish: the coarse red tomato sauces and tartare sauce may go well with fish fingers, but as you have paid the price of gold for crabmeat, the flavour must stand alone.

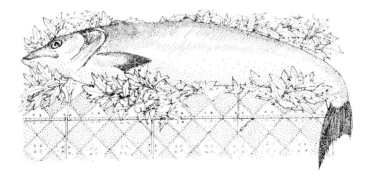

Fish Parmigiana

Serves 4

4 cod steaks, coley fillets, or halibut

8 oz (225 g) homemade tomato sauce (p. 147), *or* Napolitan sauce (see Appendix)

Salt, freshly ground black or white pepper

2 oz (50 g) Parmesan cheese, grated

Scant 1 oz (25 g) melted butter

San Franscisco's Italian colony has innumerable good ways of serving fish – this is a very quickly cooked dish and makes even rather dull fish fillets delightful.

Preheat oven to 425°F (220°C), Gas 7.

1. Put the fish fillets or steaks in a shallow ovenproof dish and season with salt and pepper. Spread on the tomato sauce and sprinkle the cheese evenly over the sauce. Pour on the melted butter.

2. Bake for about fifteen to twenty minutes, until the fish flakes easily.

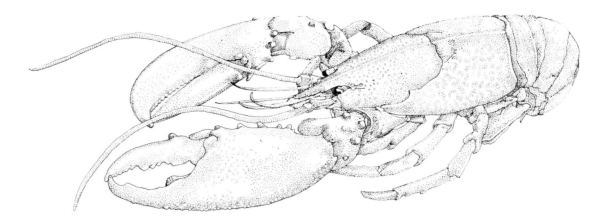

Lobster Newburg

Serves 4

Two 2 lb (1·8 kg) lobsters, killed and
cleaned

2 oz (50 g) butter (*not* margarine)

4 tbsp olive oil

8 fl. oz (225 ml) dry white wine

3 tbsp brandy

6 fl. oz (175 ml) fish court bouillon or
light chicken stock skimmed of all
fat

½ pt (275 ml) single cream

1 oz (25 g) beurre manié (see p. 42)

1. Cut the lobsters in halves. Heat the butter and oil in a
large deep frying pan, but do not let it brown. Toss the
lobster pieces in the pan until the shells redden and the meat
is lightly browned. Remove, and keep warm on a hot platter.
2. Turn up the heat under the frying pan, add the wine and
brandy and boil rapidly until it reduces to half its original
volume. Lower the heat, stir in the court bouillon or stock,
add the cream, and return the lobster pieces to the pan.
Cover and simmer on very low heat for ten minutes.
3. With a slotted spoon, take out the lobster pieces and pick
the meat from the shells. Put it in a warmed casserole.
Simmer the sauce until it is slightly reduced, then stir in the
pieces of beurre manié. When it is smoothly thickened, taste
for seasoning, stir the sauce into the lobster, and serve at
once. Toast triangles or crisp, hot French bread are the usual
accompaniments.

Baked Breaded Fish

Serves 6

1 tbsp salt

8 fl. oz (225 ml) milk

1½ lb (675 g) fish fillets

3 oz (75 g) fine dry breadcrumbs

½ tsp fresh rosemary, finely chopped, or
a good pinch of dried rosemary

2 oz (50 g) melted butter

½ tsp or more paprika

Thinly sliced lemon

Preheat oven to 475°F (245°C), Gas 9.
1. Mix the salt and the milk. Cut the fish into serving-sized
pieces. Thoroughly mix the breadcrumbs with the rosemary.
Dip the fish first into milk and then roll it in the crumbs.
2. Put the fish in a buttered shallow dish and pour on the
melted butter. Bake near the top of the oven for about twelve
to fifteen minutes. Scatter the paprika over the fish, and
serve with lemon slices.

*Opposite Seafood coast to coast. Top Chesapeake crab
cakes (Maryland); Centre Halibut baked with Spinach
(Oregon); Bottom Oysters Bienville (Louisiana)*

Oregon Baked Halibut with Spinach   *Serves 4–6*

1½ lb (675 g) halibut steaks

2 oz (50 g) butter

½ pt (275 ml) milk

1 oz (25 g) plain flour

½ tsp salt

Freshly ground black pepper

Pinch of freshly grated nutmeg

2 oz (50 g) Parmesan cheese, grated

10 oz (275 g) packet of frozen chopped
   spinach, cooked and drained

½ tsp paprika

Preheat oven to 300°F (150°C), Gas 2.
1. Remove the skin and bones from the halibut and cut into serving-sized pieces. In a small heavy saucepan combine butter, milk, flour, salt, pepper, and nutmeg. Bring to the boil, stirring well, then turn down the heat and simmer, stirring, another minute or two until the sauce is thick and smooth. Stir in half the grated cheese.
2. Mix the spinach with half the sauce and spread it on the bottom of a shallow baking dish. Arrange the fish pieces on the spinach, and pour on the remaining sauce. Sprinkle with paprika and remaining cheese, and bake about twenty-five to thirty minutes.

Fish Fried in Cornmeal   *Serves 4*

4 fillets of white fish (cod or large
   whiting)

2 oz (50 g) fine yellow cornmeal

Salt, freshly ground black pepper

Mixture of butter and clean bacon
   drippings, about 3–4 oz (75–100 g)

1. Mix cornmeal, salt, and pepper, and turn the fish fillets over in the mixture until well coated. If you do this an hour before cooking, and chill the fish, the coating seems to stay on better.
2. Heat the fat in a frying pan until it sputters but do not let it brown, lay the fish fillets in and cook them about three to five minutes, browning on one side, then turn over and cook them for a slightly shorter period. Remove the fish at once, drain on kitchen paper, and serve with lemon wedges.

Salmon or Tuna Loaf   *Serves 6*

12 oz (350 g) cooked or tinned salmon
   or tuna

1 egg, size 3

¼ pt (125 ml) evaporated milk

4 oz (100 g) soft fresh breadcrumbs

1 small onion, finely chopped

¼ tsp celery salt

½ tsp salt

Dash of hot pepper sauce

Pinch of dry mustard

*Opposite Chicken from the exotic to
the simple. Top Chinese Chicken with
Peanuts; Right Iowa Chicken Pie; Left
Chicken Divan*

Preheat oven to 350°F (180°C), Gas 4.
1. Flake the salmon in a mixing bowl. Whisk the egg; stir the milk and breadcrumbs into the salmon, add the egg and remaining ingredients, and mix lightly with your hands.
2. Butter a bread tin or oblong ovenglass casserole and lightly spoon the mixture into it. Bake for about forty minutes until the centre is firm. Serve with Dill Sauce (see p. 146), or a simpler one which is merely 8 oz (225 g) of béchamel heated and mixed with two tablespoons of flaked almonds.

This very simple dish can be made rather fancier by separating the egg, mixing the yolk with the salmon mixture, whisking the egg white stiff, and folding it in lightly.

Western Baked Salmon

Serves 6 or more

3 lb (1·35 kg) salmon

1 medium onion, thinly sliced

4 rashers lean streaky bacon

2 tsp prepared mustard

Salt, freshly ground black pepper

This is a recipe from Washington State.

Preheat oven to 350°F (180°C), Gas 4.
1. Remove the head of the salmon and clean well. Spread the inside with mustard, salt, and pepper. Tuck the slices of onion into the cavity.
2. Put the salmon in a buttered baking dish, cover with the bacon strips, and bake for forty-five minutes, or until fish flakes easily when a fork is inserted.

Scalloped Tuna (or Salmon)

Serves 4

12 cream crackers

3 stalks celery, leaves removed

2 eggs, size 3

Two 7½ oz (210 g) tins tuna or salmon

1 medium mild onion, finely chopped

1 medium green pepper, seeded and diced

1 small clove garlic, crushed with 1 tsp salt

4 oz (100 g) butter or margarine, melted

Freshly ground black pepper

Scant 1 oz (25 g) cold butter or margarine

A nice little all-American favourite, quickly and easily made.

Preheat oven to 375°F (190°C), Gas 5.
1. Coarsely crush the cream crackers with a rolling pin. Dice the celery. Lightly whisk the eggs. Drain the tuna or salmon, break it into chunks, and gently mix with the onion, green pepper, and celery, stir in the crackers, garlic, and melted butter. Season with black pepper.
2. Butter a 1½ pt (1 litre) casserole, put the mixture into it, and cut the cold butter in flakes over the top. Bake half an hour until it is brown and bubbling.

Tuna and Noodles

Serves 3–4

4 oz (100 g) good egg noodles

7½ oz (210 g) tin of good tuna

10½ oz (285g) tin condensed mushroom soup

Milk or single cream

Salt, freshly ground black pepper

A little freshly grated nutmeg

One of these dishes that is so simple that the recipe is very seldom written down – it's comforting, cheap, and something to fall back on when you don't feel like real cooking.

Preheat oven to 350°F (180°C), Gas 4.
1. Cook the noodles in boiling salted water until tender and drain well. Put them in a casserole, flake the tuna lightly, and mix it in. Dilute the condensed soup with about 3–4 fl. oz (75–100 ml) milk or cream, and stir in well. Season.
2. Bake for about thirty to forty-five minutes until the top is brown and bubbling. Serve with a salad – crisp greens mixed with cooked sliced beans and some tinned red pimientos, perhaps – and something light and tart for a pudding, nothing rich or heavy.

New England Seafood Stew

Serves 4, 6, or 8

4 oz (100 g) salt belly of pork, or a piece of unsmoked bacon

2 oz (50 g) butter or margarine

$\frac{1}{2}$ tsp salt

$\frac{1}{2}$ tsp paprika

$\frac{1}{2}$ tsp celery salt

1 tsp Worcestershire sauce

$\frac{3}{4}$ pt (425 ml) water or fish stock

1 lb (450 g) cod or halibut steaks

8 oz (225 g) cooked, peeled shrimp or prawns

8 oz (225 g) cooked lobster meat

1 pt (550 ml) milk

8 fl. oz (225 ml) single cream

Freshly ground black pepper

This is one of those meals in a tureen which is characteristic of New England cooking. It is very filling, and can be served as a starter, fish, or main course.

1. Dice the salt pork or bacon, and parboil it in boiling water for ten minutes. Drain and dry well, then fry it until it is crisp and brown. Drain off the fat and set the pork aside.
2. In the large saucepan, bring the butter or margarine, seasonings, and water or fish stock to the boil, add the fish, shrimp, and lobster and simmer until the fish is tender. Add the reserved pork, the milk and cream and reheat but do not boil. Grind on black pepper to your taste.

Oysters Bienville

Serves 4 as main course, 6 as starter

6 spring onions, white parts only

3 oz (75 g) mushrooms

Generous 1 oz (25 g) butter

6 cooked, shelled, large prawns

3 tbsp flour

3 fl. oz (75 ml) chicken stock

2 fl. oz (50 ml) dry vermouth

4 fl. oz (100 ml) single cream

1 egg yolk, size 3

Good pinch of salt

Pinch of cayenne

24 large oysters, with their bottom shells

Rock salt, at least 2 lb (900 g)

Topping:

3 oz (75 g) soft breadcrumbs

2 oz (50 g) Parmesan cheese, grated

With its mixture of prawns and oysters, this is one of the most luxurious dishes ever produced by that Mecca of good food, New Orleans.

Preheat oven to 450°F (220°C), Gas 8.
1. Chop the spring onions finely; chop the mushrooms, but not too finely. Melt the butter in a medium-sized heavy saucepan, and stir-fry the spring onions and mushrooms for about three minutes. Chop the prawns and add to the frying pan, stir-fry one minute more.
2. Blend in the flour, chicken stock, vermouth, and cream, and heat gently, stirring, until the mixture is just thickened. Remove at once from the heat.
3. Whisk the egg yolk lightly and stir in a tablespoon of the mushroom mixture, then stir this into the frying pan. Season with salt and cayenne.
4. Put a layer of rock salt in two roasting tins (about 13 × 9 in. or 28 × 23 cm), and put in the oven for five minutes. Arrange the oysters on their shells in the salt, bedding them in firmly. Spoon some of the mushroom mixture on top of each, and sprinkle on some of the topping. Bake for about seven minutes until brown and bubbling, and serve immediately.

San Francisco Oyster Loaf

Serves 4

18 oysters, shelled

Seasoned flour

6 oz (175 g) butter

Loaf of good firm unsliced white bread

Chopped parsley

Lemon wedges

In the gold-rush days of California, many a husband slinking home from a binge in the bars made his peace with an oyster loaf; and the self-same story is told of goings-on in New Orleans before the War Between the States. Wherever all this took place, the recipe is identical. These days, the guilty conscience would be about the cost and not the cause.

Preheat oven to 350°F (180°C), Gas 4.
1. Cut a thick slice from the top of the loaf and scoop out the crumbs, leaving a wall about ½ in. (1·5 cm) thick all around. Put the loaf, and the top piece separately, in the oven and let them get quite brown, brushing several times inside the loaf and lid with about half the butter, melted.
2. Heat the remaining butter in a frying pan, toss the oysters in seasoned flour, and fry them quickly. Sprinkle with the parsley and fill the loaf with oysters, pour on the hot butter, clap on the lid. Serve in slices, with lemon wedges.

Hangtown Fry

Serves 4–6

8 large oysters, opened

3 oz (75 g) plain flour

6 eggs, size 2

3 tbsp single cream

1 oz (25 g) Parmesan cheese, grated

4 tbsp parsley, finely chopped

Salt, freshly ground black pepper

This is a recipe from the early gold-rush days in California, when oysters were two a penny and the appetites of the miners were exceedingly robust – this was a breakfast dish for them. Today, we would consider it an extravagant but delicious Sunday supper.

1. Dip the oysters in the flour and let them stand for a few minutes. Heat the butter until very hot in a frying pan, but do not let it brown, and sauté the oysters lightly. Whisk the eggs, cream, cheese, parsley, and seasoning, pour over the oysters, lower the heat, and cook until the egg mixture is set and looks like custard. Heat the grill very hot.
2. Slip the frying pan under the grill for about one minute, until the top of the Hangtown Fry is lightly gilded. Serve from the frying pan or, a little more elegantly, slip the 'Fry' out onto a heated serving plate. If you like, you can decorate it all with strips of crisply fried streaky bacon.

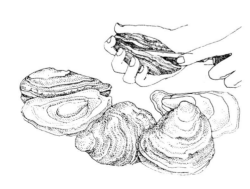

Avocado Stuffed with Shrimp

Serves 4

2 large ripe avocados

2 tbsp lemon juice

1 medium tomato, peeled

½ tsp caster sugar

½ tsp salt

Freshly ground black pepper

2 spring onions, finely chopped

½ tbsp cider vinegar

½ tbsp cold water

2 tbsp olive oil

8 oz (225 g) cooked, peeled shrimp or
  prawns

Watercress

1. Cut the avocados in half and scoop out the pulp, being careful not to break the shells. Brush the inside of shells with the lemon juice (reserving any unused juice to add to the dressing). Dice the tomatoes and the avocado pulp. Mix all the remaining ingredients except the prawns and watercress.

2. Pour the dressing over the tomato and avocado, and lightly mix in the prawns. Taste, and if necessary add some lemon juice. Pile the mixture into the shells, decorate with some well-washed watercress sprigs, and chill, covered with plastic film, until ready to serve.

Baton Rouge Gumbo

Serves about 6

1 lb (450 g) okra

Scant 1 oz (25 g) margarine

2 tbsp flour

1 large onion, finely chopped

2 stalks celery, diced

1 bayleaf

14 oz (400 g) tin Italian peeled tomatoes

1 tbsp parsley, finely chopped

¼ tsp ground thyme

1 large clove garlic, crushed

2 pts (generous litre) water or chicken
  stock

1 tsp sea salt

1 lb (450 g) cooked, peeled shrimp or
  prawns

Freshly ground black pepper

Optional: Filé powder if available, or 1
  tsp cornflour mixed with 1 tbsp cold
  water

A gumbo is a highly-seasoned Creole dish which takes its name from a derivation of the Bantu word for okra. 'Filé powder', a staple of Louisiana cooking, is a seasoning and thickening ingredient made of powdered sassafras leaves – if you should ever acquire any from an American source, be advised that it must be added very gradually to the boiling liquid after the pan has been removed from the heat, otherwise the whole thing will turn into a stringy mass. In default of filé powder, thicken the gumbo with about a teaspoon of cornflour.

1. Wash okra well, then trim the ends. Heat the margarine in a large heavy saucepan or flameproof casserole, and stir in the flour until it is a smooth paste. Add the okra, onion, celery, bayleaf, tomatoes with their juice, parsley, thyme, and garlic. Bring slowly to the boil, lower the heat and cook for ten minutes, stirring often. Add the water or stock and salt, cover, and simmer for an hour.

2. When it is the consistency of a thick soup, add the shrimp and cook for another ten minutes. If it seems too thick, put in another ½ pt (125 ml) of hot water or stock when you add the shrimp. Taste for seasoning, add pepper. Stir in the cornflour if needed; if using filé powder, sprinkle that into each serving at the table.

Shrimp à la Creole

Serves 6

6 tbsp plain flour

3 oz (75 g) butter or good margarine

1 pt (550 ml) water

2 bayleaves, broken up

3 good dashes of Tabasco

2 lb (900 g) unshelled, raw prawns

6 spring onions, coarsely chopped

4 oz (100 g) home-made tomato sauce
(see p. 147)

2 small green peppers, seeded and
coarsely chopped

1 tsp sea salt, or to taste

Freshly ground black pepper

Along with gumbo, jambalaya, Oysters Rockefeller, and French Market Crullers, Shrimp in the Creole style is a central pillar of Louisiana cooking. There are endless recipes, but as this comes from a great cook from Baton Rouge, I take it to be the classic 'rule'.

1. Begin with a classic brown *roux*: preheat the oven to 250°F (120°C), Gas 1. Spread the flour on a baking sheet and brown it, shaking the sheet occasionally, until it is medium brown but not scorched. Heat the butter in a large frying pan and stir in the flour, then cook it – stirring well – until it is the colour of hazelnuts. Turn off the heat.

2. Prepare a *court-bouillon*: bring the water, bayleaves, and Tabasco to the boil in a large saucepan, and simmer for ten minutes. Add the prawns and simmer for five minutes. Remove and peel the prawns, strain and reserve the liquid.

3. Heat the *roux* again, add the onions, tomato sauce, and green pepper. Cook for fifteen minutes on a moderate heat. Measure out 6 fl. oz (175 ml) of the *court-bouillon*, and stir it into the vegetable mixture. Simmer, stirring from time to time, about forty-five minutes. Add more of the *court-bouillon* if the mixture seems too thick. Taste, add the salt, and as much pepper as you like.

4. Stir in the shrimp and cook for ten minutes on a low heat. Add more Tabasco just before serving if you have real 'Creole' tastes. Serve with steamed long-grain white rice.

Henry's Jambalaya

Serves 4–6

4 oz (100 g) good butter or margarine

1 medium onion, finely chopped

2 cloves garlic, crushed

Scant 2 tbsp flour

2 tbsp parsley, finely chopped

2 small bayleaves

Good pinch of thyme

$\frac{1}{4}$–$\frac{1}{2}$ tsp chili seasoning (not Indian chili
or cayenne. See Appendix)

2 tbsp tomato purée

3 medium tomatoes, peeled and
coarsely chopped

1. Heat the butter in a large heavy saucepan, gently sauté the onion and garlic until they are pale gold but not brown. Stir in the flour, and cook the mixture on a very low flame, stirring often. Add the parsley, bayleaves, thyme, chili seasoning, tomato purée, chopped tomatoes, and the seasonings. Simmer on fairly low heat for ten minutes.

2. Take the saucepan from the heat, cover, and let it stand in a cool place for about two or three hours (or even overnight).

3. Add the beef stock, bring the jambalaya to the boil, lower the heat, and simmer for two hours on the lowest possible flame. Take the saucepan off the cooker, cover, and let it stand two to three hours. In fact, if it is more convenient for you, you can do Steps 1 and 2 up to this point the day before serving, and keep the jambalaya in a cool place overnight before proceeding.

Salt, freshly ground black pepper

Large dash of Tabasco or other hot
  pepper sauce (to your taste, of
  course)

2 pts (generous 1 litre) beef stock

8 oz (225 g) long-grain rice

1½ lb (675 g) peeled cooked shrimp, *or*
  1 lb (450 g) shrimp and 8 oz (225 g)
  cooked crabmeat

4. Bring the jambalaya to the boil once more, stir in the rice, and simmer on a low to medium heat for fifteen minutes, until the rice is cooked but not mushy. You will have to pick out a few grains from time to time and try them – various kinds of rice from the Patna to the American Carolina rice available in Britain will need different cooking times. Add the seafood and raise the heat so that the mixture is gently simmering, and cook only five minutes longer.

Shrimp Boiled in Beer

Serves 4–6

2 lb (900 g) prawns in their shells

1 pt (550 ml) lager

1 clove garlic, peeled and cut in slivers

2 tsp sea salt

2 bayleaves

1 tsp celery seed

Juice of one small lemon

4 black peppercorns

Dash of Tabasco or other hot pepper
  sauce

This wonderful Southern dish takes only about ten to fifteen minutes from beginning to end. My Louisiana friends say that it's a perfect dish for a barbecue party, as apparently it can be cooked over a charcoal fire, on a very hot hibachi grill, or even on the less picturesque Camping Gaz picnic cookers. Note that when Americans say 'beer' they are talking about something more like lager than even the lightest English beer. And English – or Irish or French – prawns are the closest thing to the big American Gulf Coast shrimp.

1. Wash the prawns well. In a large saucepan, bring all the other ingredients to the boil, add the prawns, and bring the mixture back to the boil. If you are cooking in your kitchen, lower the heat until the mixture just simmers. On less-controllable heat such as a charcoal grill or hibachi, you may need to use a 'flame tamer' or asbestos pad under the saucepan, or devise some way to raise the pan from the source of heat so that the contents are simmering but not boiling. Cook for two to three minutes, until the prawns turn pink.

2. Each person peels his or her own prawns, of course – provide plenty of paper table napkins, or some damp face flannels – and you may want to have quite a lot of French bread on hand to be dipped into the sauce. Lemon wedges, or a little jug of lemon juice, and a big black-pepper mill, are the traditional accompaniments. You might also add a bowl of 'drawn butter' (see p. 145).

3. To serve cold: let the shrimp cool in their beer sauce, drain them, and provide a huge bowl of mayonnaise sharpened with lemon juice or spiked with garlic.

Poultry

Acapulco Chicken

Serves 4

3 lb (1·35 kg) chicken, cut into joints

2 small cloves garlic, crushed with
  1 tsp sea salt

1 medium onion, finely chopped

1 tsp dried oregano

1 tsp (or more, to taste) chili seasoning

½ pt (275 ml) dry sherry

Boiling water

16 black olives, stoned

Preheat oven to 350°F (180°C), Gas 4.

1. Wash and dry the chicken pieces, put in a deep casserole, add garlic, chopped onion, chili seasoning, oregano, and 4 tbsp of the boiling water. Cover tightly and cook for forty-five minutes. Add the sherry, olives, and more salt if needed. Bake until the chicken is tender.
2. Thicken the gravy, if you like, after removing the chicken and olives to a warmed serving dish, by stirring in about 2 tbsp of beurre manié (see p. 42), returning to the oven, and cooking another ten minutes.

Chicken Divan

Serves 4

4 lb (just under 2 kg) chicken

1½ tsp salt

2 tbsp flour

12 fl. oz (350 ml) milk

Scant 1 oz (25 g) butter

Freshly grated nutmeg

2 8 oz (225 g) packages of frozen
  broccoli, *or* 1 lb (450 g) fresh broccoli

3 fl oz (75 ml) double cream

2–3 oz (50–75 g) Parmesan cheese,
  grated

4 oz (100 g) Hollandaise sauce

1½ tsp dry sherry

½ tsp Worcestershire sauce

This is a creation from the nineteen-twenties, originally from a New York restaurant named Divan Parisian, and is now a favourite from the East Coast to the Midwest to California. It's most luxurious when made only with meat from the breast and thigh of the chicken. This recipe begins with poaching a whole chicken – use the choicest portions for Chicken Divan, and make the rest into something equally delicious such as Chicken Hash (see p. 68). Turkey escalopes may be used in the same way.

1. Simmer the chicken in just enough water to cover, with the salt, until it is tender but not cooked to rags. Cool the chicken in the stock. Drain and reserve the stock for another dish.
2. Combine the butter, flour, and milk in a small heavy saucepan, and bring it to the boil, stirring vigorously. Lower the heat and simmer for two minutes, stirring. Stir in the nutmeg. Keep the sauce hot while you cook the broccoli until it is just tender. Drain it very well. Whisk the cream stiff.
3. Preheat the oven to 450°F (230°C), Gas 8. Slice the breast and thigh meat from the chicken. Arrange the broccoli in a single layer in a shallow oven dish, and sprinkle it with some of the Parmesan. Lay in the chicken slices. Stir the Hollandaise sauce into the warm sauce of Step 2, add the sherry and Worcestershire sauce, and fold in the whipped cream. Pour the sauce over the chicken and scatter with the remaining Parmesan. Bake on the top shelf of the oven about five to ten minutes and serve at once.

Baked Chicken with Herbs

Serves 4

3 lb (1·35 kg) chicken joints

1 egg, size 2 or 3

2 fl. oz (50 ml) milk

4 oz (100 g) soft fresh breadcrumbs

Salt, freshly ground black pepper

3 tsp fresh tarragon, chopped, or 1½ tsp
    dried tarragon

3 tsp finely chopped parsley

3 tsp finely chopped chives

3 fl. oz (75 ml) lemon juice

3 oz (75 g) butter or margarine

3 fl. oz (75 ml) dry sherry

Preheat oven to 300°F (150°C), Gas 2.

1. Wash and dry the chicken pieces. Beat the egg and milk together. Combine the breadcrumbs, salt, pepper, and herbs. Dip the chicken pieces first in the egg mixture, then roll in the crumbs until well coated. Put the chicken in a shallow baking dish.

2. Melt the butter with the lemon juice and sherry. Cover the baking dish tightly with aluminium foil and bake, on the middle oven shelf, for twenty minutes, then baste with the butter mixture every twenty minutes for another hour.

3. Increase the oven heat to 400°F (200°C), Gas 6, remove the foil, and turn the chicken pieces over. Put the dish on the top rack of the oven and cook another fifteen to twenty minutes until it is lightly browned. Add a little more butter and sherry or water, if necessary, to make a sauce in the dish.

Bott Boi

(Pennsylvania Dutch Chicken Pie)

Serves 6

For the chicken

3 lb (about 1·35 kg) chicken, cut in
    serving pieces

4 medium potatoes, peeled and diced

1 large stalk celery, coarsely chopped

1 large mild onion, peeled and diced

2 tbsp parsley, chopped

1 tsp sea salt

½ tsp freshly ground black pepper

Good pinch of saffron, if possible

For the noodles

7 oz (200 g) plain flour

½ tsp salt

1 tsp baking powder

2 tbsp lard

1 egg, size 3

This is really a version of chicken and dumplings – with freshly made egg noodles (a great speciality of the good cooks in the Amish country of Pennsylvania) cooked in the boiling chicken broth. You can either make your own noodles or buy them.

1. Poach the chicken pieces, in just enough water to cover, for an hour until just tender. Add the potatoes, celery, onion, parsley, salt, pepper, and saffron. Cover and simmer for twenty minutes. Remove chicken and strip the meat from the bones.

2. While the chicken is cooking, make the noodles. Sift the dry ingredients together, cut in the lard until it feels like coarse crumbs, stir in the beaten egg, and mix lightly with a fork. Add enough cold water to make a dough that will hold together. Roll it out paper-thin on a floured board, and cut into 2 in. (5 cm) squares. Lay them on a large clean cloth for half an hour or so.

3. Strain the broth and bring it back to the boil in the washed-out saucepan. Drop the noodles, one by one, into the boiling broth and let them cook until just tender. Return the chicken and vegetables to the broth and reheat, and serve from a big heated tureen or from the saucepan.

Brunswick Stew

2 oz (50 g) butter or margarine

3 lb (1·35 kg) chicken, or chicken pieces

2 medium onions, thinly sliced

¾ pt (425 ml) chicken stock

8 oz (225 g) tinned Italian peeled tomatoes, drained *or* two ripe tomatoes, peeled and chopped

2 tbsp parsley, finely chopped

3 tsp salt

1 tbsp Worcestershire sauce

Dash of hot pepper sauce

1 bayleaf

Optional: 4 fl. oz (100 ml) Madeira

8 oz (225 g) corn kernels (fresh, or tinned whole-kernel)

Optional: 8 oz (225 g) okra

8 oz (225 g) frozen small broad beans

3 tbsp plain flour

The original recipe for Brunswick Stew, from Tennessee, I think, specifies squirrel or wild rabbit, but most people now make it with chicken or with thawed, frozen rabbit pieces.

1. Heat the butter in a big flameproof casserole or heavy saucepan, brown the chicken pieces on all sides. Add the onion and cook until soft and limp but not brown.
2. Add the stock, tomatoes, parsley, salt, Worcestershire sauce, hot pepper sauce, bayleaf, and Madeira (if used). Bring to the boil. Cover, lower the heat, and simmer for half an hour.
3. Add the tinned or fresh corn, washed and trimmed okra if used, and the frozen broad beans, stir well, and cook for another twenty minutes. Taste for seasoning. Take out about three tablespoons of the hot liquid and blend to a paste with the flour, gradually stir it back in, raise the heat, and simmer until the sauce is slightly thickened, stirring from time to time.

California Spitted Chicken

4 oz (100 g) butter

3 tbsp fresh rosemary, chopped

3 tbsp fresh tarragon, chopped

(*or* 2 tbsp dried rosemary, crumbled and mixed with an equal amount of dried, crumbled tarragon)

¼ pt (125 ml) white wine

3½–4 lb (1·8–2 kg) roasting chicken

1 tsp sea salt

Freshly ground pepper

Rôtisserie cooking, indoors or out, is a great California thing, and this delicious, delicate recipe combines fresh herbs and a dry white California wine from the Almaden vineyards.

1. Mix the butter with the herbs and blend well. (If using dried herbs, marinate them in about 2 tbsp of wine for an hour, strain, and reserve the liquid.) Sprinkle the inside of the chicken with salt and pepper and spread about 1 tbsp of the herb butter wherever your fingers can reach. Loosen the skin over the breast and press in about 1 heaped tbsp of herb butter.
2. Truss the bird and secure it on the spit. Melt the remaining herb butter and mix with the wine. Brush the chicken well with this mixture. Roast for about two and a half hours, basting often; put a pan under the chicken to catch the delicious drippings. Carve the chicken and pour a little of the herb-and-wine juice over each piece.

Chicken and Dumplings

Serves 4

2½ lb (1·125 kg) chicken joints

1 medium onion, coarsely chopped

½ bayleaf

2 slices of lemon

Salt, freshly ground black pepper

1 stalk of celery, with leaves

1 carrot, scraped and thinly sliced

Boiling water

Dumpling batter

4 oz (100 g) flour

1½ tsp baking powder

½ tsp salt

1 egg, size 2

About 3 fl. oz (75 ml) milk

1. Wash the chicken joints, put them in a heavy saucepan, and add the onion, bayleaf, celery, and carrot. Sprinkle with salt and pepper, and pour on boiling water just to cover. Cover the pan and bring to the boil. Lower the heat and simmer about an hour, until the chicken is tender. Remove the lemon slices and bayleaf.
2. To make the dumplings: sift the flour, baking powder, salt, and nutmeg together. Beat the egg with the milk and add to the dry ingredients to make a rather stiff dough. Add a little more milk, cautiously, if the mixture is dry.
3. Raise the heat under the saucepan until the mixture comes to the boil, drop in the dumplings by teaspoonfuls, cover tightly, and simmer for fifteen minutes. Serve at once.

Chinese Chicken with Peanuts

Serves 4 with other Chinese dishes

2 whole chicken breasts, or 4 thighs

1 egg white, size 3

1 tbsp plus 1 tsp cornflour

2 tbsp soy sauce

3 tbsp water

1 tsp light brown sugar

½ tsp salt

1 tsp cider vinegar

1 tsp sesame oil (see Appendix),
   or 1 tsp sesame seeds

4 spring onions

½ pt (275 ml) groundnut oil

¼ tsp dried crushed red pepper flakes

2 oz (50 g) salted peanuts

1. Cut the chicken in ½ in. (1·5 cm) cubes. Mix the egg white, 1 tbsp cornflour, 1 tbsp soy sauce, 1 tbsp water, and stir well. Mix with the chicken cubes, cover, and let stand in the refrigerator for half an hour.
2. Stir together the sugar, salt, remaining cornflour, remaining soy sauce, vinegar, sesame seeds or oil, and 2 tbsp water, and set them aside. Put a big strainer on top of a heatproof bowl. Cut the spring onions in thin slices.
3. Heat the groundnut oil in a *wok* or heavy frying pan to 300°F (150°C). Stir the chicken mixture well, tip it into the frying pan, and stir-fry until the chicken cubes are opaque. Pour the oil and chicken into the strainer. Reheat the frying pan and return 2 tbsp of the strained oil. Put in the red pepper flakes, spring onions, and chicken, and stir-fry for one minute.
4. Stir in the cornflour and vinegar mixture, and cook and stir on a high heat for about one more minute, until the sauce suddenly thickens and clears. Stir in the peanuts and serve very hot, with steamed rice, Chinese Plum Sauce, and Dragon Mustard (see p. 146).

Chickenburger

Serves 6

1 lb (450 g) raw chicken, boned

1 lb (450 g) pie veal, well trimmed

3 thin slices of white bread, crusts removed

4 fl. oz (100 ml) milk

6 tbsp sherry

¼ pt (125 ml) single cream

Salt, freshly ground black pepper

Freshly grated nutmeg

The original name of this pleasant unpretentious dish is 'chicken cutlet à la Pojarski'. It's a New York recipe, and was christened with its American name in an inspired moment by Craig Claiborne of The New York Times. *It should be served with some chilled soured cream, or, if you like it better, a hot mushroom sauce.*

1. Cut the chicken and veal into small pieces, and mince finely in a meat mincer or with a very sharp knife. Don't attempt this in a food processor as it makes too fine and soft a mince. Soak the bread in the milk, squeeze it dry, and mix with the meat.
2. Add all the other ingredients, and form the mixture into flat oval or round cakes. Grill under a very hot grill, or sauté in hot butter, browning well on both sides.

Iowa Chicken Pie

Serves 4–6

For the chicken

5 lb (about 2·5 kg) boiling fowl, cut up

1 large carrot, scraped and cut up

1 large onion stuck with 5 cloves

2 tsp salt

8 oz (225 g) mushrooms

2 oz (50 g) butter

Additional 2 oz (50 g) butter or margarine

3 tbsp flour

6 fl. oz (175 ml) single cream

For the biscuit dough

8 oz (225 g) white or light brown flour

2½ tsp baking powder

1 tsp salt

3 oz (75 g) margarine

About 6 fl. oz (175 ml) milk

1. Wash the chicken pieces and put in a large saucepan with water to cover, with the carrot and onion. Bring slowly to the boil, and skim any scum from the surface. Cover, and simmer gently about an hour. Add salt, and continue to simmer until the chicken is tender.
2. Remove the chicken and keep warm. Take the meat off the bones, in as large pieces as you can manage. Sauté the mushrooms in 2 oz (50 g) of butter and add to the chicken.
3. Strain the broth and skim the fat. Bring the broth to the boil and cook until it is reduced by about one quarter. Melt the additional 2 oz (50 g) of butter in a small heavy saucepan, add the flour, and cook, stirring, until smooth. Then add about 12 fl oz (350 ml) of the chicken stock, and the cream. (Strain the remaining stock and freeze.) Cook the sauce until it is smooth and thick. Preheat the oven to 450°F (230°C), Gas 8. While the sauce is cooking, make the biscuit dough.
4. Sift the flour, salt, and baking powder together. With a knife or pastry blender, cut in the fat until it feels like coarse breadcrumbs.
5. Add the milk slowly, stirring lightly with a fork, to make a soft but not sticky dough. Knead on a floured board until smooth. Pat, do not roll out, to about ½ in. (1·5 cm) thick, in a shape that will fit your casserole.
6. Put the chicken, mushrooms, and the sauce in a deep casserole. Top with biscuit dough and bake about twenty minutes, until the crust is browned.

Chicken Fricassee

Serves 6

4 lb (just under 2 kg) boiling chicken

1 large onion

1 large carrot, scraped

3 or 4 sprigs of parsley

6 black peppercorns

2 tsp sea salt

Generous 1 oz (25 g) butter or margarine

3 tbsp plain flour

6 fl. oz (175 ml) single cream

1. Cut up and wash the chicken. Put in a large saucepan with the onion, carrot, parsley, peppercorns, and water to cover. Bring slowly to the boil, then lower the heat, cover, and simmer until the chicken is tender but not falling off the bones. Add the salt about an hour after cooking starts.

2. Remove the chicken, put in a very slow oven – 200°F (95°C), Gas ½ or less. Strain the broth and skim the fat. Measure out about ¾ pt (450 ml) of broth. Melt the butter, stir in the flour, and very gradually add the hot broth. Stir in the cream, and cook, stirring, until the sauce is thick and smooth. Taste for seasoning. Pour over the chicken and serve with fluffy mashed potatoes or good egg noodles.

Florida Lime Chicken

Serves 6

For the marinade

4 fl. oz (100 ml) fresh or bottled lime juice *not* Lime Juice Cordial

4 fl. oz (100 ml) good salad oil (not olive oil)

1 small onion, very finely chopped

1 tsp sea salt

Dash of hot pepper sauce

6 chicken portions

Salt, freshly ground black pepper

This is also a good recipe for outdoor cooking over a charcoal fire.

1. Blend the sauce ingredients and marinate the chicken pieces, turning from time to time, for about two hours. Strain off the sauce and reserve.

2. Preheat the oven to 400°F (200°C), Gas 6. Put the chicken pieces on a rack in a shallow roasting tin, and roast for about an hour. Turn the chicken once. Spoon the reserved barbecue sauce over the chicken five or six times during roasting.

Sagebrush Chicken

Serves 6

For the chicken

1 oz (25 g) plain flour

1½ tsp ground sage

1½ tsp salt

Plenty of freshly ground black pepper

2 lb (900 g) chicken joints

1 fl. oz (25 ml) groundnut oil

This recipe comes from Amarillo, Texas, and is sometimes called Yorkshire Chicken Pudding, since the batter that bakes with the chicken is rather like the English pudding mixture.

1. Mix the 1 oz (25 g) flour, sage, salt, and pepper in a plastic or paper bag, and toss the chicken joints in it until well-coated. Heat the oil and brown the chicken, turning often, on a moderate heat, until it is almost completely cooked. Put in

For the pudding

4 oz (100 g) plain flour

1 tsp baking powder

1 tsp salt

3 eggs, size 3

12 fl. oz (350 ml) milk

2 oz (50 g) melted butter or margarine

a deep 3 pt (1½ litre) casserole. This step can be done in advance, and the chicken refrigerated, but bring it back to room temperature before baking. Preheat oven to 350°F (180°C), Gas 4.

2. For the pudding, sift the 4 oz (100 g) flour with the baking powder and salt. Whisk the eggs, milk, and melted butter together, stir in the flour and whisk until very smooth. Pour it over the chicken and bake, uncovered, about an hour until the 'pudding' is well-risen and brown.

Okra and Chicken Gumbo
Serves about 4

1 tbsp butter or margarine

12 oz (350 g) cooked ham

1½ lb (675 g) chicken pieces

1 small onion, finely chopped

½ tsp dried red pepper flakes, *or* one
very small chili pepper

12 oz (350 g) tomatoes, peeled, plus ¼ pt
(125 ml) tomato juice *or* 12 oz (350 g)
tinned Italian tomatoes

8 oz (225 g) okra

2½ pts (1·5 litres) water

Small bayleaf

Salt, pepper, good pinch of cayenne

1. Heat the butter in a large heavy saucepan and sauté ham and chicken, covered, for about fifteen minutes. Stir in the onion, red pepper flakes, and peeled, chopped tomatoes or well-drained tinned tomatoes (save the juice). Cook about five minutes, stirring from time to time.

2. Wash the okra well, top, tail, and slice it. Add to the ham and the chicken mixture and simmer for about ten minutes, stirring. Then add the tomato juice, water, and bayleaf, season, and cook slowly, covered, for about an hour.

3. Remove the meat from chicken bones, discard the bones, and stir the meat back into gumbo. Reheat if necessary, and serve with fluffy white rice.

Roast Chicken with Ham Stuffing
Serves 6

5 oz (125 g) butter or margarine

1 medium onion, finely chopped

3 stalks celery, with leaves, coarsely
chopped

Salt

8 oz (225 g) cooked ham, chopped

6 oz (175 g) soft fresh breadcrumbs

Freshly ground black pepper

Good pinch of dried tarragon

4 lb (just under 2 kg) roasting chicken

5 fl. oz (125 ml) white wine

Preheat oven to 400°F (200°C), Gas 6.

1. Melt 3 oz (75 g) of butter in a small heavy saucepan and cook the onion until soft and translucent but not brown. Add the celery and salt and cook for about one minute. Mix with the ham, breadcrumbs, black pepper, and tarragon, and stir in the remaining 2 oz (50 g) softened butter.

2. Stuff the chicken loosely and secure the vent with skewers or cocktail picks. Roast for twenty minutes on its back. Pour the wine into the tin, turn the chicken over, baste with the wine and drippings. Continue to roast, basting occasionally, until the thigh joint moves easily in its socket when gently pulled.

Chicken Hash

Serves 4

1 medium onion, finely chopped

1 level tbsp butter

4 fl. oz (100 ml) dry white wine

¾ pt (450 ml) béchamel sauce (see p. 48)

Freshly grated nutmeg

12 oz–1 lb (350–450 g) cooked chicken,
    cut in small cubes

2 oz (50 g) flaked almonds

2 egg yolks, size 3

4 fl. oz (100 ml) dry sherry

4 fl. oz (100 ml) single cream

This recipe came to me from the chef of the old Ritz-Carlton Hotel in New York, long since vanished, and it's the best of any of the many chicken hash recipes I have ever made or tasted. It should be served on crisp toast triangles with, if possible, a border of purée of peas, somewhat on the dry side.

1. Sauté the onion in hot butter in a large saucepan until translucent but not brown. Add the wine, stir, and then stir in the béchamel. Grind a little nutmeg (about a saltspoon of it, if you want to measure) into the sauce. Stir in the chicken and almonds.
2. Put the saucepan on an asbestos mat and simmer very slowly for about ten minutes. Beat the egg yolks with sherry and cream, stir into the chicken, and cook for another five minutes until just heated through. Taste for seasoning.

Chicken in the Pot

Serves 4

1 oz (25 g) butter or chicken fat

4 lb (just under 2 kg) boiling fowl

3 rashers streaky bacon, without rinds

1 onion, thinly sliced

1 carrot, thinly sliced

2 stalks celery, roughly chopped

Salt, freshly ground black pepper

2 fl. oz (50 ml) dry white wine or water

1. Heat the butter or chicken fat in a large heavy frying pan and brown the chicken gently on all sides. Remove, pour away the fat (strain and save for another dish). Put the bacon in the bottom of a heavy flameproof casserole, set the chicken in, surround with the vegetables, season, and pour in the wine.
2. Tightly lid the casserole, set it on a medium heat until you can hear a gentle bubbling, then lower the heat to the minimum and cook for at least three hours. At the end of that time, remove the lid and move the chicken leg, the thigh should move freely and the juices should run clear with no tinge of pink. When the chicken is cooked, remove to a heated platter, surrounding it with its vegetables.
3. Skim the fat from the gravy, and thicken it slightly with beurre manié if you like (see p. 42). Carve the chicken and put it in a warmed casserole, pour in the gravy, and serve with boiled or steamed potatoes.

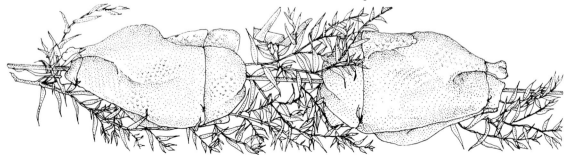

Chicken Jambalaya

Serves 6

3 lb (1·8 kg) chicken, or chicken joints

3 oz (75 g) plain flour

Salt, pepper, a good dash of cayenne

3 level tbsp lard (generous 1 oz or 25 g)

3 large onions, finely chopped

5 stalks celery, coarsely chopped

2 cloves garlic, crushed

Half small red sweet pepper, seeded and chopped

12 oz (350 g) long-grain rice

½ pt (275 ml) lager

1 pt (550 ml) water

2 level tsp salt

1. Cut the chicken into joints and toss in seasoned flour. Melt the lard in a large heavy frying pan and brown the chicken pieces on all sides. Remove. In the same fat, kept hot, cook the onions, garlic, celery, and pepper until softened.
2. Put the chicken joints back in the frying pan, cover, and cook slowly for about half an hour until the chicken is tender and no red juices run when the thickest portion is pierced with a fork. Add the rice, and cook, stirring, for two minutes. Add lager and water, and stir well. Add salt. Cover, and cook another half an hour until the rice is soft.

Southern Barbecued Chicken

Serves 4

Two 2½ lb (1 kg each) chickens, split in half for grilling, with backbones removed

Salt, freshly ground black pepper

3 fl. oz (75 ml) salad oil (groundnut or soya)

10 tbsp ketchup

4 fl. oz (100 ml) cider or white wine vinegar

8 tsp Worcestershire sauce

3 oz (75 g) light or dark brown sugar

1 tbsp dry mustard

2 tbsp chili seasoning (see Appendix)

1 tsp fresh ginger root, grated, or ½ tsp ground ginger

1 clove garlic, finely chopped

1 oz (25 g) butter or margarine

2 thick slices lemon

Note from my friend Harris Jackson of Baton Rouge, Louisiana: 'This has all the ingredients of a traditional barbecue sauce plus ginger which is an interesting addition. One important point: if you haven't the charcoal-grill facilities, put together the sauce, simmer for ten minutes, then pour over the chicken cut in serving pieces. Let it marinate for half an hour, an hour, as you please, then bake in a 350°F (180°C), Gas 4 oven until done, turning once or twice. Just as good as the outdoor one.'

1. Pound the four halves of the chicken with a meat hammer or the bottom of a heavy frying pan, to make them lie flat for grilling. Sprinkle with salt and pepper, and rub all over with oil.
2. Mix all the remaining ingredients and cook in a saucepan over a medium heat until smooth and well-blended. This can be done well in advance, and the sauce and chickens refrigerated until you are ready to barbecue.
3. Prepare the grill or *hibachi* (there should be no flames, and the charcoal should be white-hot). Brush sauce over the skin of the chicken halves and put them skin-side facing the heat. Cook for about ten minutes, turn, and baste the other side. Continue turning and basting every ten minutes, until the chickens are completely cooked. Brush the remaining sauce over them at the very end.

Day-Before Duck

Serves 6

Two 5 lb (2·25 kg each) ducks, ready to roast

2 tsp salt

Freshly ground black pepper

5 oz (125 g) onion, finely chopped

1 large clove garlic, crushed

1 lb (450 g) mushrooms

2 fl. oz (50 ml) olive oil, or olive and groundnut oil mixed

2 oz (50 g) butter

2 tbsp plain flour

8 fl. oz (225 ml) chicken stock

I think this is an Italian recipe, but no one can tell me for sure. It's a very good two-stage dish, as most of the preparation can be done twenty-four hours before cooking time: it was given me by a New York friend who does a balancing act with two jobs, two sons, two houses, and about two thousand hungry friends.

Preheat oven to 375°F (190°C), Gas 5.

1. *The day before:* Rub the ducks well with salt and pepper. Set them on a rack in a large roasting tin and roast for two hours, spooning or syphoning off the fat from the roasting tin about every half hour. Cool the ducks and cut into serving pieces. Refrigerate, wrapped in plastic film, overnight. Mix the onion and garlic and wrap tightly in plastic film and refrigerate.

2. *Forty-five minutes before serving:* Slice the mushrooms thinly, and mix with the onion and garlic. In a large heavy frying pan, heat the oil with half the butter, and sauté the vegetables until the mushrooms are soft. Stir from time to time. Put the vegetables and the duck in a very large heavy saucepan or flameproof casserole. Melt the remaining butter in the frying pan, slowly stir in flour until smooth, then gradually add the chicken stock and stir well. Pour over the duck, and simmer for about half an hour. Serve with rice or good egg noodles.

73rd Street Duck

Serves 2–3

3½–4 lb (1·5–2 kg) duck

2 stalks celery, coarsely chopped

1 large tart apple, peeled and quartered

6 oz (175 g) apricot jam

2 oz (50 g) runny honey

2 tbsp strained orange juice, *or* 1 tbsp orange liqueur

This recipe came from a Czechoslovakian restaurant on the Upper East Side of New York, hence the rather odd name. This combination of duck, apricot, and honey seems to be uniquely Central European.

Preheat oven to 450°F (230°C), Gas 8.

1. Wipe and dry the duck and stuff the cavity with the celery and apple. Put it on a rack in a roasting tin and set it in the hot oven. Reduce the heat at once to 350°F (180°C), Gas 4, and cook until it is tender, allowing about twenty minutes to the pound.

2. Mix the apricot jam, honey, and orange juice or liqueur and spread most of it onto the duck. Return it to the oven and cook another ten to fifteen minutes until the glaze is dark gold. Every five minutes, brush on more of the reserved glaze, until it is used up.

The stuffing of this bird is rather uninteresting and gets fat-saturated – but eat it if you feel so inclined.

Roast Turkey and the Trimmings

Americans roast turkey in very much the same way the British do, but it is served with slightly different 'extras' – no bread sauce, no rolls of bacon, no tiny sausages. Instead, there is giblet gravy and usually two kinds of cranberry sauce.

GIBLET GRAVY

Giblets from the turkey

Drippings from turkey-roasting tin

1–2 oz (25–50 g) plain flour

Salt, freshly ground black pepper

4 fl. oz (100 ml) top of milk

1. While the turkey is roasting, wash the giblets well, trim them, and simmer in about one pint (550 ml) of slightly salted water until tender. Strain off the stock and set aside. Chop the giblets.
2. Put the turkey on a warm serving dish to rest until it is carved. Spoon about four tbsp of fat from the roasting tin into a saucepan (add butter if there is not sufficient fat). Pour one pint (550 ml) of the giblet stock into the roasting tin and swirl it around, picking up the brown bits. Stir the flour into the fat in the other pan and cook until browned, stirring often. Gradually stir in the stock from the roasting tin and cook until thickened and smooth.
3. Stir in the giblets, salt, and pepper, bring to the boil, remove from the heat, and blend in the milk.

CRANBERRY MOULD

$\frac{3}{4}$ pt (425 ml) water

1 lb (450 g) cranberries

12 oz (350 g) caster or granulated sugar

1. Bring the water and cranberries to the boil and cook for five to ten minutes, until all the cranberries have popped open. Strain them through a fine sieve, pressing pulp and juice through.
2. Return to the saucepan, add the sugar, and boil for about three minutes. Pour the sauce into a decorative mould, cool, and refrigerate for three to four hours until the cranberries have set. Unmould at serving time.

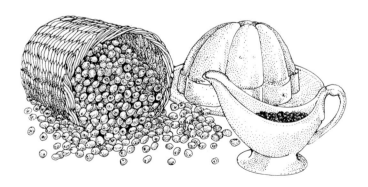

WHOLE CRANBERRY SAUCE

6 oz (175 g) caster sugar

8 fl. oz (225 ml) water

10 oz (275 g) cranberries

1. Mix the sugar and water, bring to the boil, and boil for five minutes. Add the cranberries which have been washed and picked over. Cook for five minutes, or until the cranberries stop popping. Do not stir.
2. Cool in the saucepan, and turn into a pretty glass dish for serving.

ALL-AMERICAN BREAD STUFFING
Enough for a 5–6 lb (2·25–2·7 kg) bird

4 oz (100 g) butter or margarine

1 small onion, finely chopped

1 stalk celery, with leaves, chopped

1¼ lb (550 g) dry, coarse breadcrumbs (or cubes)

1–2 tsp sage leaves *or* 1 tsp dried sage

½–1 tsp salt

Freshly ground black pepper

Water or giblet stock to moisten

1. Heat the butter in a frying pan and sauté the onion and celery until they are just limp but not brown. In a large bowl, mix together the breadcrumbs (or cubes), sage, salt, pepper, then stir in the onion, celery, and butter. Handle it lightly, and add just enough liquid to give a slightly moist but not soggy feeling.
2. Stuff the cavity of the chicken or turkey, and lightly stuff the neck skin, if any of the mixture is left over.

For a *Southern Stuffing*, instead of breadcrumbs, use crumbled cornbread (see p. 159), and bacon drippings instead of butter.
For a *Sausage Stuffing*, brown 4 oz (100 g) of good sausage meat in a little butter, remove, and sauté the onions and celery as above. Finish as in the basic recipe.

There are at least twenty other regional recipes for stuffings, ranging from Maryland Oyster, to Oregon Apple, Florida (with grated orange peel), and even Mexican (with chopped olives and rice), as well as the more conventional chestnut and mushroom stuffings.

Turkey Triangles
Serves 6

1 small onion, finely chopped

3 tbsp butter or margarine (generous 1 oz or 25 g)

½ pt (275 ml) milk

Good pinch of curry powder

Salt, freshly ground black pepper

1 lb (450 g) cooked turkey, coarsely chopped

Preheat oven to 425°F (220°C), Gas 7.
1. Blanch the onion in boiling water for two minutes, drain well. In a small heavy saucepan, mix the butter, flour, and milk, and bring to the boil, stirring constantly. Simmer for one minute after the sauce reaches boiling point. Add the onion, curry powder, salt, and pepper. Mix with the turkey and cool. Taste for seasoning.

8 oz (225 g) shortcrust pastry

A little beaten egg

2. Roll out the shortcrust pastry as for a pie and cut into six even-sized squares. Put a heaped tablespoonful of turkey mixture on one half of each square, moisten the edges with cold water, and press together firmly. Cut a decorative slash in the top of each. Brush with beaten egg.

3. Put the triangles on lightly buttered baking sheets and bake about half an hour; look at them after fifteen minutes and lower the heat if they are browning too swiftly. Serve with a bowl of cranberry sauce or jelly.

Viennese Turkey Escalope

Serves 4

1 lb (450 g) boned turkey breast

Salt, freshly ground black pepper

1 egg, size 3

2 tbsp water

4 tbsp plus 1 tsp groundnut or soya oil

5 tbsp plain flour

4 oz (100 g) fine soft breadcrumbs

4 thin slices of lemon

4 rolled anchovy fillets

Finely chopped parsley

2 oz (50 g) butter

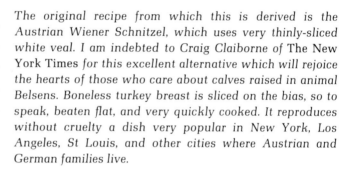

The original recipe from which this is derived is the Austrian Wiener Schnitzel, which uses very thinly-sliced white veal. I am indebted to Craig Claiborne of The New York Times *for this excellent alternative which will rejoice the hearts of those who care about calves raised in animal Belsens. Boneless turkey breast is sliced on the bias, so to speak, beaten flat, and very quickly cooked. It reproduces without cruelty a dish very popular in New York, Los Angeles, St Louis, and other cities where Austrian and German families live.*

1. With a very sharp knife, thinly slice the turkey breast, against the grain of the meat, into four equal pieces. Put them between pieces of greaseproof paper and lightly beat them out very thin and flat, without breaking the flesh. Sprinkle with a little salt and pepper.

2. Whisk the egg lightly with water, 1 tsp oil, more salt and pepper, and pour it into a shallow dish. Put the flour and the breadcrumbs separately on two flat plates. Dip each turkey slice into flour, egg, and crumbs alternately, turning over to coat both sides. Pat lightly with the flat side of a heavy cook's knife, to make the crumbs adhere. Heat the oven to 350°F (180°C), Gas 4.

3. Heat 2 tbsp oil in a heavy frying pan and cook the escalopes one at a time, about a minute and a half on each side, until golden brown. Remove and keep warm on a heated platter in the oven until all are finished. Add more oil to frying pan if necessary. Put a lemon slice on each escalope and a rolled anchovy fillet in the centre of the lemon. Dust with parsley.

4. Melt the butter in the hot frying pan and heat until it is lightly browned, pour at once over the turkey, and serve.

Meats

Chili Con Carne Verde

Serves 6

3 lb (1·35 kg) good stewing steak

Lard for frying

8 oz (225 g) tinned green chilis, drained

3 garlic cloves, crushed with 1 tsp salt

1 lb (450 g) tomatoes, peeled, or 1 lb (450 g) tinned Italian peeled tomatoes, drained

¾ pt (425 ml) broth from the meat

This recipe, from New Mexico, is the most wonderful change from the more usual red chili. It is said that the first chili dishes were cooked by the missionaries who followed the conquistadores from Spain to Mexico, and into what later became the American Southwest. They found the hot little red and green chilis grown by the Indians, and the rest is history. Like most chilis, this is better the second day.

1. Simmer the meat in enough water to cover it until it is just tender but not over-cooked. Drain, reserving the broth. Dry the meat, cut it in 1 in. (2·5 cm) cubes, heat the lard very hot in a big frying pan, and sauté the meat until it is quite brown.
2. Scrape out the seeds from the chilis, handling with rubber gloves and throw the seeds away. Chop the chilis finely, then stir them, the garlic, and tomatoes into the broth. Put the meat in a large casserole or heavy saucepan, pour in the tomato mixture, and simmer slowly, covered, until the meat is tender. Taste for seasoning. Serve with red kidney beans and a dish of cooked cornmeal.

Rockbottom Chili

Serves 4

½ tbsp lard

1 lb (450 g) lean minced beef

1½ tbsp chili seasoning (see Appendix)

1 large clove garlic, crushed

1 medium onion, finely chopped

4 tbsp plain flour

¾ pt (425 ml) water

1½ tsp salt

Freshly ground black pepper

½ tsp ground cumin

14 oz (400 g) tin red kidney beans

I must preface this recipe by saying that real chili purists insist that chili is never made with minced meat, and never includes beans. This one commits both sins. However, it comes from San Antonio, Texas, where certainly they should know about chili. It's agreeably spicy but not burning hot, and can be made in less than half an hour. For chilis made the traditional way, go on to Three Alarm Chili.

1. Heat the lard very hot in a heavy frying pan and brown the meat, stirring it often. Push it to one side of the pan and if necessary add a little more lard. Stir in the chili seasoning and cook for one minute, then blend with the meat. Add garlic and onion, and flour, mix well, pour in the water, and bring to the boil. Add salt, pepper, and cumin.
2. Simmer on a low heat, stirring once in a while, for about fifteen to twenty minutes. Add the undrained tinned kidney beans, and simmer until they are heated through. Serve with fluffy white rice.

Three-Alarm Chili

Serves 8–10

4 fl. oz (100 ml) olive oil, or olive and soya oil mixed

4 lb (just under 2 kg) good braising beef

2 oz (50 g) wholewheat flour

2 oz (50 g) Texas chili seasoning (see Appendix)

2 tsp dried oregano

2 tsp ground cumin

3 large cloves garlic, crushed with 2 tsp sea salt

2 pts (1·125 litres) beef stock

Freshly ground black pepper

In American parlance, a three-alarm fire is one that is raging out of control. Very descriptive of the intense heat and flavour of this recipe from Amarillo, Texas. Start it the day before it is to be served, as it is even tastier if reheated. It must cook at least four or five hours, on the very lowest simmer, or in an electric slow-cooker as long as ten to twelve hours. Texans say that a real chili is always made like this with cubed beef, never with mince, and that beans are to be served on the side and not mixed in.

1. Heat oil in a large, heavy frying pan. Cut the meat in 1 in. (2·5 cm) cubes, and brown them, in batches, very well. Remove the meat as it is browned and drain on kitchen paper. You may need more oil, it all depends on the meat.
2. Put the meat in a huge, heavy casserole with a tight lid, stir in the flour and chili seasoning, and turn it over and over with a big spoon until the meat is well coated. Add the oregano, cumin, garlic, salt, and beef stock. Bring it to the boil, cover, and simmer very slowly for four to five hours or even longer.
3. Taste for salt, and add freshly ground black pepper just before serving.

Accompany this with a big dish of yellow cornmeal (see Polenta, p. 110), cooked red kidney beans, some sliced, very ripe tomatoes and, of course, plenty of cold lager.

I am told that this chili freezes well, but that it may need more chili seasoning and salt stirred in after thawing and before reheating.

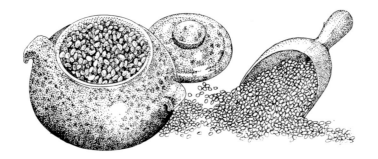

Tamale Pie

Serves 6

2 tbsp salad oil (groundnut for choice)

1 medium onion, chopped

1 clove garlic, crushed

1 medium green pepper, seeded and coarsely chopped

1 lb (450 g) lean beef, minced

½ lb (225 g) lean pork, minced

28 oz (793 g) tin Italian peeled tomatoes, drained

4 oz (100 g) black olives, pitted

1–1½ tsp chili seasoning

1 tsp salt, or to taste

2 level tbsp yellow cornmeal

1¼ pts (750 ml) boiling water

6 oz (175 g) yellow cornmeal

12 oz (350 g) tin whole-kernel corn

2 oz (50 g) sharp Cheddar cheese, grated

1. Heat the oil in a heavy frying pan, sauté the onion, garlic, and green pepper until soft. Remove, increase heat, and brown minced meats lightly, stirring. Add the tomatoes, olives, seasoning, the two tbsp cornmeal and cook slowly for an hour. Preheat oven to 350°F (180°C), Gas 4.

2. In boiling water, cook the 6 oz (150 g) cornmeal until thickened, then stir in the whole-kernel corn with its juices.

3. Butter a casserole or large deep pie dish, pour in the corn and cornmeal mush. As it cools, shape it to look like a thick pie crust, and then fill it with the meat mixture. Sprinkle with grated cheese and bake about half an hour until bubbly.

Swiss Steak

Serves 4

1½ lb (675 g) topside, cut about 1½ in. (4 cm) thick

About 2 tbsp flour

Salt, freshly milled black pepper

About 1½ tbsp butter and oil, mixed

1 large onion, thinly sliced

1 tbsp soy sauce

One of those all-American recipes that pops up everywhere, under various names including Grandmother's Steak, Smothered Steak, and Chuckwagon Steak. It can be simmered on top of the cooker, or casseroled in the oven.

1. Cut the meat in serving-sized pieces and slash the fat along the edges. With a meat hammer, pound in the flour, salt, and pepper until the steak is flattened and the flour well beaten in. Heat a large, heavy frying pan very hot, put in the butter and oil, and, when it is spitting but not brown, put in the steak and brown it very well on both sides.

2. Put the meat with the onion slices in a heavy saucepan or casserole, pour about ¼ pint (125 ml) of hot water into the frying pan, swirl it around, scrape up the brown bits, and pour it all over the meat. Add the soy sauce. Cover tightly and simmer about one and half hours until meat is tender. Taste for seasoning. The gravy will be bright brown, and very full of flavour, and should not need any more thickening.

If you prefer to do it in the oven, preheat to 325°F (165°C), Gas 3, and cook, tightly covered, for about an hour and a half.

The National Hamburger

*While the origin of the hamburger is undoubtedly German –
in Larousse Gastronomique, there's a recipe for 'bifteck à
l'Hambourgeoise', subtitled 'a German steak' – it is just as
undoubtedly America's national dish. I've read that the idea
of a meat patty inside a hamburger bun (rather like a bap)
was introduced at the St Louis World's Fair in 1904, where
many a fast-food creation was born, including ice-cream
cones! Chains of hamburger shops quickly spread across the
country, vying with each other for size, juiciness, and variety
of 'relishes' served alongside – from the humble ketchup
bottle on to pickled cucumbers, tomatoes, 'hamburger
relish', potato chips (crisps), and so on. Then it went up-
market, and in good restaurants is elegantly described as
'Hamburger Steak', or 'Grilled Minced Beef'. Cheeseburgers,
blue-cheese-burgers, tomato-and-cheese-burgers, now the
variety has become endless.*

*Nothing is simpler to make at home, nothing more
delicious in its own unpretentious way – equally, nothing is
nastier than an over-cooked hamburger. Having seen served
to hapless customers in Britain some of the most appalling
concoctions labelled, brazenly, hamburgers – thin, grey, and
squashed between two flattish rolls – I burn with an
evangelical flame to describe real hamburgers. No bread or
breadcrumbs. No chopped onion. Nothing but good, freshly
minced, lean beef with enough fat to make it juicy. Once
you've established the ground-rules, you can indulge in any
fancy-work you like.*

For each person, you will need from 4 to 8 oz (100 to 225 g) of
that good minced beef. Shape lightly into a cake about 1 in.
thick by 4 in. across (2·5 × 10 cm). Heat a heavy frying pan
(preferably well-seasoned cast iron) so hot that it looks
dangerous. Sprinkle a thin layer of salt evenly over the
surface; it will begin to brown at once. Add the beef, cook
until it is well-browned. Turn it over. For a *rare* hamburger,
cook about one more minute, lowering the heat to medium.
For *slightly better-done*, cook four minutes. For *well-done*,
six minutes, turning once more. Remove, season with freshly
ground black pepper. That's all.

If you have a grill that you can make very hot, with an
evenly distributed source of heat, by all means grill the
hamburgers, as this usually makes a fine dark, crusty
exterior – but watch them closely as they can catch fire
easily. Charcoal-grilled meat is delicious but unless you can
put a pan under them you will lose the excellent drippings.

Don't be tempted to buy round steak or fillet or such
luxuries for hamburgers – they are too lean and the taste is a

bit sawdusty. Good chuck, or even lean braising steak, minced or ground by an obliging butcher, is your best bet. If you can cut away all the tendons and connective fibres from shin of beef, and mince it yourself, the flavour is perfection, but it is a tricky and time-consuming job. Despite the joys of a food processor, I have found that mincing beef for hamburgers is the one thing it doesn't do well – the texture is too fine and even, and the patties crumble in the cooking.

There are many ways of varying the basic hamburger recipe, and here are a few.

HAMBURGER AU POIVRE

Serves 4

2 lb (900 g) beef, minced

4 level tsp coarsely ground black pepper

4 level tsp butter

Worcestershire sauce and hot pepper sauce to taste

1 tbsp lemon juice

Chopped parsley

Chopped chives

1. After shaping the raw beef patties, press the pepper evenly all over the meat and let them stand in the refrigerator for half an hour.
2. Cook hamburgers as above. Then put one level tsp of butter on each hamburger in the pan, add some Worcestershire sauce and some hot pepper sauce, and stir in the lemon juice.
3. Put the hamburgers on a hot serving plate, lower the heat, swish the sauce around, and scrape up the brown bits with a wooden spoon. Pour over the hamburgers, and sprinkle with parsley and chives.

RED WINE HAMBURGERS

Serves 4

1¼ lb (550–75 g) lean beef, minced

4 fl. oz (100 ml) red wine

1 heaped tbsp chives, finely chopped

Pinch of dried thyme

Salt, freshly ground black pepper

1 oz (25 g) butter

1. Mix the meat with 2 fl. oz (50 ml) of the wine, chives, thyme, salt, and pepper and let stand at room temperature for an hour. Shape into patties.
2. Heat the butter in a heavy frying pan and sauté the hamburgers for about one minute on each side. Add the remaining 2 fl. oz (50 ml) wine and cook gently for two more minutes on each side, or longer if you like them better done. Taste for seasoning, put the hamburgers on a hot serving plate, and pour on the sauce.

MADALYNNE REUTER'S HAMBURGERS WITH CAPERS

Serves 4

1½ lb (675 g) lean beef, minced

2 oz (50 g) capers, drained

3 tbsp iced water

Salt, freshly ground black pepper

Mix the meat with the capers and iced water, let stand half an hour at room temperature. Heat a heavy frying pan very hot, and coat it with a thin, even layer of salt, put in the hamburger patties and brown on one side on a high flame, turn, and cook for one or two minutes more depending on the degree of done-ness you like.

Hemingway's Hamburgers

Serves 4

2 lb (900 g) best-quality lean beef, minced

4 fl. oz (100 ml) cheap red wine

2 tbsp capers, drained

1 medium onion, very finely chopped

1 tsp sage

1 tsp oregano

1 tsp chili seasoning

2 eggs, size 3

A little oil for frying

I don't know whether these wonderful hamburgers have anything to do with the mighty writer, mighty hunter – but they are certainly larger than life-size as he was.

1. Mix the beef with everything except the eggs and oil, and let stand, covered, at room temperature for two or three hours, or in the refrigerator for five hours. Then mix in the eggs thoroughly, with your hands. Make four huge patties, 6 in. (15 cm) in diameter and about 1½ in. (4 cm) thick.
2. Heat a very large frying pan (or two big ones) very hot. Put in about ⅛ in. oil and heat it until a small cube of bread, dropped in, browns in thirty seconds. Cook the hamburgers on one side for about four minutes, until crusty and very brown. Turn and cook the other side for two minutes. They should be dark brown outside and pink-rare inside. Serve with creamy mashed potatoes and good bread for mopping up the pan gravy, which is one of the glories of this dish.

Hamburgers '21'

Serves 2, luxuriously

1 tbsp butter

4 in. (10 cm) piece of celery heart, finely chopped

1 lb (450 g) sirloin steak, minced

Sea salt

2 tbsp Béarnaise sauce

This recipe is said to come from the very expensive New York restaurant '21'. I can't vouch for that part of it, but it's certainly costly enough to make the story plausible. What with minced sirloin and Sauce Béarnaise, it's quite a production.

1. Heat the butter in a small frying pan and sauté the celery for about three minutes. Mix it with the beef, and with wet hands shape two large oval cakes about 1 in. (2·5 cm) thick. Heat a well-seasoned cast-iron frying pan until it is spitting hot, cover the surface lightly with sea salt, and fry the hamburgers without any fat, to the degree of rareness you prefer.
2. Just before serving, put a tablespoon of Béarnaise sauce on each.

QUICK BLENDER BÉARNAISE

Makes 8 oz (225 g)

2 tbsp white wine

1 tbsp tarragon vinegar

2 tsp fresh tarragon, chopped, or 1 tsp dried tarragon

2 tsp shallots, chopped

1. In a small, heavy saucepan or frying pan, mix the wine, vinegar, tarragon, shallots, and black pepper. Bring to the boil and cook until the liquid has almost completely evaporated.
2. In another saucepan, heat the butter very hot, but don't let it brown. Put the egg yolks, lemon juice, salt, and cayenne

Freshly ground black pepper

4 oz (100 g) butter

3 egg yolks, size 3

2 tbsp lemon juice

¼ tsp salt

Pinch of cayenne

in the blender or food processor and blend for two seconds. Pour in the bubbling butter slowly, with the motor running. Then add the wine and herb mixture, and blend for about two to four seconds until the mixture is thick and smooth.

Corned Beef Hash

Serves 3–4

12 oz (350 g) tin of corned beef

8 oz (225 g) potatoes, peeled and cooked

1 small onion, finely chopped

1 tbsp butter or margarine

Optional: Poached eggs

A traditional American, and very good, dish is corned beef hash with one poached egg perched on top for each person. It is always served with ketchup or chili sauce (see p. 144) on the side.

1. Dice the potatoes and chop the corned beef as finely or coarsely as you choose. Mix both with the onion and toss everything lightly together. Heat a heavy frying pan (about 8 in. or 20 cm in diameter) very hot, melt the butter, and press the corned beef mixture firmly into the pan. Fry without stirring it, on a high heat, until a good crust forms on the bottom. Lift one bit with a palette knife to check.
2. Put a plate over the frying pan, quickly invert, then flip the hash back into the pan and continue to cook, on a moderate heat, until the bottom is well-crusted. If it is more convenient, you can do this second step in the oven at 400°F (200°C), Gas 6.

Steamboat Hash

Serves 6–8

6 big potatoes, washed but not peeled

1 very large onion, about 12 oz (350 g)

3 lb (1·35 kg) best-quality beef, minced

1 pt (550 ml) light ale

Sea salt

Plenty of freshly ground black pepper

A good pinch of dried rosemary

This is a great sloppy, unrefined dish, wonderful cold-weather fare, and only to be served to those who will mop up their plates with large chunks of French bread.

1. Grate the potatoes on the medium side of the grater, and coarsely chop the onion. In a large, heavy saucepan or flameproof casserole with a good tight-fitting lid, combine all the ingredients and bring slowly to the boil.
2. Lower the heat, and cook on a slow simmer for about two to two and a half hours, digging down with a big spoon every half hour or so and stirring it all around well. Taste for seasoning, and serve with kosher dill pickles, a green salad, and a big wedge of cheese.

Red Flannel Hash

Serves 4

12 oz (350 g) cooked corned beef (tinned, or the Corned Beef below)

1 small onion, finely chopped

3 medium beetroots, cooked and chopped

3 medium potatoes, steamed, peeled, and coarsely chopped

2 tbsp single cream

1 oz (25 g) butter or margarine

1. Cut the corned beef into cubes, then with a sharp knife chop it finely and mix with the onion. Add the coarsely chopped beetroot and potatoes, and cream, and with your hands gently mix everything together. Taste for seasoning.

2. Melt the butter or margarine in a heavy frying pan until it begins to sizzle but don't let it brown (don't substitute oil here, as it seems to make the hash greasy). Put in the hash mixture, press it down with a palette knife or fish slice, and cook on a fairly high heat for about fifteen minutes.

3. Put a plate the same size as the frying pan over the top, and with a quick twist invert the pan so that the hash slides out on the plate. Then slip it back into the pan and cook for another fifteen minutes, and again do the plate-and-pan trick. Cut in four wedges and serve hot, with the traditional American garnishes of dill pickles, American Chili sauce (see p. 144), and thinly sliced tomatoes.

Corned Beef

Serves 8–10

To corn

3 lb (1·35 kg) brisket of beef, boned and rolled

4 oz (100 g) saltpetre (sodium nitrate), from the chemist

4 tbsp coarse sea salt

A large earthenware, glass, or enamel-lined bowl or crock

To cook

Corned beef as above

2 large onions, thinly sliced

2 carrots, thinly sliced

1 stalk celery, coarsely chopped

6 black peppercorns

1 large bayleaf

3 whole cloves

3 fl. oz (75 ml) cider or wine vinegar

In the early days of the country, drying or 'corning' (salting) of beef was the only way to make sure of a supply in the lean winter months. While one can often find a good butcher who makes his own corned beef, now, the flavour can't compare with home-corned meat. It will take a week or more, so be warned.

Mix 3 oz (75 g) of the saltpetre with 2 tbsp salt in about 4 fl. oz (100 ml) boiling water, then cool the mixture. Prick the meat all over with a sharp fork and put in in the container. Pour the mixture over it, add cold water to cover, and weight it down with a piece of board or a brick wrapped securely in a clean cloth. The brine should come about two inches above the meat. Turn it once a day for three days, then pour off the salt mixture. Mix the remaining 1 oz (25 g) of saltpetre and 2 tbsp salt in about half a teacup of boiling water, pour it over the meat, cover with cold water, weight down and let it stand a further three or four days, turning each day. Pour off the brine, put the meat in a bowl of cold water for five minutes, and drain well.

1. Put the meat in a saucepan with enough cold water to cover, bring slowly to the boil, pour off the water, Cover with fresh cold water and add all the other ingredients, bring to the boil again, skim, and simmer about two or three hours until it is tender.

2. Discard the vegetables, and cook some carrots and whatever else you like to accompany the corned beef. Serve hot with horseradish sauce and mustard.

Or let the beef cool in its liquid, then slice thinly and serve on good, dark rye bread – with dill pickles and a choice of mustards, you now have real New York Corned Beef on Rye.

Maya Burrito

Serves 4 with other Mexican dishes

4 flour tortillas (see p. 168)

4 tbsp lard

8 oz (225 g) lean beef, minced

4 tbsp refried beans (see p. 117)

4 tbsp Red Chili Sauce (see p. 145)

4 tbsp soured cream

2 oz (50 g) mild Cheddar cheese, grated

Burritos are warm, soft tortillas filled with something lively and spicy – meat, beans, tomatoes, cheese, and so forth. This is a recipe from a Mexican restaurant in Denver, Colorado.

1. In a heavy frying pan, heat one tablespoon of lard very hot and cook the beef, stirring constantly, until it loses its red colour. Then stir in the refried beans, and continue to cook gently. In a large shallow saucepan or frying pan, heat the remaining lard very hot and quickly fry the tortillas until they are soft. Take them out with tongs.
2. Put a tortilla on each plate, spread with the beef and bean mixture, and add a tablespoon of Red Chili Sauce. Roll them up and cover each with a tablespoon of soured cream, and a scattering of grated cheese. Serve at once.

The Great Meat Loaf

Serves 4–6

2 tbsp bacon dripping or lard

1 medium onion, finely chopped

1 large clove garlic crushed with $1\frac{1}{2}$ tsp salt

1 lb (450 g) lean beef, minced

1 lb (450 g) lean pork, minced (shoulder or leg)

4 oz (100 g) soft breadcrumbs, brown or white

$\frac{1}{2}$ oz (about 4 rounded tbsp) parsley, washed and very finely chopped

$\frac{1}{2}$ tsp freshly ground black pepper

$\frac{1}{4}$ tsp ground allspice

1 egg, size 3

2 fl. oz (50 ml) brandy

2 rashers streaky bacon

Preheat oven to 350°F (180°C), Gas 4.
1. Heat the bacon dripping or lard in a frying pan and sauté the onion and garlic until soft but not brown. In a large mixing bowl, mix meats, crumbs, parsley, onion and garlic, brandy, pepper, allspice, and the well-beaten egg. Mix it well with your hands – do *not* use a machine as this over-mixes.
2. Pack into an oblong loaf pan (about $1\frac{3}{4}$ pts or 1 litre), and stretch the bacon rashers along the top. Bake in the centre of the oven for about one and a half hours. Let it stand in the tin for about twenty minutes before removing and slicing, so that it will not crumble.

To serve cold as pâté: put another loaf tin on top, weight it down with tins of food, and chill.

Russian Hill Bitki

Serves 6

1 thick slice white or rye bread, crusts removed

4 fl. oz (100 ml) milk

1 egg, size 2

1 small onion, very finely chopped

½ tsp salt

Good grinding of black pepper

Some freshly grated nutmeg

1 lb (450 g) best quality lean beef, minced

1 tbsp butter (*not* margarine)

½ pt (275 ml) soured cream

I am told that this recipe is of Russian origin, and appropriately enough it comes from the lovely San Francisco district called Russian Hill. It's a very good way of making one pound of beef into a supper dish for six people. Dress it up with a California-style salad as a starter, and finish with a luxurious pudding like Caramella (see p. 197).

1. Break the bread into small pieces and mix with the milk and egg beaten up together, soak it for ten minutes, then force through a food mill (or do all this in a blender or food processor). Mix with the onion, salt, pepper, and nutmeg, and gently but thoroughly mix in the beef. Shape it into six oval cakes.
2. Heat a heavy frying pan very hot, add the butter and let it sizzle but not brown; put in the *bitki*, and cook until brown on both sides. Remove them to a hot platter, lower the heat, stir in the soured cream, and scrape up the brown bits, and very quickly pour the sauce over the meat.

Mulligan Stew

Serves 4–6

6 fl. oz (175 ml) wine vinegar

2 fl. oz (50 ml) olive oil

4 juniper berries

1 medium onion, sliced

8 cloves

6 black peppercorns

2 lb (900 g) beef (or venison), chuck or bottom round

2 oz (50 g) butter or margarine

14 oz (397 g) tin Italian peeled tomatoes, drained

1 small swede, peeled and diced

12 pickling-size onions, peeled

6 oz (150 g) tinned whole-kernel corn

4 carrots, scraped and sliced

3 stalks celery, roughly cut up

2 tbsp salt

Optional: 8 oz (225 g) runner beans, topped, tailed, and sliced

A pioneer recipe from Colorado, originally cooked over the camp-fire.

1. Mix the vinegar, oil, juniper berries, onion, cloves, and peppercorns, and leave the meat in this marinade in a glass or enamel bowl overnight. Drain, dry, and cut the meat into 1½ in. (4 cm) cubes. Heat the butter or margarine in a heavy flameproof casserole and brown the meat. Add enough cold water to cover, and bring to the boil. Lower the heat and simmer about an hour and a half to two hours, until the meat is tender.
2. Add all the other ingredients and simmer, covered, until the vegetables are tender. Taste for seasoning.

Opposite American beef in many forms. Top *Corned Beef from New York; Centre* Red Flannel Hash *from the Midwest; Bottom* Yankee Pot Roast *from Maine*

Picadillo

2 tbsp olive oil, or olive and groundnut oil mixed

1 large clove garlic, crushed with 1 tsp salt

4 spring onions, finely chopped

12 oz (350 g) lean beef, minced

4 oz (100 g) minced pork

12 oz (350 g) tinned Italian peeled tomatoes, drained

1 tsp cider vinegar

½ tsp ground cumin

Pinch of powdered cloves

3 oz (75 g) raisins or sultanas

2 fl. oz (50 ml) beef stock

2 oz (50 g) flaked almonds

Cuban immigrants into Florida brought this delicious spicy-sweet dish with them. Serve it with boiled black beans and fluffy white rice – mixed together, this is called Moros y Cristianos.

1. In a deep heavy frying pan or heavy saucepan, heat the oil and sauté the crushed garlic and onions for about one minute. Mix in the beef and pork and sauté, stirring constantly, for about five minutes until it begins to brown slightly.
2. Add all the other ingredients except the almonds, breaking up the tomatoes well with a fork. Bring the mixture to the boil, reduce the heat, and simmer slowly for about half an hour. Turn out on a large warmed meat plate, surround with black beans and rice, and scatter the flaked almonds over the meat.

New England Boiled Dinner

4 lb (less than 2 kg) salt beef (brisket) *or* corned beef (see p. 82)

1 large onion stuck with 3 cloves

1 large bayleaf

3 black peppercorns

Water

3 medium carrots, scraped

3 medium potatoes, peeled

1 medium swede, peeled and sliced *or* 4 peeled white turnips

1 medium head firm white cabbage, quartered

There's a theory that this wonderful winter dish came down over the border from French Canada in the eighteenth century. Certainly it's not unlike a pot-au-feu, without the usual boiling fowl. It is endlessly variable: with or without potatoes, with small onions or one huge one, with cloves or not, with white turnips or a cut-up swede (rutabaga in American cookery). The Boiled Dinner can simmer for three or four hours, or cook in a very moderate oven, or spend the day in an electric slow-cooker. The broth makes glorious soup, and any leftover beef is tomorrow's lunch.

1. Wash the meat, put in a heavy deep saucepan with the bayleaf, peppercorns, and the clove-studded onion. Cover it with water and bring to the boil, then lower the heat and simmer, covered, about an hour. Pour off the water, replace it with fresh cold water, bring to the boil and cook slowly until the beef is tender, about two hours more.
2. Put in the carrots, potatoes, swede, or turnips and cook another forty-five minutes. In the last twenty minutes, add the quartered cabbage and cook until it is just tender but still retains some crispness. Strain off the broth and keep it. Serve the beef on a warmed meat plate ringed with vegetables, and accompanied by mustard, horseradish, and coarse sea salt.

Opposite Top *Hemingway's Hamburgers;* Centre *Chili Dogs;* Bottom *Rockbottom Chili*

Pastrami or something very like it

Serves 12

To corn

5 lb (2·25 kg) silverside of beef, well marbled with fat

2 large cloves of garlic, slivered

2 tsp ground allspice

4 oz (100 g) sea salt

1 tbsp black peppercorns, crushed

4 oz (100 g) dark brown sugar

1 oz (25 g) saltpetre (sodium nitrate) from the chemist

To cook

2 medium onions cut in eighths

2 carrots, sliced

Large bayleaf

Pinch of ginger

4 cloves

$\frac{1}{2}$ tbsp black peppercorns, coarsely crushed

Hot pastrami sandwiches! This spicy, densely pressed beef is a New York (and Hollywood) joy. Those who like it love it, and those who don't are equally vehement. It is Roumanian in origin, by way of the Jewish immigrants of the nineteenth century. I am told that real pastrami is smoked after being 'corned' in brine with spices and sugar. But this one will do quite well.

Pierce the beef all over with a sharp fork, or cut slits in it with a knife, and press thin slivers of garlic well in. Mix the rest of the spices and rub them hard all over the meat. Put it in a deep, well-fitting casserole and refrigerate for about a week. Every day, turn the meat and rub the spices into the surface.

1. Put the beef in a deep saucepan, cover with cold water and bring slowly to the boil, then pour off the water. Cover it with fresh cold water and add the vegetables and spices, except the crushed peppercorns. Bring to the boil, skim the surface, and simmer, covered, about four hours until the meat is tender. Let it cool in the liquid, then remove and roll the entire surface of the meat in the cracked pepper, pressing it well into the fat.
2. Put the meat in a bowl with a plate and a weight (a brick or several tins of food) on top, and refrigerate. Cut it in thin slices for sandwiches, or thicker ones to serve with potato salad and coleslaw. For hot pastrami, reheat over boiling water.

Steak Diane

Serves 1

6–8 oz (175–225 g) sirloin steak

1$\frac{1}{2}$ tbsp butter (scant 1 oz or 25 g)

2 tbsp dry sherry

1 tbsp brandy

1 tbsp unsalted butter, creamed with 1 tsp very finely chopped chives

This is tricky to do for more than two or three people, as you will need a really big, heavy frying pan. In American restaurants it is often a table-side spectacular, with an alcohol burner, a beautiful copper pan, and blue flames shooting around.

1. Trim the meat very well and beat it to flatten it slightly. In a heavy frying pan heated very hot, melt the butter and heat it until it just begins to brown. While it is heating, warm the brandy in a small saucepan.
2. Cook the steak quickly in the hot butter, turning it only once, to the degree of rareness you like. Put it on a heated plate, swirl the sherry round the pan and pour it over the steak. Pour the brandy into the pan and light it. When the flames die, stir in the butter and chives, and pour onto the steak. Serve at once.

Sauerbraten

Serves 4–6, with delicious leftovers

4 fl. oz (100 ml) red wine

4 fl. oz (100 ml) wine vinegar

1 tbsp dry mustard

$\frac{1}{2}$ pt (275 ml) water

1 onion, very thinly sliced

2 tbsp light brown sugar

3 cloves

8 black peppercorns

Optional: 6 allspice berries

4 lb (just under 2 kg) silverside, boned
   and rolled

2 tbsp beef dripping

Flour (see method)

This kind of sweet and spicy beef dish is most probably of German origin, as its name would indicate. The recipe here came from the Pennsylvania-Dutch country, although I think the addition of red wine in the marinade is probably a New York idea.

1. Heat all ingredients together, except the meat, dripping, and flour, to just below boiling point. Cool and pour into an earthenware dish or casserole that will be a fairly tight fit for the beef. Put in the meat, spoon the marinade around and over it several times, cover with plastic film, and set in the refrigerator or a cold larder to marinate for at least two days, preferably three. Turn it over twice a day, Pour off the marinade and save it.
2. Wipe the beef very dry with kitchen paper. Heat the dripping very hot in a large flameproof casserole, and sear the meat on all sides. Add the marinade and bring to the boil, lower the heat, and simmer until the beef is tender – at least two and a half hours, and more probably three hours. Remove the meat and keep warm.
3. Pour off the liquid, strain it, and measure out as much as you like for a sauce: for every 10 fl. oz (275 ml), you will need two level tablespoonfuls of flour. Mix a little of the hot liquid into the flour, stir it smooth, return it all to the pan, and bring it to the boil. Stir well, and simmer the sauce until it is slightly thickened. Pour it over the meat.

A bowl of soured cream, horseradish sauce, and small dumplings or noodles are usually served with Sauerbraten.

The next day, slice the leftover meat thin and serve with potato salad in a mustardy mayonnaise.

Serves 4

Teriyaki

$1\frac{1}{2}$ lb (675 g) sirloin or rump steak, cut
   thin (about $\frac{1}{4}$ in. or 0·75 cm)

6 fl. oz (175 ml) soy sauce

2 fl. oz (50 ml) dry sherry or dry cider

1 large clove garlic, crushed with 1 tbsp
   caster sugar

6 very thin slices of ginger root

1 small onion chopped very, very finely

Thin wood or bamboo skewers

A recipe from one of America's newest states, Hawaii: it's ideal for cooking on a hibachi or barbecue, or it may be done under a very hot grill.

1. Cut the meat against the grain in thin strips. Mix all the marinade ingredients together in a deep earthenware or glass bowl. Add the meat and stir it well, making sure that it is completely covered. Marinate for two hours, stirring two or three times. Pour off the marinade and save it.
2. Heat the barbecue or grill very hot. Weave the meat on to skewers. Grill it quickly, basting with marinade when you turn the skewers. Serve with the remaining marinade as a sauce, and with fluffy white rice.

Yankee Pot Roast

Serves 6–8

1 tbsp lard

4 lb (1·8 kg) beef brisket, boned and rolled

Sea salt

4 tbsp boiling water

1 medium onion, thinly sliced

1 small white turnip, peeled and diced

3 carrots, scraped and diced

2 stalks celery with their leaves, diced

3 oz (75 g) mushrooms

4 oz (100 g) cooked peas

1 tsp butter or good margarine

1 tsp flour

A recipe from Maine: don't be tempted to increase the amount of liquid under any circumstances. You will need a heavy flameproof casserole with a good tight lid, or a very heavy saucepan.

1. Heat the lard very hot in a frying pan, or in your flameproof casserole if that's what you are using. Wipe the meat dry, and brown it on all sides. Sprinkle it well with salt. Put a rack or an old saucer, upturned, in the bottom of your casserole or saucepan, and set the meat on it. Distribute the onion slices around it and pour on the boiling water. Cover and simmer for about four hours.

2. Add all the other vegetables except the peas and mushrooms, and simmer another half an hour until they are tender. Remove the meat and keep it warm. Work the flour and butter together and drop in nut-sized pieces into the simmering sauce, stirring well after each addition, and cook until it is smooth and thick. Slice the mushrooms and stir them into the pot with the peas, put back the meat, cover, and cook another ten minutes. Taste for seasoning. Slice the meat as thinly as you can, and serve on a heated *deep* meat plate surrounded by vegetables and gravy.

Swedish Meat Balls

Serves 4–6

8 oz (225 g) fresh brown bread, crusts removed, cubed

4 fl. oz (100 ml) milk

1½ lb (675 g) lean beef, minced

2 tsp sea salt

¾ tsp freshly grated nutmeg

2 tsp sweet Spanish paprika

1 tsp mixed herbs – oregano, basil, dried parsley flakes

1 tsp dry mustard

3 eggs, size 3

1 medium onion, finely chopped

4 tbsp butter or good margarine

1 small clove garlic, crushed

4 tbsp plain flour

This is a sophisticated version of a recipe that originated in the Swedish colony in Minnesota – great loggers, hunters, and eaters.

1. Soak the bread cubes in the milk, drain, and press lightly to dry them a bit. Mix with the beef, salt, nutmeg, herbs, paprika, and mustard. Whisk the eggs and mix with the meat.

2. Heat 2 tbsp of the butter in a large heavy frying pan and sauté the onion until it is soft and pale gold. Mix the onion with the beef mixture, wipe out the pan with kitchen paper, and heat the remaining 2 tbsp of butter.

3. With floured hands, roll the meat into balls about 1 in. (2·5 cm) in diameter. Brown well in the hot butter, remove, and keep warm.

4. Stir into the drippings in the frying pan the garlic, flour, and tomato paste, scraping up all the richly-flavoured crusty bits around the pan. Slowly, stirring all the time, add the beef stock, and cook over low heat until it begins to thicken.

2 tsp tomato paste

$\frac{3}{4}$ pt (425 ml) good beef stock

8 fl. oz (225 ml) soured cream

Freshly ground black pepper

Now you have a choice of finishing methods:

Oven. Preheat to 300°F (150°C), Gas 2. Put everything into a heavy casserole with a tight lid, and cook from one to two hours to your convenience. Taste for seasoning.
Cooker top. Return the meatballs to the gravy in the frying pan, stir around, cover tightly with a double thickness of aluminium foil, and simmer for about an hour and a quarter on a very low heat. Correct the seasoning. Remove from oven or from direct heat, and stir in the soured cream.

Tacos with Tex-Mex Filling

Serves 4–6

Taco shells

4 oz (100 g) light brown flour (81% or 85% type)

3 tbsp fine cornmeal

$\frac{1}{2}$ tsp salt

Scant 1 oz (25 g) white fat

2–4 fl. oz (50–100 ml) warm water

Taco filling

2 tbsp olive oil (or olive and groundnut oil mixed)

$1\frac{1}{2}$ lb (675 g) lean beef, minced

1 small onion, finely chopped

1 large clove garlic, crushed

3 sprigs of parsley, chopped

2 tbsp chili seasoning (or less, to your taste)

2 tsp ground cumin

$\frac{1}{2}$ tsp salt

Good pinch of dried basil

6 oz (175 g) tomato purée

8 fl. oz (225 ml) water

Topping

4 oz (100 g) Cheddar cheese, coarsely grated

3 oz (75 g) onion, very finely chopped

About half a medium cos lettuce, shredded

1 large ripe tomato, diced

This recipe comes from San Antonio, Texas, and includes a very good Taco sauce-filling.

1. Mix the flour, cornmeal, and salt, and cut in the white fat until it feels like fine breadcrumbs. Slowly add the water, just enough to make a soft but not sticky dough. Wrap in plastic film and refrigerate for an hour or more.
2. Divide the dough in ten pieces, and roll each between your hands into a ball. Lightly flour a pastry board, flatten the ball of dough between your palms, and roll out to 6 in. (15 cm) in diameter.
3. Very lightly grease a heavy frying pan or griddle (girdle), and heat it until drops of cold water dance and bounce on the surface. Fry each taco about one to two minutes on each side, until dry and brown-spotted. Fold each in half as soon as it is cooked.
4. Heat the oil in a heavy frying pan, and sauté the meat until it loses its red colour. Remove, and if the pan looks dry add a little more oil. Sauté the onion and garlic until lightly browned and soft. Put the meat back in the pan, add the parsley, chili seasoning, cumin, salt, basil, tomato purée, and water. Simmer for fifteen minutes and taste for seasoning.
5. Open each taco shell, fill with some of the sauce, and top with the cheese, lettuce, onion, and tomato. Eat in your hands.

Barbecued Lamb

Serves about 6

5 lb (2·25 kg) leg of lamb, boned

Dry mustard

Freshly ground black pepper

4 oz (100 g) butter or margarine

1 garlic clove, crushed

1 small onion, finely chopped

1 oz (25 g) fresh mint leaves

With the great and growing popularity of charcoal grilling, this simple method of cooking a leg of lamb has become an American classic. Instead of the simple mint sauce in the recipe, any of the barbecue sauces in this book may be used. I should think that this recipe could be adapted for oven-barbecueing – if you decide to try that, preheat the oven to the highest possible setting, then reduce the heat to 400°F (200°C), Gas 6, and cook the lamb to the desired degree of done-ness.

1. About two hours before you are ready to start cooking the lamb, flatten it, cut off the parchmenty 'fell', and rub the entire surface with mustard and black pepper. It is hard to be exact about the quantities needed – use enough to coat the surface lightly.

2. Heat the charcoal to the white-hot stage. In a small saucepan, heat 2 oz (50 g) of the butter and cook the garlic and onion for about ten minutes on a low heat. Add the mint leaves and the remaining butter and remove from heat.

3. Brush some of the sauce over the lamb and grill it for about twenty minutes on one side, basting once or twice with the sauce. Turn and grill on the other side. Allow about forty-five minutes overall grilling time, for pink-rare lamb. Well-done lamb should take about an hour, but of course these times depend on the heat of the charcoal and the type of your grill.

If using any of the other barbecue sauces, heat well before basting the lamb.

Barbecued Lamb Steaks

Serves 4

8 fl. oz (225 ml) dry red wine

4 fl. oz (100 ml) red wine vinegar

3 cloves garlic, crushed with 1½ tsp salt

1 tsp freshly milled black pepper

Good pinch of cayenne

2 fl oz (50 ml) vegetable oil

2 tsp lemon juice

1 tsp dried oregano

4 large lamb steaks (or chump chops), about 2¼ lb (1 generous kg)

This Californian wine marinade for meat is a very good tenderising and flavouring one, and is also excellent for beef, with minor variations (see below). The marinade keeps well, tightly covered, in the refrigerator for at least a month.

1. Mix the marinade mixture. Slash the fat around edges of the chops or steaks, put them in a shallow pan and pour on 8 fl oz (225 ml) of the marinade. Cover and let stand for two hours, turning once.

2. Lift out the meat, reserving any marinade that is left. On a barbecue or *hibachi* that is ready to use, grill the lamb, turning several times and brushing with marinade, until it is done to your taste: about twelve minutes on each side for

medium-rare. The chops can be done under a grill, but they must be about 3 in. (8 cm) from the flame.

For beef: mix the ingredients as above, but instead of lemon juice and oregano, add 1 tsp rosemary, 1 tsp Worcestershire sauce, and 1 tbsp Dijon mustard.

Lamb Hash

Serves 4

About 1¼ lb (550 g) cold, cooked lamb

1 medium cooked potato, diced

1 tbsp flour

2 tbsp parsley, finely chopped

Sea salt

1 level tbsp butter or margarine

1 large onion, chopped

3 tbsp tomato purée

4 fl. oz (100 ml) light stock

Preheat oven to 350°F (180°C), Gas 4.
1. Dice the lamb in cubes about ½ in. (1·5 cm) square, and mix with the cold diced potato. Stir in the flour, parsley, and quite a lot of salt, to your taste. Melt the butter in a small heavy frying pan and gently sauté the onion until just pale golden. Mix with the tomato purée and the lamb. Then pour on the stock.
2. Press into a greased shallow casserole and bake, about one hour, until brown and crusty.

The New York Times Cookbook, in which I have great faith, has a recipe much like this, but after the baking period, the hash is scooped into four small individual casseroles, 8 fl. oz (225 ml) of double cream is divided between them, and about 1 oz (25 g) grated Parmesan cheese is scattered over the top. Then they go under the grill to 'colour up'. It sounds very luxurious, making a Sunday supper-party dish out of rather prosaic ingredients.

Braised Shoulder of Lamb

Serves 4–6

2 lb (900 g) boned, rolled shoulder of lamb

2 garlic cloves

4 fl. oz (100 ml) good salad oil (olive and groundnut mixed, for choice)

4 fl. oz (100 ml) soy sauce

2 fl. oz (50 ml) dry or medium sherry

½ tsp ground ginger

12 small onions

A few sprigs of parsley

1. Pierce the skin of the lamb with a very sharp knife in about twenty places. Cut the garlic in very thin slivers and press them into the slits. Rub about two tablespoons of oil over the skin. Mix the soy sauce, sherry, and ground ginger in a deep bowl or casserole, put in the meat, turn it over once or twice. Cover and let it marinate three hours or more, turning it from time to time.
2. Preheat the oven to 300°F (150°C), Gas 2. Pour off the marinade and save it. Dry the lamb well on kitchen paper. Heat the remaining oil in a heavy frying pan and brown the lamb on all sides.
3. Put the lamb in a casserole that will hold it rather tightly, arrange the onions around it, strew on the parsley, pour on the marinade, and cover. Bake for about two hours until the lamb is very tender. Slice it and serve in its juices, with something bland like Polenta (see p. 110) or mashed potatoes.

Lamb Stew with Dill

Serves 4

2 lb (900 g) shoulder or meaty breast of lamb, cut in serving-sized pieces

8 small onions, peeled

2 large white turnips, peeled and diced

¾ pt (425 ml) boiling water

1 tsp Marmite

1 tsp sea salt

4 black peppercorns

1 bayleaf

¾ tsp dried dillweed *or* two large fronds of fresh dill

For the sauce

2 tbsp butter (scant 1 oz or 25 g)

2 tbsp flour

¾ pt (425 ml) stock from stew

1 tsp dried dillweed

1 tbsp cider vinegar

1 tbsp caster sugar

Salt, freshly ground black pepper

1 egg yolk, size 3

1. In a large heavy saucepan, bring the meat, onions, turnips, and water to the boil, and skim well. Add all the seasonings, cover, and cook for about an hour, on a low heat, until the lamb is tender. Pour off the stock, retaining it, and if necessary add some hot water to make it up to the required ¾ pt (425 ml) for the sauce.

2. For the sauce, melt the butter in a small saucepan, stir in the flour, and slowly add the stock. Cook it, stirring, until it is thick and smooth. Add the dillweed, vinegar, sugar, salt, and pepper, and cook for about four minutes longer. Beat the egg yolk and stir into it one tbsp of the hot sauce, then stir it all back into the simmering sauce. Pour over the lamb.

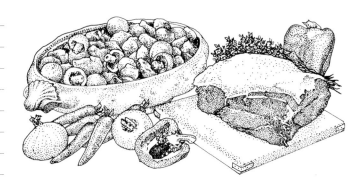

Stuffed Double Lamb Chops

Serves 4

4 very thick lamb cutlets (or chump chops)

4 tbsp olive oil

1 small clove garlic, crushed with ½ tsp sea salt

1 tbsp butter

3 oz (75 g) mushrooms, chopped

3 oz (75 g) cooked ham, coarsely chopped

1 oz (25 g) fresh soft breadcrumbs

Grated rind of one small lemon, or half a large one

Preheat oven to 350°F (180°C), Gas 4.

1. Marinate the lamb cutlets or chops in the oil and garlic for about two hours. Cut a deep slit sideways through the meat, almost back to the bone.

2. In a small frying pan, heat the butter and sauté the mushrooms for about two minutes, stirring, until they are just beginning to brown. Add ham, breadcrumbs, lemon rind, and mix. Stuff the chops with the mixture, and secure with cocktail sticks.

3. Pour any remaining marinade into a shallow baking dish, let it get hot in the oven, then put in the chops. Bake, uncovered, for about one hour, turning them over at the halfway stage.

These chops may also be grilled, with caution, for about fifteen minutes each side, but must be kept about 2 in. (5 cm) from the flame as they burn easily.

California Lamb Pot Pie

Serves 4–6

2 lb (900 g) shoulder of lamb, boned

A little flour

4 tbsp good vegetable oil

8 fl. oz (225 ml) chicken stock (can be a cube)

Half small lemon, thinly sliced

2 large mild onions, coarsely chopped

1 bayleaf

1 level tsp sea salt

6 black peppercorns

2 carrots, thinly sliced

For the topping

1 lb (450 g) freshly mashed potatoes

1 egg, size 2

3 tbsp butter

Salt, freshly ground black pepper

1. Cut the lamb in 1 in. (2·5 cm) pieces and toss it in the flour. Heat the oil in a heavy frying pan and brown the lamb cubes well. Put them in a large saucepan with the stock, lemon slices, onions, bayleaf, peppercorns, and salt and bring to the boil. Lower the heat and simmer gently for one and a half hours.
2. Add the carrots, and cook for another half an hour. Heat the oven to 400°F (200°C), Gas 6.
3. Turn the lamb and vegetables into a deep 2 pt (generous litre size) casserole. Whisk the mashed potatoes, egg, butter, and seasonings together, and drop by big spoonfuls around the edges of the casserole. Or – prettier – force it through a large pastry bag fitted with a star tip. Bake for fifteen minutes on the shelf above the centre of the oven.

Boston Irish Stew

Serves about 6

4 lb (1·8 kg) best end of neck mutton, or lean lamb shoulder

9 medium potatoes, peeled

6 medium onions, peeled

1 large stalk celery

½ lb (225 g) streaky bacon, coarsely chopped

1 bayleaf

1 tsp dried thyme

Salt, freshly ground black pepper

This tasty stew can be simmered in a heavy saucepan on top of the cooker, or cooked slowly in the oven at 350°F (180°C), Gas 4. It's a perfect dish for an electric slow cooker, too.

1. Trim as much fat as possible from the mutton or lamb, and cut in neat serving pieces. Slice the potatoes and onions, but not too thinly. Arrange a layer of meat in the bottom of a saucepan or casserole, add a layer of potatoes, one of onions, and scatter in some chopped bacon. Season with salt, pepper, thyme, and bayleaf. Continue to make layers, ending with one of meat. Pour in just enough water to cover.
2. Tightly cover the saucepan or casserole, and simmer or bake until the meat is tender – this will take anywhere from two to three hours, depending on the age and tenderness of the meat. You can sprinkle a handful of chopped parsley over the top if you feel like it.

Serve with hot baking-powder biscuits (see p. 154) and a crisp green salad for contrast.

Kentucky Burgoo

4 lb (just under 2 kg) smoked bacon
(collar if possible)

3 lb (1·8 kg) chicken, giblets removed

½ level tsp cayenne

12 oz (350 g) carrots, scraped and diced

12 oz (350 g) potatoes, peeled and diced

2 large onions, coarsely chopped

10 oz (275 g) frozen broad beans

8 oz (225 g) cabbage, shredded

12 oz (350 g) fresh corn kernels, or
frozen whole-kernel corn

6 stalks celery, coarsely chopped

14 oz (400 g) tin Italian tomatoes

10 oz (275 g) tinned okra, drained, or
frozen (or fresh) okra

2 tbsp Worcestershire sauce

1 medium green pepper, seeded and
diced

2 oz (50 g) parsley, finely chopped

This is an immense bubbling stew served up out of huge copper cauldrons at parties for the Kentucky Derby. As you can see, it contains just about everything but a horseshoe, and I wouldn't be too sure about that! It can be made in a half-sized recipe, of course.

1. In a large saucepan, put the bacon and chicken, with enough water just to cover. Bring to the boil, cover, and simmer for an hour and a half, until the chicken is tender. Remove the chicken and continue to cook the bacon for another hour until it is tender. Remove the meat, and leave the stock in a cool place until the fat rises to the top. Skim off.
2. Measure out 5 pts (about 2·5 litres) of the stock and return it to the washed-out saucepan. Add the cayenne, potatoes, carrots, onions, and broad beans, bring to the boil and simmer for fifteen minutes. Remove skin from the chicken and ham, strip the meat off the bones and dice it.
3. Add the cabbage, corn, celery, tomatoes, okra, and Worcestershire sauce to the mixture, and cook for another fifteen minutes until the vegetables are tender but not mushy. Stir in the green pepper, parsley, and the diced meats, reheat just to the boil but do not cook any further.
4. Keep the Burgoo simmering on an electric hot tray, and ladle it into deep soup bowls. Cornbread (see p. 159) with Burgoo is a tradition but there are those who prefer French bread or crusty rolls to dip into the sauce.

Ilka Toth's Hungarian Pork Chops

4 large loin pork chops, about 1½ lb
(675 g)

½ pt (275 ml) dry cider or white wine

2 large carrots, scraped and sliced

1 medium mild onion, peeled and sliced
very thinly

2 oz (50 g) butter or margarine

1 heaped tbsp brown flour

1 heaped tbsp Hungarian paprika

4 tbsp dry brown breadcrumbs

Salt, freshly ground black pepper

1. Marinate the chops in the cider or wine, with carrots, and onion. Leave them, covered, in a cool place for ten to twelve hours. Strain off the marinade and set it aside.
2. Dry the chops well. Heat the butter in a heavy frying pan and brown the chops on both sides. Stir the flour into the pan, let it brown slightly, then slowly add 8 fl. oz (225 ml) of the marinade. Bring to the boil, lower the heat, and simmer for twenty minutes.
3. Preheat the oven to 350°F (180°C), Gas 5. Mix the paprika with the extra marinade, add to the sauce, and cook on for about five minutes while the oven is heating. Put the chops in a casserole in one layer, press on the breadcrumbs evenly, and season to taste. Bake for about twenty minutes, until the breadcrumbs are lightly browned.

Chinese Pork and Prawns   *Serves 4 with other Chinese dishes*

1 tbsp soy sauce

1 tsp sesame seed oil

$\frac{1}{2}$ tsp hot chili sauce (see Appendix)

$1\frac{1}{2}$ tsp tomato purée

$1\frac{1}{2}$ tsp cider vinegar

4 tbsp water

3 tsp (or more if needed) groundnut oil

1 clove garlic, crushed

$\frac{1}{2}$ cucumber, peeled and coarsely diced

4 oz (100 g) pineapple cubes – if tinned, drain them well

3 small tomatoes, peeled and diced

12 oz (350 g) lean boneless pork

4 oz (100 g) cooked peeled prawns

1 egg, size 3

4 level tsp cornflour

1 tbsp cold water

$\frac{1}{2}$ tsp salt

Extra 4 tbsp cornflour

3 fl. oz (75 ml) groundnut oil (for frying)

The list of ingredients may look formidable, but in fact it is a very easy recipe to prepare, and like all stir-fried Chinese food it cooks in a matter of minutes. This sweet-sour dish goes well with other simple Chinese food such as stir-fried bean sprouts, plain steamed rice, and spring rolls (very good frozen ones are available). Cantonese restaurants in America serve Chinese Plum Sauce and Dragon Mustard (see p. 146) with this kind of food.

1. Mix the soy sauce, sesame oil, hot chili sauce, tomato purée, vinegar, and 4 tbsp water. In a large heavy frying pan, heat the 3 tsp groundnut oil very hot, and fry the garlic until it is golden, stirring constantly. Add the cucumber, pineapple and tomato, and stir-fry for one minute. Add more groundnut oil if the mixture begins to stick. Pour in the soy sauce mixture, lower the heat, and bring to the boil, stirring. Cook for one minute and remove the pan from the heat.
2. Cube the pork, and if the prawns are very large, cut them in half. Make a batter of the egg, 4 tsp cornflour, water, and salt. Dip the pork and prawns in the batter, then toss them in a plastic bag with the remaining cornflour. Let them stand a few minutes. Heat the 3 fl oz (75 ml) of groundnut oil in a deep saucepan to 380°F (190°C) and fry the pork and prawns quickly. Remove with a slotted spoon and drain on layers of kitchen paper and keep warm.
3. Reheat the sauce mixture gently on a low heat. Reheat the oil in the saucepan to its initial temperature, drop in the pork and prawns, and fry for two minutes. Drain very well and stir into the warmed sauce.

Chinese Baked Spareribs   *Serves 4 with other Chinese dishes*

8 fl. oz (225 ml) soy sauce

3 tbsp cider or red wine

6 fl. oz (175 ml) water

1 tbsp light brown sugar

1 large clove garlic, crushed with $\frac{1}{2}$ tsp salt

4 lb (just under 2 kg) lean sheet spareribs of pork

1. Mix the soy sauce, cider or wine, water, sugar, and garlic. With a very sharp knife, cut partway through the separations between the ribs. Put the meat in a roasting tin and pour on the marinade, let stand for an hour or more, turning once or twice. Pour off the marinade in a jug and save. Preheat oven to 350°F (180°C), Gas 4.
2. Put the ribs on a rack over a roasting tin and bake, basting often with the marinade, for about one and a half hours, or until crisp but not blackened.

Serve with Chinese Plum Sauce and Dragon Mustard (see p. 146).

Chinese Pork with Bean Sprouts

Serves 4 with other Chinese dishes

3 tbsp good vegetable oil

1 medium onion, finely chopped

8 oz (225 g) roast pork

2 oz (50 g) white mushrooms, wiped

7 oz (200 g) fresh, washed bean sprouts
(or good tinned ones)

1 tbsp dark soy sauce

2 tbsp water

2 level tbsp cornflour

$\frac{1}{4}$ tsp sugar

1. In a *wok* or heavy wide frying pan, heat the oil and sauté the onion until it is translucent but not browned. Cut the pork in matchstick-sized pieces, slice the mushrooms thinly. Add the pork, mushrooms, and bean sprouts, and cook, stirring, for five minutes.

2. Mix the soy sauce, water, cornflour, and sugar and stir into the pork. Cook, stirring constantly, until the sauce thickens and clears. Taste for seasoning, and add freshly ground black pepper if you like.

Virginia Baked Ham

About 8 lb (3·5 kg)

The whole subject of what is ham, and what is bacon, in British terms, is a minefield. So many parts of Britain have their own way of cutting and curing pork that it's difficult to be very specific. However, taking a deep breath, one plunges in. The best cut to use to approximate American-style baked ham would probably be a whole or half gammon. If it is the mild-cure type, it may not need soaking.

To boil: Allow twenty-five minutes to the pound (450 g) plus twenty minutes more. Put the gammon in a large saucepan, just cover with cold water, and bring slowly to the boil. Then add 3 tbsp cider vinegar, 6 cloves, 1 bayleaf, and 4 peppercorns. Simmer, removing the scum from time to time. Drain, carefully cut off the rind, leaving a good layer of fat, and cool.

Score the fat with a very sharp knife (the invaluable Stanley kitchen knife) in a diamond pattern. Rub the fat with a mixture of 5 oz (125 g) soft brown sugar and 2 tsp dry mustard, moistened with a little bit of the ham stock. (This would do for about a 10 lb or 4·5 kg ham.) Set a whole clove in the corner of each diamond. Preheat oven to 400°F (200°C), Gas 6. Put the ham on a rack in a roasting tin and cook about twenty-five minutes until the sugar is glazed and the fat is crisp.

Heretical Ham. In place of the water and spice mixture above, boil the gammon in 2 litres of Coca Cola, diluted with about 1 pt (550 ml) of water. The flavour is remarkably good, no doubt due to all those secret ingredients in Coke.

Ham Baked with Peaches and Bourbon

Serves 10 with leftovers

6 lb (about 2·75 kg) gammon

2 oz (50 g) light soft brown sugar

A little dry mustard

14 oz (400 g) tin peach halves

4 fl. oz (100 ml) bourbon whisky

1 oz (25 g) butter

The original of this recipe comes from James Beard, and is adapted to suit British cuts of gammon or ham.

1. Boil the ham as in the Virginia Baked Ham recipe, allowing twenty minutes to the pound. Remove from water, drain well, and cut off the rind. Pat dry with kitchen paper. Rub the sugar mixed with mustard over the surface. Preheat the oven to 400°F (200°C), Gas 6.
2. Drain the juice from the peaches and mix with bourbon. Put the ham on a rack in a roasting tin in the oven. Baste every ten minutes for fifty minutes with the bourbon mixture. In the last five minutes before serving, lay the peach halves in a shallow grill pan, sprinkle with a very little brown sugar (about 1½ tbsp is enough), cut the butter in flakes over the top, and grill under a hot flame until brown and slightly caramelised. Put around the ham on a heated platter.

Red Rice with Ham

Serves 4

2 tbsp bacon drippings, or good oil

1 large onion, coarsely chopped

2 stalks celery, leaves removed, finely diced

8 oz–1 lb (225–450 g) cooked ham, diced

6 oz (175 g) long-grain rice

28 oz (793 g) tin very good Italian tomatoes, undrained

¼ level tsp salt

Medium green pepper, seeded and finely diced

Pinch of dried sage

About 8 fl. oz (225 ml) water

This very old recipe comes from Charleston, South Carolina, the country devastated by the War Between the States, when it was necessary to feed a family on as little meat and as much rice as one could. It's best made with leftover baked gammon or very good boiled, smoked bacon.

1. Heat the bacon drippings or oil and gently sauté the onion and celery until soft. Stir in the ham and cook until it browns slightly. Add the rice slowly, and keep stirring around with a wooden spoon until it is translucent. Add the other ingredients, cover, and simmer until the rice is cooked.
2. If the tomatoes are very juicy, use less than 8 fl. oz (225 ml) of water; you can always add more as the dish cooks. Depending on the rice, it will probably take about half an hour. The finished dish should have very little liquid showing, yet should not be dry.

Puchero (Mexican Bean and Pork Stew)

Serves 4

8 oz (225 g) brown 'pinto' beans (see Appendix)

1 lb (500 g) salt belly of pork

1 large onion, peeled and sliced

1 large carrot, scraped and sliced

2 cloves garlic crushed with $\frac{1}{2}$ tsp salt

2 tbsp oil or margarine

4 black peppercorns

1 level tsp dried red pepper flakes, *or* $\frac{1}{4}$ small chili, de-seeded and chopped

1 Bayleaf

1 pt (550 ml) water

4 fl. oz (100 ml) cider vinegar

8 oz (225 g) ripe tomatoes, or the equivalent in peeled, tinned Italian tomatoes, drained

6 oz (150 g) chorizos, or other dry spiced Spanish sausage

1. Wash the beans, put in a saucepan with enough cold water to cover, bring to the boil, simmer for two minutes, cover, and let stand for two hours. Drain and cover with fresh cold water, bring to the boil and simmer for one and a half hours. In a separate pan, cover the belly of pork with cold water, bring to the boil, lower the heat, and simmer for one hour.

2. Sauté the onions, carrots, and garlic in the hot oil or margarine, stir in the beans, black peppercorns, red pepper flakes or chili, bayleaf, water, and vinegar. Bring to the boil, add the meat, and stir well. Simmer until the meat and beans are tender; add the tomatoes after the dish has been cooking for about an hour, then half an hour later add the chorizos.

3. Remove the meat and sausages, slice them, and put everything into a heated casserole for serving. Taste for seasoning, and serve with cooked cornmeal (see Polenta, p. 110), and beer.

Salt Pork and Cream Gravy

Serves 4

1 lb (450 g) salt belly of pork

1 egg, size 3

4 tbsp plain flour

8 fl. oz (225 ml) soured cream

4 fl. oz (100 g) single cream

It must be explained that American salt pork – so widely used in New England and the South – is much leaner than the variety sold under that name in delicatessens here. Salt belly of pork answers very well in this recipe. Cut off the rind and any bones.

1. Cut the pork in thin slices and parboil for ten minutes. Drain it well and dry on kitchen paper. Heat a heavy frying pan very hot, and cut off about 1 oz (25 g) of the pork fat, put it in the pan, and let it melt well.

2. Beat the egg, and dip the pork slices first in egg and then in the flour. Keep aside any flour that is not clinging to the meat. Fry in hot fat until crisp and brown. Remove the meat, keeping it warm in a hot dish, and pour off all but two tablespoons of the pan drippings. Stir in the reserved flour, and scrape around the pan to pick up any brown bits. On the lowest possible heat, very gradually stir in the soured cream and the single cream – do *not* let it boil. Taste, and season with black pepper if you like. Pour over the pork.

Jacket potatoes and some tart apple purée are very good with this.

Scalloped Ham and Potatoes

Serves 8

2 oz (50 g) butter or margarine

1 large mild onion, finely chopped

3 tbsp flour

1 tsp salt·

Freshly ground black pepper

1 tsp dry mustard

12 fl. oz (350 ml) milk

4 oz (100 g) mild Cheddar cheese, grated

4 large potatoes, sliced about ¼ in. (0·75 cm) thick

14 oz–1 lb (400–450 g) cooked ham, diced

4 large stalks celery, sliced

1 medium green pepper, de-seeded

This is such a good buffet party dish that I give the larger quantities, but the recipe may be halved for four.

Preheat oven to 350°F (180°C), Gas 4.

1. Melt the butter in a large saucepan and sauté the onion until soft but not browned. Stir in the flour, salt, pepper, dry mustard, then take the pan off the heat and gradually add the milk, stirring constantly. Return the pan to the heat and bring to the boil, lower the heat, and stir until the sauce thickens. Stir in the cheese.

2. In a 3 pt (2 litre) casserole, well buttered, make layers of the potato, ham, celery, green pepper, and cheese sauce. End with the cheese sauce. Cover and bake for one hour, remove the cover and bake for another thirty to forty-five minutes until the potatoes are cooked and the sauce bubbles and browns on the top.

Yucatan Peninsula Roast Pork

Serves 4–6

2 dry hot red chilis, carefully de-seeded and washed

5 black peppercorns

1 large bayleaf, crumbled

4 cloves

8 allspice berries, crushed

2 fl. oz (50 ml) cider or wine vinegar

2 large cloves garlic, crushed with 1 heaped tbsp sea salt

1 tsp whole cumin seed

2 lb (900 g) boneless pork

Serve this pork dish with something cool – avocado slices on cos lettuce, or thinly sliced tomatoes – and a loaf of French bread. This isn't very Mexican, but is useful for blotting. Something bland like hominy grits goes well with this spiced pork.

Very important: be careful when handling chilis as they can burn. Use rubber gloves, and do not rub your face or your eyes after de-seeding the chilis.

1. Pour boiling water over the chilis in a cup and steep for thirty minutes. Drain and discard the water. In a blender or food processor, blend the chilis with the bayleaf, peppercorns, cloves, allspice, vinegar, garlic, salt, and cumin seed.

2. With a thin, very sharp knife, stab the pork deeply, all over, and turn it over in the chili mixture. Wearing your rubber gloves, rub and press the mixture into the slits. Let the pork stand under a plastic film wrap in the refrigerator overnight.

3. Preheat the oven to 350°F (180°C), Gas 4. Put the meat in a deep casserole and cook for one and a half hours, turn it, and cook for another forty-five minutes. Stir in 4 fl. oz (100 ml) of hot water, and scrape to loosen the drippings. Cover and cook for another hour until the meat is completely tender. Skim the fat from the sauce, slice the meat and serve, passing the sauce separately.

Czechoslovakian Pork with Horseradish

Serves 4–6

2 lb (just under 1 kg) lean pork, from the leg, cut in 1½ in. (4 cm) cubes

2 tbsp butter or margarine (or clean pork dripping)

¾ pt (425 ml) water

8 fl. oz (225 ml) cider or white wine vinegar

1 medium onion, peeled, and stuck with 3 cloves

1 medium carrot, scraped and thickly sliced

2 large stalks celery, cut in 1 in. (2·5 cm) lengths

1 level tbsp sea salt

1 tsp caraway seeds

½ tsp freshly ground black pepper

2 level tbsp porridge oats

2 oz (50 g) grated horseradish

Soured cream

Potatoes

1. Brown the pork well in hot butter in a large flameproof casserole or saucepan, and add all the other ingredients except the oats and horseradish. Bring to the boil, lower the heat and simmer, covered, for one and a half hours until the pork is tender. Add the oats for the last fifteen minutes.

2. Remove the meat with a slotted spoon and put into a hot serving dish. Sieve the stock, then liquidise it with the vegetables, and pour this sauce over the meat. Spoon the horseradish over and around the meat, and stir it into the sauce.

Serve with steamed or boiled potatoes, and a bowl of soured cream.

Opposite *American ways with pork.* Top *Chinese Spareribs; Dragon Mustard and Plum Sauce;* Centre *Seventh Avenue Delicatessen Coleslaw;* Bottom *Virginia Baked Ham*

Overleaf *A barbecue and all its trimmings.* Clockwise from top centre *Arizona Barbecued Lamb, Golden Gate Salad, Cornbread, California Spitted Chicken, Grilled Hamburgers, Corn on the Cob, Oregon and Lemon Barbecue sauces*

Vegetables and Pasta

Scalloped Aubergine

Serves 4

1 aubergine, about 1½ lb (675 g)

4 fl. oz (100 ml) boiling water

1 small onion, about 4 oz (100 g), very finely chopped

2 oz (50 g) butter

4 fl. oz (100 ml) milk

2 eggs, size 3

2 oz (50 g) fresh soft breadcrumbs, brown or white

½ tsp salt

2 oz (50 g) Cheddar cheese, grated

The eggplant (aubergine) journeyed from India through the Middle East to Spain, and on to the Spanish colonies in the Americas. In colour, it can range from almost white (the earliest ones must have looked like giant eggs), to the glossy deep purple we know. This is a recipe from Texas, where those handsome vegetables grow in profusion.

Preheat oven to 375°F (190°C), Gas 5.

1. Peel and dice the aubergine and simmer in boiling water until tender but not mushy. Drain it very well in a colander, then put into a bowl. Melt 1 oz (25 g) of butter in a heavy frying pan, and sauté the onion until it is pale gold. Stir it into the aubergine.

2. Whisk the eggs and milk together and lightly mix into the aubergine. Melt the remaining butter and mix it with the crumbs and salt in a separate bowl. Put a layer of aubergine in the bottom of a baking dish, cover with a layer of crumbs, and continue, ending with crumbs. Sprinkle the surface with the cheese, and bake for about half an hour.

New Orleans Baked Aubergine with Shrimp

Serves 4 or 8

2 large aubergines, or 4 small ones

1½ lb (675 g) uncooked prawns

3 oz (75 g) butter

1 tbsp vegetable oil

1 large onion, finely chopped

1 clove garlic, finely chopped

1 thick slice white bread, soaked in a little milk

1 bayleaf, torn up

1 tsp dried thyme

2 tbsp parsley, chopped

2 tbsp tomato purée

Salt, freshly ground black pepper, a good pinch of cayenne

2 rounded tbsp fresh breadcrumbs

This may be served warm (not hot) as a main dish for four, or cooled, on a bed of soft lettuce as a starter for eight.

Preheat oven to 350°F (180°C), Gas 4.

1. Cut the aubergines in half lengthwise. Boil in enough water to cover for about fifteen minutes until tender. Test carefully with a fork, but don't break the skins. Drain with the flesh side down. Carefully remove the flesh but leave about ¼ in. (0·5 cm) in the shell.

2. Roughly cut up the aubergine flesh and put in a sieve to drain. Boil the prawns for three minutes and shell them. Heat the oil and 1½ oz (35 g) of butter in a frying pan and sauté the onions until they are translucent, stirring well. Add the garlic and sauté another minute or two.

3. Squeeze the bread and mix with the aubergine flesh, prawns, and all the seasonings. Stir into the onion and garlic mixture and cook for two minutes. Put aubergine shells in a buttered baking dish, close together, and fill with prawn mixture. Spread evenly with breadcrumbs and dot the remaining butter over the shells. Bake for fifteen minutes.

Boston Baked Beans

Serves 4–6

1 lb (450 g) dried white haricot beans

12 oz (350 g) salt belly of pork, or bacon ends

Scant tsp salt

1 large onion peeled

3 oz (75 g) black treacle

2 tsp dry mustard

1 tsp freshly ground black pepper

'So here's to good old Boston,
The home of the bean and the cod,
Where the Cabots speak only to the Lowells,
And the Lowells speak only to God.'

Beans were being grown in the coastal states of the Eastern part of America, long before it was colonised. The Indians knew that legumes would flourish even in poor soil, could be dried for winter storage, and were good eating any time of the year. Even before those other two Boston institutions – the Cabots and the Lowells – became famous, baked beans, with molasses and fat salt pork, were probably being made all through the New England colonies.

Baked beans used to be served with Boston Brown Bread (see p. 157), on Saturday nights, then reheated for Sunday supper – proper Bostonians did not cook on the Sabbath. They (the beans, not the Bostonians) can cook all day in an electric slow cooker or slow oven.

1. Soak the beans overnight in enough cold water to cover very generously. Drain well. (Or: bring them to the boil in 1½ pts – a scant litre – of cold water, boil for two minutes, remove from the heat, and let stand, covered, for two hours before draining.)

2. Blanch the salt pork or bacon for five minutes in boiling water, and drain. Put the beans and a pinch of the salt in a large saucepan and add enough cold water to cover the beans to a depth of 2 in. (5 cm). Bring to the boil, lower the heat, simmer until the beans are barely tender. Drain well. Mix the black treacle, mustard, and pepper and add to the beans. Preheat the oven to 250°F (120°C), Gas 1.

3. Put the peeled onion in the bottom of a large casserole, or in the traditional round-bellied brown bean pot – whichever you use, it must have a tight lid. Cut up the pork. Put a layer of beans in the pot, add half the pork, the rest of the beans, and the remaining pork. Pour in boiling water just to cover, and bake for about six hours, adding fresh hot water from time to time.

4. Take off the lid, raise the heat to 350°F (180°C), Gas 4, and bake for another thirty to forty-five minutes, until the pork bits brown and the beans are slightly crusted on top. Taste for salt and add it if it is necessary. The beans are always served out of the bean pot at the table, and everyone should have a bit of the mahogany-brown pork and a scrap of onion.

Florentine Cannelloni

Serves 6 as a main dish

8 oz (225 g) very broad noodles

For the filling

8 oz (225 g) mushrooms

1 small clove garlic

3 tbsp olive oil, or olive and soya oil mixed

5 oz (125 g) cooked chicken, finely chopped

1 hard-boiled egg, finely chopped

Pinch of dried thyme

Pinch of dried basil

2 tbsp single cream

For the sauce

1 oz (25 g) butter

2 tbsp flour

8 oz (225 ml) chicken stock

4 fl. oz (100 ml) single cream

3 tbsp Parmesan cheese, grated

A considerable confusion exists about cannelloni – traditional cannelloni noodles are wide squares, which are filled, rolled, and baked. However, sometimes one finds in London shops a form of tube-shaped hard pasta also called cannelloni. Whether you use the wide square noodles or the shaped hard pasta, this filling from Tuscany is very simple and extremely good.

1. Cook the noodles in a large quantity of boiling water for about five to seven minutes and drain well. If using tube-shaped pasta, follow makers' directions.
2. Chop the mushrooms and garlic, heat the oil, and brown them lightly. Add all the other ingredients to the pan and mix lightly. Cool for about five minutes. Put about one tbsp of filling on each square, and roll it up like a cigar. Put the cannelloni seam-side down in a shallow gratin dish. Heat the grill very hot.
3. Blend the butter, flour, and *cold* chicken stock in a saucepan, bring to the boil, stirring vigorously, then lower the heat and let the sauce simmer for about two minutes until it is thickened and smooth, stirring from time to time. Add the cream. Taste for seasoning and add salt, and freshly ground pepper if necessary. Stir in the grated Parmesan.
4. Spread the sauce evenly over the cannelloni and put the dish under the grill. Cook only until the top is golden and the cheese sauce bubbles. For an even crustier top, sprinkle with about two tbsp grated Parmesan before putting the dish under the grill.

If you can make your own pasta, so much the better – then you can cut the squares to any size and shape you like. Home-made pasta should be cooked only about three to four minutes before draining and proceeding as in the recipe.

Harvard Beets

Serves 4

4 oz (100 g) caster sugar

1 oz (25 g) cornflour

3 fl. oz (75 ml) red wine vinegar

3 medium beetroots, cooked and peeled – about 1 lb (450 g) after cooking

2 oz (50 g) butter or good margarine

This is a dish long loved in New England. I have read somewhere that the odd name may be a reference to the traditional red of the Harvard College football team jerseys – the 'Crimson', which is also the name of the student newspaper. Harvard beets can be absolutely dreadful to eat – a thick, pinkish sweet sauce blanketing the honest slices of cooked beetroot – or it can be as delicious as this is.

1. In a double boiler, mix the cornflour with the vinegar and sugar. Cook it over boiling water, stirring, until it is smoothly thickened. Slice the hot cooked beetroots, and add them to the sauce. Lower the heat, and let the beetroot cook a little more in the hot sauce, while the red colour blends in. It should take about ten minutes.

2. At the last minute, stir in the butter so that the sauce looks glossy and rich but not oily.

Broccoli in Cheese Custard

Serves 4

10 oz (275 g) packet frozen broccoli, or fresh broccoli

½ pt (275 ml) milk

4 oz (100 g) Gruyère (or Jarlsberg) cheese, grated

2 eggs, size 3

2 tbsp lemon juice

1 oz (25 g) melted butter or margarine

1 tsp salt

Freshly ground black pepper

Preheat oven to 350°F (180°C), Gas 4.

1. Cook the broccoli until just tender but still slightly crisp. Cut it up roughly, not too fine. Whisk all the other ingredients well together.

2. Butter a casserole (about 8 in., 20 cm), put in the broccoli, and pour the egg and milk mixture over it. Set the casserole in a roasting tin and pour in about 1 in. (2·5 cm) of hot water. Bake for forty to fifty minutes, until a thin-bladed knife thrust in the centre comes out clean.

If you want to make this rather more elegant, separate the eggs, whisk the whites to soft peak stage, mix the beaten yolks with the rest of the ingredients, and then gently cut and fold in the whites; bake as above.

Corn Fritters

Serves 4–6

4 oz (100 g) plain flour

1 tsp baking powder

½ tsp salt

2 eggs, size 3

11 oz (300 g) tin whole-kernel corn

4 fl. oz (100 ml) milk

Oil for frying

Serve these with fried chicken, or with the Herb-Breaded Chicken (see p. 62). In some parts of the South, corn fritters are dished up for Sunday breakfast with corn syrup (the nearest English equivalent would be golden syrup) and crisply fried bacon. In other parts of the country, they are called Corn Oysters.

1. Sift the dry ingredients together. Separate the eggs and whisk the yolks well, stir into the drained corn, and mix with the dry ingredients. Add the milk and mix thoroughly. Whisk the egg whites stiff, and cut and fold into the corn mixture.

2. Heat the oil in a deep-fryer to 380°F (190°C) and drop in the mixture by tablespoons, cooking until light brown on both sides. If you prefer, shallow-fry the fritters in about 1 in. (2·5 cm) of oil in a hot frying pan. Drain on kitchen paper and serve hot.

Corn Pie

Serves 6

4 oz (100 g) cream crackers, crushed finely

4 oz (100 g) margarine, melted

½ pt (275 ml) milk

12 oz (350 g) frozen corn, cooked, or tinned whole-kernel corn, drained

½ tsp salt

Freshly ground black or white pepper

1 tbsp chopped onion

2 tbsp flour

2 eggs, size 3

½ tsp paprika

Preheat oven to 400°F (200°C), Gas 6.
1. Mix the crushed cream crackers with the margarine, set aside about one-third of the mixture. Press the remaining crumbs firmly into an 8 in. (20 cm) pie tin or quiche dish.
2. Mix 8 fl. oz (225 ml) of the milk, the corn, salt, pepper, and onion in a saucepan and bring to the boil, then lower the heat and simmer gently for three minutes. Whisk the flour into the remaining milk and gradually stir it into the corn mixture. Cook, stirring, until it thickens, then remove from the heat and cool slightly.
3. Whisk the eggs well, stir about 2 tbsp of the hot mixture into the eggs, blend, and stir it back into the corn. Pour into the pie tin, sprinkle with the remaining crumbs and paprika. Bake for about fifteen minutes. Cut into wedges to serve.

Cornmeal

Serves 4–6

4 cups water

1 cup cornmeal, fine or medium, not coarse

1 tsp salt

1 tbsp butter or margarine

Corn (maize) runs like golden thread through America's history: corn, squash (marrow), and pumpkins were known to the Indians before the Pilgrims landed on Plymouth Rock. Dried and ground into meal, corn is a food of at least one hundred uses – in bread, as a substitute for potatoes or rice, in cakes and puddings. Cooked cornmeal is not only an early-American dish, but is served as polenta by Italian Americans, mamaliga by those of Romanian origin, and is the basis for tamale pie in the Southwest.

Here is the fundamental, bed-rock cornmeal recipe, and some ideas for its use. For once, I must express the measures in cups rather than ounces/grams, as cornmeal available in Britain varies as to its texture and volume. Use a large cup (or a cottage-cheese container) which holds 8 fl. oz (225 ml) of water, as your measure.

In a large saucepan, bring water to the boil, then trickle the cornmeal very slowly through your fingers, stirring the mixture with a wooden spoon, so that it doesn't curdle into lumps. Lower the heat to the barest simmering point, and cook until it is smooth and thick, stirring often. Cook for about twenty minutes more; it may be easier to do all this in the top of a double saucepan over boiling water, in which case cook in all for about forty-five minutes. Stir in salt and butter.
Polenta. Scoop the cornmeal into a ring on a heated serving plate, and fill the centre with your favourite Italian meat-and-tomato sauce.

Cornmeal Mush. Stir in an additional 3 oz (75 g) butter and serve as a vegetable with fried chicken, pork chops, or chili.
Fried Cornmeal Mush. Put the cooked cornmeal into a mould or bread tin and chill well, then cut it in slices and fry in hot fat until it is crisp and brown. In New England and Pennsylvania, this is a breakfast dish often served with maple syrup; in the South, slices of fried cornmeal go with pan-fried quail, squirrel, or fish.
Tamale Pie. This is a dish based on cooked cornmeal, and for the recipe, see p. 77.

Gnocchi (Semolina or Cornmeal)

Serves 2–4

1 pt (550 ml) milk

4 oz (100 g) semolina *or* fine cornmeal

1 oz (25 g) butter or good margarine

4 tbsp Parmesan or Cheddar cheese, grated

1 tsp salt

Several gratings of fresh nutmeg

1 egg, size 3, beaten

1 tbsp melted butter or margarine

Every Italian restaurant in America seems to have gnocchi on its menu; pronounced as near as possible as N'Yawki, but I've heard it said G-Knocki or Yonnkee. Forget the pronunciation and enjoy the light and subtle texture and flavour. These quantities serve two as a light supper dish, or four as a vegetable.

1. Bring the milk to simmering point and very slowly trickle in the semolina or cornmeal. Lower the heat as much as you can, and cook, stirring, until it thickens and is smooth. Add the butter, half the cheese, the salt, and nutmeg. Remove from the heat, stir again, and when slightly cooled whisk in the beaten egg and stir vigorously until it smooths out again.
2. Pour onto an oiled marble slab, about $\frac{3}{8}$ in. (1 cm) thick, or into a shallow buttered roasting tin. Smooth and spread it evenly and let it get cold and set. Preheat oven to 350°F (180°C), Gas 4.
3. With a small thin-edged glass dipped frequently in hot water, cut circles about 2 in. (5 cm) in diameter, and lay them, overlapping, in a buttered shallow gratin dish. Scatter the rest of the cheese evenly over them, pour on the melted butter, and bake for about fifteen to twenty minutes until lightly crusted and bubbly.

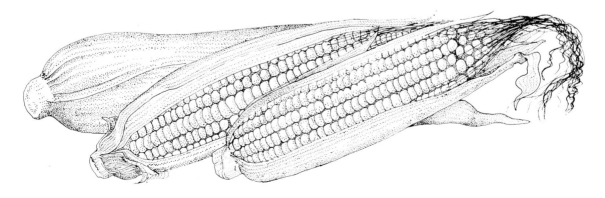

Mississippi Corn Pudding

Serves 4

12 oz (350 g) tinned cream-style corn

½ tbsp caster sugar

½ tsp salt

1 oz (25 g) butter or margarine, melted

3 eggs, size 3

½ pt (275 ml) milk

½ tbsp cornflour

½ tbsp cold water

'Cawn puddin' – this recipe comes from the Millbrook Plantation, built by slave labour in the eighteen-forties, and was written down by a cook whose great-great-grandmother cooked in that house before the Civil War (1860–65).

Preheat oven to 350°F (180°C), Gas 4.

1. Mix the corn with the sugar, salt, and butter, or margarine. Whisk the eggs with the milk and blend with the corn. Mix the cornflour with the cold water to a smooth paste, and stir into the corn mixture.
2. Lightly butter a shallow 1½ pt (850 ml) casserole, pour in the mixture, and bake about an hour until it is a firm custard.

Grits, or Hominy Grits

Serves about 4

6 oz (175 g) grits

1 tsp salt

1½ pts (850 ml) boiling water

Scant 1 oz (25 g) butter

In certain rather up-market English shops, one sometimes sees packages of grits – which makes transplanted Southerners fall about with laughter, especially when they see the price. Grits, you see, started life as rockbottom, end-of-the-month, empty-purse food. It is cornmeal that has been treated with lye to make it very white. It's the best background for various 'trimmings' that can be imagined. I have had grits with red gravy, with fried catfish, baked in a sort of soufflé, with fried chicken, and for breakfast with light molasses (rather like golden syrup). Harris Jackson of The Associated Press started life in Baton Rouge, Louisiana, went on to Singapore, and has been known to dish up grits with curry.

1. Pour the grits in a steady stream, through your fingers, into the boiling salted water, stirring with a long wooden spoon. When it boils again, turn down the heat and simmer about forty-five minutes, stirring every few minutes, and making sure to scrape all around the bottom of the saucepan.
2. Put in a heated serving dish and add the butter. Serve in place of potatoes with any fairly highly-seasoned dish.

Fried hominy grits. Pour any leftover grits into an oiled loaf tin and chill. Cut in slices about ⅜ in. (1 cm) thick, dip them in milk, and fry in hot fat until brown on both sides. Serve with any sauce or gravy, or with golden syrup.

Barley and Mushroom Casserole

Serves 4

1 large onion, finely chopped

8 oz (225 g) mushrooms, sliced

2½ oz (50–60 g) butter or margarine

6 oz (175 g) pearl barley

1 pt (550ml) beef or chicken stock

Preheat the oven to 350°F (180°C), Gas 4.

1. Gently sauté the onion and mushrooms in melted butter until the onion is soft. Stir in the barley, raise the heat, and cook until it browns slightly, stirring from time to time.
2. Pour the mixture into a buttered casserole and add ½ pt (275 ml) of the stock. Cover, and bake about thirty minutes. Add the remaining stock and bake, covered, another twenty minutes to half an hour until the liquid is absorbed and the barley is tender.

I have omitted any mention of salt or pepper, as this depends on the seasoning of the stock. Taste the mixture half way through the cooking time and correct the seasoning if necessary.

San Diego Zucchini

Serves 4–6

12 courgettes, about 5 in. (13 cm) long

Salt

2 eggs, size 3

Flour

Margarine for frying (about 1½ oz or 25–35 g)

¾ pt (425 ml) soured cream

4 oz (100 g) sharp Cheddar cheese, grated

This creamy-topped courgette dish from California will serve four as a light luncheon main course, or six as a vegetable. The courgettes must be young, firm, and all the same size.

1. Wash the courgettes and cut off the blossom end. Cook in just enough boiling salted water to cover them, until barely tender. Drain well and cool. Whisk the eggs with about ¼ tsp salt. Roll the courgettes in flour and let them stand while you heat the margarine in a heavy frying pan. Dip the courgettes quickly in the egg, and fry until brown, turning them over several times. (The amount of margarine depends on the size of the courgettes.)
2. Put the courgettes in one layer in a shallow heatproof dish or grill pan, pour on the soured cream, and sprinkle with the cheese. Grill under a hot flame until the topping bubbles and browns.

French-fried Courgettes

Serves 6

2 lb (900 g) even-sized courgettes

1 clove garlic, crushed with ½ tsp salt

About 3 oz (75 g) plain flour

Oil for frying

1. Wash the courgettes and cut them in ¼ in. (0·75 cm) slices, or if you have a chip-cutting gadget, cut them as though you were making chips. Mix the garlic salt with flour in a plastic bag, and toss the courgette pieces well.
2. Heat the oil to 375°F (190°C) in a deep-fryer and cook the courgettes, in batches, for about two minutes. Drain on kitchen paper, taste one, and if you like, sprinkle with salt and freshly ground black pepper. Serve at once.

Chili Con Queso

14 oz (400 g) tin Italian peeled tomatoes, drained

4 oz (100 g) tin mild or hot green chilis, drained

1 small onion, finely chopped

1 oz (25 g) butter or good margarine

Pinch of light brown sugar

½ tsp salt

3 black peppercorns

Bayleaf

8 oz (225 g) mild Cheddar cheese (the nearest thing to Monterey Jack cheese)

This is a chili and cheese combination served with French bread, tortillas, or good home-made white bread – a wonderful recipe from Taos, New Mexico, often served as an accompaniment to drinks, or as an appetiser. It's almost like a fondue mixture, and can be made in a fondue pot and kept warm over a very low heat so that people can spear a piece of French bread and dip it into the chili mixture.

1. Chop the tomatoes and chilis. Heat the butter in a heavy frying pan or fondue pot, and sauté the onion until it is soft and transparent. Add the tomatoes, chilis, sugar, salt, perppercorns, and bayleaf and simmer for fifteen minutes.
2. Add the cheese, and as it begins to melt lower the heat and cook until it is well-blended with the tomatoes. Keep it warm as you serve it, for it goes stringy when it cools.

Hoppin' John

3 oz (75 g) black-eyed peas

12 fl. oz (350 ml) water

Pinch of salt

1 small onion, coarsely chopped

A ham bone with some meat still on it, or about 2 oz (50 g) of salt belly of pork or smoked bacon ends

Good pinch of cayenne

Freshly ground black pepper

3 oz (75 g) long-grain rice

Generous 1 oz (25 g) butter or margarine

Another recipe from the Deep South, I think from Georgia. 'Cow peas', black-eyed beans, dried butter beans, hominy (lye-bleached corn kernels), and red beans, are among the thrifty, filling, and protein-rich foods that came out of the country cooking of Georgia, Alabama, and the Carolinas. Hoppin' John is black-eyed peas with rice, and is usually served with cornbread (see p. 159), spread with plenty of cold butter.

1. Wash the peas and pick them over. In a saucepan with a tight lid, bring the peas to boil with enough water to cover them, boil them for two minutes, cover tightly, and let stand for two hours. Drain them, and cover with the 12 fl. oz (350 ml) of fresh cold water. Add the salt, onion, and the ham bone or salt pork or bacon ends.
2. Cover and bring to the boil, lower the heat and simmer about one and a quarter hours, until the peas are tender and the water is almost absorbed. If there is too much liquid at the end of the cooking time, pour it away. Strip the meat off the ham bone if used, and stir it back into the peas. Taste, and season with as much or as little black pepper and cayenne as you like.
3. Let the peas cook on the very lowest heat while you boil or steam the rice. Stir the butter into the rice, mix it with the peas, and raise the heat to high, stirring round with a wooden spoon just until everything is heated together.

Lima Beans in Curry Sauce

Serves 4

15 oz (425 g) tinned butter beans

Milk or single cream

1½ oz (25–35 g) butter or margarine

1 small onion, finely chopped

2½ tbsp flour

½ tsp salt

½–¾ tsp mild curry powder

These plump, slightly curved beans are a true native of the Americas, first found in Peru – but they're pronounced Lyma, not Leema. Both fresh and dry, they were a staple of the American Indians centuries ago. They need abundant sunshine and rain, so have never been grown in any quantity in Europe. Tinned or dried butter beans may be substituted for dried limas in almost any recipe; fresh or frozen small broad beans, while not quite the same, are acceptable in recipes that specify fresh or frozen lima beans.

Preheat oven to 350°F (180°C), Gas 4.

1. Drain the beans and reserve the liquid: make it up to ½ pt (275 ml) with milk or cream. In a small heavy saucepan, melt the butter or margarine, and sauté the onion until it is pale gold. Stir in the flour, and cook, stirring, until it bubbles. Add the salt and curry powder, and cook for five minutes on a very low heat.
2. Gradually add the milk and bean liquid mixture, and cook, stirring, until it is smooth and thick. Taste, and add more curry powder if you like. Stir in the beans, and put everything in a shallow casserole. Bake for about half an hour until brown and bubbling.

Mrs Mannucci's Green Beans with Lemon

Serves 4

1 lb (450 g) whole green beans

1 large clove garlic, crushed

3 tbsp olive oil

2 tbsp lemon juice

Rind of half a large lemon, very finely chopped

Freshly ground black pepper

Salt

4 tbsp Parmesan cheese, grated

I don't know who Mrs Mannucci is (or was), I do know that her recipe makes a wonderfully fresh-tasting, lively dish to serve with something simple like roast pork, or to accompany Chicken Hash (see p. 68).

1. Top and tail the beans, or if using frozen beans, thaw them. Steam them, if possible, until just tender, about ten to twelve minutes. Do not overcook. If you haven't a steamer, cook them in just enough boiling salted water to cover, and drain very well.
2. Sauté the garlic in hot olive oil in a large heavy frying pan or heavy saucepan – do not let it brown. Stir in the beans, reduce the heat, and stir them around so that they are coated with the oil. Add the lemon juice and rind and a lot of black pepper (my recipe says about three-quarters of a teaspoon). Taste and add salt if necessary.
3. Put in a hot serving dish and sprinkle with Parmesan, turn the beans over lightly with a fork and serve at once.

Mushrooms Stuffed with Crabmeat   *Serves 4*

16 large flat mushrooms

6 oz (175 g) cooked crabmeat (or shrimp)

2 oz (50 g) fine dry breadcrumbs

2 eggs, size 3

1 tbsp chives, chopped

1 tbsp parsley, chopped

Salt, freshly ground black pepper

2 oz (50 g) butter

1–2 tbsp Parmesan cheese, grated

Preheat oven to 375°F (190°C), Gas 5.

1. Cut off the stems of the mushrooms and save them for soup. Wipe the mushroom caps. Mix the crabmeat, breadcrumbs, eggs, parsley, chives, salt, and pepper lightly together.

2. Reserve 1 tbsp of the butter, melt the rest, and brush some of it over each mushroom cap, using what is left to grease a large shallow baking dish. Put in the mushrooms, lightly mound some of the crabmeat mixture into each cap, and sprinkle with cheese. Melt the reserved tbsp of butter and pour it over the mushrooms. Bake for about fifteen to twenty minutes or until the mushrooms are just tender. If they seem to be too dry while baking, baste with a little additional butter, or a few tablespoons of chicken stock.

French-Fried Onion Rings   *Serves 4*

4 large onions, peeled

3 fl. oz (75 ml) milk

About 3 tbsp flour

Salt, freshly ground black pepper

Oil for deep frying

1. Slice the onions about $\frac{1}{4}$ in. (0·75 cm) thick, and separate carefully into rings. Dip them in the milk, then toss in flour well-seasoned with salt and pepper. You may need more flour, it all depends on the size of the onions.

2. Heat the oil in a deep-fryer to 375°F (190°C). Test it by dropping in one ring: if it quickly rises to the surface with bubbles, the temperature is right.

3. Fry the rings in small batches, keeping the oil temperature constant. Drain them on kitchen paper and keep them hot if you can in the oven until all are fried, and serve as quickly as possible.

Frijoles   *Serves 3–4*

6 oz (175 g) dried black or red kidney beans

1 large onion, finely chopped

1 bayleaf

1 clove garlic, crushed with 1 tsp salt

$\frac{1}{2}$ small dry hot red chili pepper, deseeded and chopped

Scant 1 oz (25 g) lard

1 large tomato, peeled and chopped

1. Wash and pick over the beans, put in enough cold water to cover, bring to the boil and boil for ten minutes, then remove from the heat and let stand, covered, for two hours. Add half the chopped onion and garlic, the bayleaf and chili, bring to the boil and simmer gently, adding more water as needed. When the beans begin to look wrinkled, add half the lard and cook on.

2. When the beans are soft, add about 1 tsp more salt, and cook for another thirty minutes until the liquid is almost cooked away.

3. Heat the remaining lard and sauté the remaining onion and garlic until soft, add the tomato, and cook for two or three minutes. Take a tablespoon of beans from the pot and with a fork mash them into the tomato mixture, then add

another tablespoon and mash, and finish with a third tablespoon. Stir this thick bean paste back into the pot and cook for a few minutes over a low heat to thicken the sauce.

Frijoles Refritos (Re-fried Beans). Start as above in Steps 1 and 2; for Step 3, use a large frying pan for sautéeing the onion and garlic, and gradually, by big spoonfuls, stir in and mash all the beans from the pot. You will probably need some more lard. Cook the mixture until it is thick and looks rather dry. Taste for seasoning, add more salt if necessary. Delicious as a spread for tortillas (see p. 168).

Deep-Dish Chicago Style Pizza

Serves 6

2 tsp dried yeast

2 tbsp hand-hot water

8 fl. oz (225 ml) boiling water

1 tbsp lard or margarine

1 tsp salt

$\frac{1}{2}$ tsp caster sugar

12 oz (350 g) strong bread flour, or '85%' light brown flour

Olive oil, or olive and soya oil mixed

Sauce as in Traditional Neapolitan Pizza (see overleaf), and same toppings

The worst pizza I have ever eaten was in Naples, the best in London – at the Chicago Pizza Pie Factory. Deep-dish pizza is unlike the traditional Neapolitan kind in that it has less dough crust and more filling. It seems to have originated in Chicago some time after World War II, and long may it flourish. This recipe came from a church group in Berwyn, Illinois, which makes pizzas by the dozen for fund-raising.

1. Dissolve the yeast in the warm water and set it aside to froth up. Stir the boiling water into the lard, salt, and sugar and whisk until smooth. Cool to lukewarm and stir in the yeast liquid. Add about half the flour and beat to a smooth batter, then mix in the remaining flour to make a soft dough. You may need a little more, depending on the flour.

2. Knead well on a floured board until the dough is firm and springy. Divide into two pieces and wrap one piece in plastic film. Roll or pat out the remaining dough to $\frac{1}{4}$ in. (0·75 cm) thickness and shape it into a round. Lightly oil a 9 in. (23 cm) round sandwich tin, about 2 in. (5 cm) deep, and press the dough into it, pulling it up around the edges and pressing down the base so it will not shrink. Brush with a little olive oil and let it rise in a warm place for about fifteen minutes. Preheat oven to 425°F (220°C), Gas 7.

3. Press the dough down lightly with your fingers so that it is even, and bake about five minutes. Fill the shell with sauce to within about $\frac{1}{2}$ in. (1·5 cm) of the top, add the sliced cheese, and any two or three other 'trimmings' that you like. Bake for about twenty minutes, until the cheese is melted and the edge of the crust is brown. Cut in wedges and serve.

The remaining dough may be chilled or frozen, and used to make other pizzas or a small loaf of bread. The reason for giving the double quantity in the recipe is that it is hard to work out a satisfactory dough with precise half-measures of all the ingredients.

Traditional Neapolitan Pizza   *For two 15 in. (28·5 cm) pizzas*

For the dough

16–20 oz (450–550 g) strong bread flour

4 level tsp dried yeast

12 fl. oz (350 ml) water

2½ tsp salt

3 tbsp olive oil, or olive and soya oil mixed

For the sauce

2 tbsp olive oil, or olive and soya oil mixed

1 large clove garlic

28 oz tin (793 g) Italian peeled tomatoes

1 tsp dried oregano

1 tsp dried basil

Dash of hot pepper sauce

For the toppings

Begin with 6 oz (175 g) of Mozzarella or German loaf cheese then add your choice of other savoury ingredients such as

Anchovies soaked in milk

Pepperoni

Mushrooms

Capers

Tiny meatballs

And always finish with grated Parmesan cheese

Nothing is more emblematic of America's many and varied ways of cooking than pizza – which of course is Italian in origin but is by now considered an absolutely all-American dish. Its coast-to-coast variations are innumerable. I have heard that there is actually one made in Arizona with tortillas as a base! Pizzas range in size from 3 in. (8 cm) cocktail miniatures, to the giant 24 in. (60 cm) family-style Sicilian type. Almost all are based on a yeast bread dough – white or wholemeal – given very little raising time after an initial 'proving'. This recipe gives two methods, one with an electric mixer, the other made in a more traditional way.

Quick electric mixer method:

1. To make the dough: combine 8 oz (225 g) of the flour with the yeast in the mixer bowl. Blend water, oil, and salt in a saucepan and heat to lukewarm. Add to the flour mixture and beat on a medium speed for three minutes. Stir in 6–8 oz (175–225 g) more of the flour, to make a stiff dough. Turn it out on a floured surface and knead until smooth. Divide the dough in half and pat each half into a flattened round.

2. Pull the dough circles out evenly to fit 15 in. (38·5 cm) round pizza tins; or form them into rounds, pinch up the edges about ¾ in. (2 cm) and put them on a lightly oiled baking sheet. Let them rest, loosely draped in oiled plastic film, for about thirty minutes before adding the filling.

3. Make the sauce by heating the oil and sautéeing the garlic until it is pale gold. Add the drained tomatoes, oregano, basil, salt, pepper, hot pepper sauce, and a little freshly ground black pepper if you like it. Cook on a moderate heat, stirring to break up the tomatoes, for about ten minutes. Cool slightly and divide the sauce between the pizza rounds. Preheat oven to 450°F (230°C), Gas 8.

4. To top the pizzas, cover with sliced Mozzarella cheese, add any or all of the other suggested ingredients, and end with a thick sprinkling of grated Parmesan. Bake for about ten to twelve minutes, until the crust is browned.

To make the dough without a mixer:

Stir the yeast into half the lukewarm water, add half a teaspoon of sugar, and let it stand to froth up. Mix the yeast liquid into the flour and salt in a basin. Stir the remaining flour and oil together and add to the flour. Mix with your hands, then turn out on a floured board and knead – about ten minutes – until smooth. Put the dough in an oiled bowl, cover with oiled plastic film, and let it rise for about thirty minutes in a warm place. Then proceed to make the dough into two rounds, letting them stand for about ten minutes before adding the topping. Finish as in Step 3 above.

Baked Potatoes (and their variations)

The most famous of American 'baking' potatoes are the Idahos, grown in a soil rich in volcanic ash. The nearest English equivalent would be Golden Wonders. Choose even-sized potatoes, scrub them well, and rub butter, margarine, or oil into the skins. Make a ½ in. (1·5 cm) slash in the skin of each, and bake directly on the shelf of the oven at about 375°F (190°C), Gas 5, for an hour or a little less, depending on the size of the potatoes. Test by squeezing very gently in a towel. Serve them at once, with the top gashed open, a nut of butter put in, salt, and black pepper. Or try one of these popular variations.

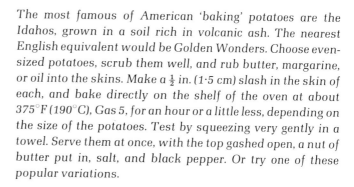

1. Top each baked potato with a spoonful of soured cream mixed with finely chopped chives.
2. Cook thin streaky bacon until very crisp and crumble it into the potato.
3. Cut a deep cross in the top of each potato, turn back the points of the skin, and put about a heaped teaspoonful of grated sharp Cheddar in each.
4. Scoop out the potato from the shell into a hot dish and quickly mix it with 1 tbsp butter, 1 tbsp grated Gruyère, ½ tsp salt, freshly ground black pepper, and ½ tbsp single cream. Fill back into the shell, put on a sheet of aluminium foil and continue to bake about ten to fifteen minutes.

And *always* eat the skin!

Potato Kugele

Serves 4

4 rashers streaky bacon

6–8 medium potatoes, peeled

1 small onion, peeled and finely chopped

2 eggs, size 3

2 tbsp flour

1 tsp salt

Freshly ground black pepper

2 tbsp bacon drippings

This North European dish was brought to America by immigrants from Russia, Poland, or possibly Germany some time in the last century. It's almost a one-dish meal as it stands, or it can be served as a vegetable with something plain like grilled lamb chops, baked ham, or sausages. Put a bowl of very cold soured cream on the table with it.

Preheat the oven to 350°F (180°C), Gas 4.
1. Fry the bacon very crisp and crumble or dice it. Grate the potatoes and press between two sieves, or roll them in a tea-towel to dry them. Mix quickly with all the other ingredients except the bacon drippings: use dripping to grease a shallow casserole. Press the potato mixture firmly and evenly into casserole.
2. Bake for about an hour until it is brown and crusty; serve at once.

Potato Knishes

4 medium potatoes

2 eggs, size 3

½ tsp salt

About 2 tbsp flour

For the filling

About 4 oz (100 g) cooked chopped
  beef, chicken, or chicken livers

1 medium onion, very finely chopped

1 tbsp chicken fat or margarine

Oil for deep-frying

Knishes are remote cousins of dumplings, and are some-times made with dough enclosing cheese, onions and/or meat; the American variety has a Roumanian origin, and is almost always made with potatoes. No politician could hope to pick up votes from the Lower East Side of New York City without being photographed eating a knish, preferably bought from a pushcart on the street.

1. Boil the potatoes until just tender, peel, and mash them and allow them to cool. For the filling, sauté the onion in a hot fat until it is lightly browned, and mix with the cold cooked meat.
2. Beat the eggs with the salt, mix well with the potatoes, then add enough flour to make a soft dough. Pat it out on a floured board to about ¼ in. (0·75 cm) thickness and divide in half. Cut out rounds (or squares).
3. Put some filling on half the rounds, cover each with another piece of potato dough, and crimp the edges well together. Heat oil to 375°F (190°C) in a deep fryer, and fry the knishes until they are brown, a few at a time. Drain on kitchen paper, and serve while hot. For a drier knish, heat the oven to 250°F (120°C), Gas 1, lay them on a baking sheet and bake for about half an hour.

Hashed Brown Potatoes

About 1½ lb (675 g) potatoes, peeled
  and cooked

About 2 oz (50–60 g) bacon drippings

Plenty of salt, freshly ground black
  pepper

1. Cut the potatoes into very small cubes, and season them highly. Heat a heavy frying pan very hot, heat the fat until it sizzles, add the potatoes and push down hard with a big metal palette knife or slice.
2. Set a lid on the frying pan, slightly askew. Lower the heat and let the potatoes cook about half an hour. Gently lift one edge with the palette knife and see whether they're browning nicely on the bottom. Invert a plate the same size as the frying pan over it, and reverse the whole thing so that the potatoes slide out smoothly, brown side up.

Home Fries. This is a much quicker version. Slice or roughly chop the potatoes, heat the fat, toss in the potatoes and cook them, stirring and turning, until they brown all over. Do this on a fairly high flame, and keep them moving so they don't burn. Turn out on a hot platter. This is a good country-and-Western breakfast dish, served with fried eggs and crisp bacon.

Potatoes Hashed in Cream

Serves 6

6 medium steamed or baked potatoes (cold)

3 oz (75 g) bacon drippings or butter

1 generous tsp salt

Freshly ground black pepper

¼ pt (125 ml) single or double cream

1. Peel the potatoes and chop them coarsely. Heat a heavy frying pan and let the fat get spitting-hot before you put the potatoes in. Fry, stirring constantly, until the potatoes are well-browned. Season well, then lower the heat and pour the cream evenly over the potatoes.

2. Cook for three or four minutes more without stirring until the cream has become crusty. Carefully loosen the potatoes with a palette knife, invert a plate over the top of the frying pan and quickly turn out the potatoes, brown side up.

Latkes (Potato Pancakes)

Serves 4

One of the great traditional Jewish dishes of America, potato latkes came at the time of the Diaspora, the last decade of the nineteenth century and the first years of the twentieth. Families have been known to stop speaking to each other for years over the question of flour, or no flour, in potato latkes. Here are two recipes which neatly straddle the problem.

LATKES 1

4 medium potatoes, peeled

1 medium onion

1 egg, size 3

1 tsp salt

¼ tsp white pepper

½ tsp bicarbonate of soda

Butter or margarine for frying

1. Soak the potatoes in cold water for at least two hours. Drain and grate finely, then press the shreds in a sieve or towel until they are quite dry. Grate the onion into the potatoes, add the egg, salt, pepper and bicarbonate, and mix well.

2. Heat the butter in a heavy frying pan, and drop in the mixture by dessert-spoons. Cook gently until golden-brown on the underside, flip over, and cook the second side. Drain on kitchen paper and keep warm while you fry the rest of the pancakes.

LATKES 2

4 medium potatoes, peeled

1 small onion, finely chopped

3 eggs, size 3 or 4

2 tbsp matzo meal *or* breadcrumbs

Salt, freshly ground black pepper

3–4 tbsp good oil for frying

1. Grate the potatoes and squeeze them dry in a tea-towel. Mix with the onion, eggs, salt, pepper, and enough matzo meal or crumbs to make a thin batter.

2. Heat the oil in a heavy frying pan and drop in the pancake mixture by spoonfuls – do not fry too many at a time, and keep the heat high. Brown both sides, drain and serve at once.

This recipe can be made without the onion, then the pancakes may be served as a dessert with cold apple purée, or lemon juice and sugar.

German Fried Potatoes

Serves 4

4 large potatoes, peeled

1 large onion, thinly sliced

3 tbsp good vegetable oil, or bacon
  drippings

1 tsp salt

Freshly ground black pepper

1. Slice the potatoes as evenly as you can, on a mandoline or with the slicing blade of a food processor: they should be about $\frac{1}{8}$ in. (0·5 cm) thick. Heat the oil or drippings in a large heavy frying pan, add the potatoes and onion, give them a good stir around.

2. Cover and let them cook, turning every few minutes, until the potatoes are tender and golden. Season well and serve at once.

Vincent Sardi's Manicotti

Serves 6

*For the manicotti batter, making 24
  5 in. (13 cm) pancakes*

3 eggs, size 3

4 oz (100 g) plain flour

A pinch of salt

8 fl. oz (225 ml) water

A little oil for frying

For the filling

8 oz (225 g) Ricotta or cottage cheese

4 oz (100 g) Mozzarella cheese, cubed

1 egg, size 3

4 oz (100 g) Parmesan cheese, grated

2 tbsp chopped parsley

Salt, freshly ground black pepper

For the sauce

$\frac{1}{2}$ pt (275 ml) home-made tomato sauce
  (see p. 147)

This recipe has travelled a long way: it came to me as a photocopy of a much-stained newspaper cutting from (I think) a San Francisco newspaper which went out of business in 1955. It had gone through many hands on its way. I'm not even sure that the dish did in fact originate in the famous theatrical restaurant on West 44th Street in New York. If not, I can only say to the charming Vincent that I apologise for borrowing his name. In any case, it's a lovely dish.

1. Mix the ingredients for the manicotti pancakes together, beat well, and let the mixture stand half an hour. Heat a shallow crêpe pan, about 5 in. (13 cm) in diameter and oil it very lightly. Pour in a thin layer of batter, tilt the pan so that it runs evenly over the surface, and cook on a high heat on one side only until the pancake begins to lift from the pan at the edges. Slip it out and lay it on greaseproof paper, uncooked side up. Repeat until all the batter is used up. Preheat the oven to 350°F (180°C), Gas 4.

2. If you are using cottage cheese, press it through a fine sieve. Mix the Ricotta or cottage cheese with the Mozzarella, egg, Parmesan, parsley, salt, and pepper. Put about one heaped tbsp on the uncooked side of each pancake. Roll the pancake and put it, seam side down, in a buttered shallow baking dish (you may need more than one dish).

3. Pour the tomato sauce over the *manicotti*, and bake it for fifteen minutes or until the sauce bubbles and begins to brown. Dust the manicotti with more grated Parmesan just before serving, if you like.

The manicotti can be made in six individual shallow gratin dishes instead of the larger one – four manicotti makes a lavish serving. In fact, this quantity will stretch to feed eight.

Scalloped Potatoes and Onions

Serves 4

4 large potatoes, peeled and thinly
  sliced

1 very large mild onion, or 2 medium
  ones, thinly sliced

3 tbsp flour

1 tsp salt

Freshly ground black pepper

1–1½ oz (25–35 g) butter or margarine

Pinch of dried thyme

¾ pt (425 ml) milk, or a little more

Pinch of mace

Preheat oven to 300°F (150°C), Gas 2.
1. Butter an oblong baking dish and put in a layer of potato slices, then a layer of onions, sprinkle with half the flour, half the salt, plenty of black pepper, repeat until the potatoes, onion, flour and salt are used up. Cut the rest of the butter in flakes over the onions.
2. Pour enough milk in to come just to the top of the layers and sprinkle the mace across the milk. Bake uncovered for about two hours until the potatoes are soft and browned.

Succotash

Serves 4–6

12 oz (350 g) tinned butter beans

12 oz (350 g) frozen corn kernels,
  cooked, or tinned whole-kernel corn

1 oz (25 g) butter

1 tsp salt

½ tsp sugar

2 fl. oz (50 ml) water

¼ pt (125 ml) single or double cream

One of the earliest native American dishes: the name comes from a Narragansett Indian word that seems to mean 'something broken in pieces'. In different parts of the country, succotash means different things: in addition to its original corn and beans, it sometimes includes tomatoes and onions. In England, it is necessarily a compromise dish, using the best tinned butter beans you can find (the kind sometimes called Golden Lima Beans).

1. Cook the vegetables until they are just tender, and mix with all the other ingredients except the cream. Simmer for about five minutes on very low heat.
2. Stir in the cream and cook for another minute or two until it is well heated.

Spaghetti with White Tuna Sauce

Serves 4

8 oz (225 g) spaghetti, cooked *al dente*

2 fl. oz (50 ml) olive oil

1 medium onion, finely chopped

1 clove garlic, crushed

Two 7½ oz (210 g) tins very good tuna

½ tsp freshly ground black or white
  pepper

Salt to taste

Spaghetti with white clam sauce is a great New York (and East Coast generally) dish – a relative newcomer is white tuna sauce, and most delicious it is.

1. Heat the oil and sauté the onion and garlic until golden but not brown. Stir in the drained tuna and simmer for five minutes. Add the pepper, and pour the sauce over the hot, drained spaghetti.
2. With large wooden forks, quickly mix the spaghetti and sauce, and add salt. Serve at once.

Spaghetti Carbonara

Serves 4–6

1 lb (450 g) spaghetti, cooked *al dente* and drained

4 oz (100 g) very lean streaky bacon, without rinds

1 oz (25 g) butter (*not* margarine)

2 oz (50 g) onion, finely chopped (or 1 clove garlic, crushed)

3 eggs, size 3

2 oz (50 g) Parmesan cheese, freshly grated

Freshly ground black pepper

Optional: 2 tbsp parsley, finely chopped

1. Keep the spaghetti hot in a colander over boiling water. Cut the bacon into matchstick-sized pieces and fry quickly in the butter. Stir in the onion or garlic and brown it slightly.
2. In a large bowl, beat the eggs with the cheese, black pepper, and parsley (if used). Mix the spaghetti in very quickly, then instantly pour on the bacon mixture, and toss it all together, rush to the table, and serve on hot plates.

Brown-Sugar Candied Sweet Potatoes

Serves 4

1½ lb (675 g) sweet potatoes or yams

Salt

3 fl. oz (75 ml) water

4 oz (100 g) light or dark brown sugar

1 oz (25 g) butter or margarine

This is an incredibly sweet, luscious dish that goes best with a 'country' ham – a good baked gammon, first boiled, then baked with a glaze of black treacle. Yams are botanically not quite the same as sweet potatoes, but in recipes they are almost interchangeable. If you live near a Caribbean or African market you will often find good yams – firm, with unwrinkled skins. Sometimes they are sold by weight, in pieces cut from a larger yam.

1. Cook the sweet potatoes (or yams) in water until tender but not mushy. Peel them, halve, and sprinkle with salt.
2. In a wide, shallow frying pan, mix the water, sugar, and butter, bring to the boil, put in the sweet potato halves and cook them for about fifteen minutes, turning them over often, until they are 'candied' and the sugar coating looks glazed.

Spring Onion and Noodle Casserole

Serves 4

8 oz (225 g) good egg noodles

Salt, freshly ground black pepper

2 oz (50 g) butter

2 tbsp good salad oil (olive and groundnut oil in equal parts makes a good mixture)

Preheat oven to 400°F (200°C), Gas 6.

1. Cook the noodles in a large saucepan of boiling salted water until they are tender but still slightly firm. Drain them well and pour into a buttered casserole. Stir in the salt and pepper.
2. Heat the butter and oil in a frying pan. Chop the spring onions coarsely, both the white and green parts, and sauté them until they begin to go limp, but do not brown the

8–10 spring onions

1 tbsp parsley, finely chopped

1 heaped tbsp Parmesan cheese, grated

onions. Stir in the parsley and at once mix the onions into the noodles, giving it all a good stir and shake. Scatter the Parmesan over the top and bake for about twelve to fifteen minutes, until golden and bubbling.

This can be made with chopped shallots instead of spring onions, but it isn't as pretty as this attractive green-flecked casserole.

Indiana Baked Tomatoes

Serves 4

4 large ripe Marmande tomatoes

2 oz (50 g) soft fresh breadcrumbs

2 tsp sea salt

1 tsp caster sugar

½ tsp dried basil

2 oz (50 g) butter or margarine, softened

2 tbsp parsley, finely chopped

Indiana is an extraordinary state that ranges from the black industrial areas of the steel town, Gary, in the north, to the beautiful rolling hills and streams of the counties that border on Kentucky. Beefsteak tomatoes – huge, sweet, rich in flavour – are a great Indiana speciality. If you can find Marmande or any of the other continental types, use them for this recipe – nothing else will do.

Preheat oven to 325°F (165°C), Gas 3.
1. Cut the tomatoes crosswise. Mix all the other ingredients and pile them lightly on the tomato halves. Set the tomatoes in one layer in a buttered shallow casserole or quiche dish.
2. Bake for about twenty-five minutes until they are soft and the crumb topping is lightly browned.

Scalloped Tomatoes

Serves 4

6–8 medium tomatoes

1–1½ oz (25–35 g) butter or margarine

2 medium onions, thinly sliced

1 generous tsp salt

Pinch of cayenne

1 tsp caster sugar

Freshly ground black pepper

2 oz (50 g) soft white or brown breadcrumbs, not too fine

Optional: Parmesan or Cheddar cheese, grated

Wherever tomatoes grow large and richly flavoured, this casserole of tomatoes, onions, and breadcrumbs is a ritual accompaniment to fried chicken, game, or pork.

Preheat oven to 375°F (190°C), Gas 5.
1. Drop the tomatoes in boiling water for one minute, drain, and slip off the skins. Cut them in quarters and remove the cores. Heat 1 oz (25 g) of the butter in a heavy frying pan and gently sauté the onions until they are limp but not brown. Lightly butter a casserole and put in a layer of tomatoes, some of the onions, sprinkle with salt, cayenne, sugar, and black pepper, and repeat until everything is used up.
2. Heat the remaining butter and brown the crumbs in it well, stirring often. Press them down on the top of the casserole. Bake for about thirty to forty minutes, and add cheese if you like in the last ten minutes of baking.

Sandwiches, Salads and Dressings

Hero Sandwiches   *(Po' Boys, Grinders, Hoagies, Submarines, Blimpies)*

1. thinly sliced salami, plus olives, tomatoes, mild cheese (Gouda or Mozzarella)

2. hot veal and peppers in tomato sauce

3. hot meatballs in Bolognese sauce

4. raw onions thinly sliced and combined with crisp lettuce and rare roast beef

5. hot eggplant parmigiana (aubergine with tomato sauce and cheese)

All these names are regional words for very much the same thing: French or Italian bread, piled with an assortment of cheeses, meats, vegetables, or whatever. In New York they're Heroes or Blimpies, New Orleans calls them Po' Boys, Philadelphia says Hoagies. On the West Coast, there's a variation named Long Boys (see p. 128).

For each person, one quarter of a long loaf of French bread, or half of a round Italian loaf, sprinkled with olive oil on the cut surfaces. Put on any of the combinations on the left.

Barbecued Frankfurters   *Serves 4*

8 frankfurters (about 12 oz or 350 g)

3 oz (75 g) sweet pickle relish

2 tbsp liquid from the relish

1 tbsp butter or margarine, melted

1 tsp prepared mustard

Pinch each of pepper, onion salt, and garlic salt

8 frankfurter rolls

1. Split frankfurters, lengthwise, about halfway through and fill with the pickle relish. Secure with cocktail sticks (wood, not plastic). Mix pickle relish liquid, margarine, mustard, and seasoning and brush the 'franks' with this mixture.

2. Cook over hot charcoal for about five to seven minutes, or under a grill (three or four inches from heat), brushing frequently with the sauce mixture. Serve on warm frankfurter rolls.

Chili Dogs   *Serves 4 very generously*

Cooking oil

8 oz (225 g) lean beef, minced

1 medium onion, finely chopped

2 level tsp chili seasoning (see Appendix)

$\frac{1}{2}$ tsp salt

6 oz (175 g) home-made tomato sauce (see p. 147), or Buitoni 'Napolitan' sauce

8 frankfurters

8 frankfurter rolls, split

3 oz (75 g) Cheddar cheese, grated

1. Heat a very thin film of oil in a small, heavy frying pan, cook the beef and half the onion until the meat loses its red colour and the onion is translucent. Stir in the chili seasoning, salt, and tomato sauce, and mix well. Simmer for five minutes.

2. In boiling water, heat the frankfurters through. Split and toast the rolls. (If you're barbecuing, cook the frankfurters over hot coals for about three minutes, and toast the rolls at the same time.) Put the frankfurters in the rolls, spread the chili down the centre, and top with remaining onion and cheese.

The Classic Club Sandwich

Serves 4

12 large slices of firm white bread

1 tbsp dry mustard

4 oz (100 g) home-made mayonnaise

12 rashers of lean streaky bacon,
    grilled

2 tomatoes, thinly sliced

4 thin slices of cooked ham

8 slices of cooked turkey breast (or
    chicken)

1 piece of cucumber, about 8 in. (20 cm)
    long, thinly sliced

Optional: pieces of crisp lettuce

Salt, freshly ground black pepper

All very Scott Fitzgerald, this. A tall stack of toast, ham, turkey, tomatoes, and so on, it's the perfect summer lunch. It goes as well with a frosty glass of iced tea with lemon as it does with a crisp dry California white wine.

1. Toast the bread. Mix the mustard with two tbsp of cold water, let it stand for five minutes, then mix with mayonnaise. Spread the toast with the mixture. Arrange three slices of bacon on each of four slices of toast. Put tomato slices and lettuce, if used, on the bacon, and top with another piece of toast, mayonnaise side up.
2. Put one piece of ham on each of these four pieces of toast, two slices of turkey, and some cucumber slices. Sprinkle with salt and pepper, and finish with the last pieces of toast, mayonnaise side down.
3. With a very sharp knife, and holding the layers firmly, slice each sandwich diagonally, then cut each triangle in half again. Secure with cocktail sticks. If you want a really nineteen-twenties effect, serve with thin slices of gherkins and potato crisps.

Western Long Boys

Serves 4

1 loaf French bread

1–1½ oz (25–35 g) butter or margarine

1 small onion, chopped

1 small green pepper, seeded and
    chopped

4 oz (100 g) cooked ham, coarsely
    chopped

4 eggs, size 3 or 4

4 fl. oz (100 ml) milk

½ tsp salt

Freshly ground black pepper

1. Cut the bread into four pieces, split it, toast it, and butter it. In a heavy frying pan, heat the remaining butter and sauté the onion, green pepper, and ham, stirring.
2. Mix the eggs, milk, salt and pepper and pour into the frying pan. Increase the heat, let the mixture set for about one minute, then scramble it all gently for two minutes. Spread the mixture on four pieces of the bread and top with the remaining four – serve at once before the scrambled-egg filling cools.

Served on white or wholewheat bread (or toast), this is a 'Western' or 'Denver' sandwich.

Reuben Sandwiches

There seem to be at least nine versions of this sandwich, which originated in a New York restaurant well patronised by film stars, sports personalities, and rather Runyon-esque

Broadway characters. The original Reuben sandwich was a tower of rye bread, corned beef (salt beef), well-drained sauerkraut, Swiss cheese (Gruyère or Emmenthal), and Russian dressing. It has evolved into a simpler but still impressive affair which starts with rye bread, adds corned beef sliced thinly, then sauerkraut and Gruyère, toasted under a hot grill to melt the cheese, and a final layer of plain or toasted rye bread. If you have one of those sandwich-grill things, you could probably assemble all the makings and toast it all together.

Dagwoods

There *is* no recipe for a Dagwood. It was named after a comic-strip character, Dagwood Bumstead, who was always raiding the refrigerator. It's whatever you can find that seems to go together: cheese, ham, hard-boiled eggs, mayonnaise, left-over roast beef, pickles, tomatoes, chutney, and at least three slices of bread, to make a sort of unrefined club sandwich.

Steak Sandwiches

Just cold, quite rare steak, sliced thinly and put on buttered toast, with plenty of mustard (Dijon or Meaux for choice). A *hot* steak sandwich is meat sliced very thinly, and put into buttered, hot French bread with some steak dripping.

Sloppy Joes

4 big sandwiches, or 6 smaller ones

1½ lb (675 g) lean minced beef

1 medium onion, finely chopped

1½ tsp salt

Freshly ground black pepper

3 tbsp flour

½ tsp Yorkshire relish or
   Worcestershire sauce, or to taste

4 fl. oz (100 ml) ketchup

Approx. ½ pt (275 ml) water

4–6 hamburger buns (baps), split and
   toasted, (see p. 163)

1. In heavy frying pan, cook the beef, onion, salt, and pepper, stirring until the meat loses its red colour. (You may need about a tablespoon of oil if the beef is very lean.) Stir in the flour, Yorkshire relish or Worcestershire sauce, ketchup, and enough water to make a thick, 'sloppy' mixture.

2. Simmer for about twenty minutes, until thick. Toast the rolls or baps and pour on the mixture. Serve with lots of paper napkins. Not a sandwich for the fastidious, but universally popular with the hungry young.

'Pigs in Blankets'

Basic biscuit dough (see p. 154)

8 frankfurters

Prepared mustard

Ketchup

Preheat oven to 400°F (200°C), Gas 6.

1. Roll out dough ¼ in. (·75 cm) thick and cut into pieces the length of the frankfurter and about 4 in. (10 cm) wide. Spread mustard and ketchup on each, then roll dough around the frankfurters, pinching together at edges.

2. Bake on a lightly greased baking sheet for about twenty minutes. For a golden, crisp finish, brush with a mixture of egg and water.

Tostadas

5 oz (125 g) lean beef, minced

1 tsp lard

1 small mild onion, finely chopped

4 oz (100 g) Salsa Fría (see p. 148), or tinned Napolitan sauce (see Appendix)

4 6 in. (15 cm) tortillas (see p. 168)

Oil for frying

Shredded cos lettuce

2 oz (50 g) mild Cheddar cheese, grated

6 oz (175 g) refried beans (see p. 117)

Tomato wedges, sliced spring onions, soured cream

Tortillas that have been crisply fried are then covered with various combinations of meat, cheese, sauces, chilis, soured cream, tomatoes, and so on – tostadas are a Mexican-American traditional favourite. All the makings can be assembled well in advance, and the tortillas fried at the last minute.

1. Fry the minced beef and onion in very hot lard, stirring until the meat loses its red colour and the onion is translucent. Mix with the Salsa Fría and set aside. Keep hot, or reheat when needed.

2. In a deep frying pan, fry the tortillas in about ½ in. (1·5 cm) of very hot oil, turning them several times with tongs until they puff up and brown. Drain on kitchen paper, and put a tortilla on each plate.

3. Spread with shredded lettuce, refried beans, cheese, meat, and top with tomatoes, spring onions, and soured cream.

Blue Cheese Moulded Salad

4 oz (100 g) blue cheese

3 oz (75 g) cream or curd cheese

½ tbsp powdered gelatine

2 tbsp boiling water

3 fl. oz (75 ml) double cream

Cos or Webb's lettuce

Mayonnaise

1. Thoroughly blend the cheeses until smooth. Put the gelatine in a cup and add the boiling water, stir until completely dissolved. Whisk the cream until it stands in soft peaks and gently stir it into the cheese mixture. Lightly mix in the gelatine.

2. Rinse a decorative mould with cold water and lightly fill with the cheese mixture. Chill until it is firm, and turn out on lettuce leaves, cut it in wedges or slices, and pass a bowl of mayonnaise with the salad.

Seventh Avenue Delicatessen Coleslaw

Serves 8

2 lb (900 g) firm white cabbage

8 oz (225 g) mayonnaise

8 oz (225 g) soured cream

1 tsp dry mustard

Salt, freshly ground black pepper, to taste

2 tbsp capers, drained

1 medium carrot, scraped and grated

This is a glorified, New York City version of an old-fashioned American country recipe.

1. Shred the cabbage as finely as you can, with a mandoline or food processor. Mix the mayonnaise, soured cream, mustard, salt, pepper, and capers together, stir in the grated carrot, taste for seasoning, and mix well with the shredded cabbage.
2. Cover tightly with plastic film, and chill for about an hour. This goes well with an American Reuben sandwich (see p. 128), and oddly enough is often served with batter-fried fish fillets or fish sticks – very good, too.

Macaroni Salad

Serves 6

1 lb (450 g) short-cut macaroni

1 small onion, finely chopped

1 small green pepper, seeded and finely diced

3 stalks celery, finely diced

Mayonnaise

Salt, freshly ground black pepper

Garnish: pickled pimientoes, hard-boiled eggs, watercress, parsley, capers, tiny 'cherry' tomatoes.

A variation of Potato Salad, and a picnic favourite almost everywhere north of the Mason-Dixon Line which divides South from North.

Cook the macaroni and drain well. Cool and mix with the onion, pepper, and celery, and stir in the mayonnaise to your taste. Season to taste. Serve with two or three of the above-mentioned garnishes arranged decoratively on or around the bowl. Pass a bowl of well-seasoned mayonnaise with the salad.

Chef's Salad

Serves 4–6

Salad greens (cos lettuce, Webb's, and soft lettuce)

6 oz (175 g) cooked chicken

2 oz (50 g) Gruyère, Emmenthal, or Jarlsberg cheese

5 oz (125 g) cooked ham

1 large stalk celery

2 eggs, size 3, hard-boiled

French dressing (see p. 140)

Salt, freshly ground black pepper

Here is the basic, All-American favourite recipe. It has many regional variations. In California, Texas, and Florida, a chef's salad may have segments of orange or grapefruit in the bowl, and very pleasant it is too.

1. Tear the salad greens into small pieces (do *not* cut them). Cut the chicken, cheese, and ham in slivers. Slice the celery as thinly as you can and cut the eggs in eighths. Combine all these, mix with the salad greens, and toss lightly with French dressing.
2. Taste for seasoning and put the salad in a large wooden or glass bowl.

California Sunshine Salad

Serves 4 or more

2 lemons

4 fl. oz (100 ml) cold water

1½ tbsp powdered gelatine

2 oz (50 g) caster sugar

8 fl. oz (225 ml) boiling water

Small tin crushed pineapple with its juice

3 medium carrots, scraped and grated

Crisp salad leaves (cos or Chinese leaves)

Mayonnaise

Moulded gelatine salads like this one, with fruit and vegetables in them, have a rather 'ladies' bridge club' sound to them, but in fact they are bright, cool, refreshing to taste, and jewel-like in colour. Discard your prejudices and think of this not as a salad in the traditional sense but as something interesting and original.

1. Grate the peel of half of a lemon and mix it with the cold water. Squeeze the juice of the lemons, scoop out the pulp, and press it through a food mill. If you have a blender or food processor: peel the lemons, pare away all the white pith, seed and quarter them, and blend the juice and pulp with the lemon peel and water mixture.
2. Stir the gelatine and sugar together in a cup, dissolve with the boiling water. Put the lemon mixture and the pineapple with its juices in a large bowl, add the gelatine and stir well. Chill until it is syrupy.
3. Stir the grated carrot into the cooling gelatine mixture, pour it into a decorative mould, and chill until it is firm. Turn it out on a bed of lettuce, and serve with a good, tart mayonnaise.

Caesar Salad

Serves 2–6

6 oz (150 g) croûtons made from best white bread

2 large crisp heads of cos lettuce

2 large cloves garlic, crushed with 3 tbsp good olive oil and ¼ tsp salt

Juice of one lemon

2 eggs, size 2

2 oz (50 g) Parmesan cheese, freshly grated

4 fl. oz (100 ml) good olive oil

Salt, black pepper

Worcestershire sauce

Julia Child, doyenne of American-French cooks, tells of a visit fifty years ago to Tijuana, Mexico, where she had the original Caesar Salad. Here is a version of her recipe. Perhaps no other salad has been so bastardised in ten thousand restaurants, with the addition of anchovy fillets, oregano, bits of avocado, bacon, and scraps of what sometimes taste like an old shoe. The real thing is elegantly simple.

1. Make the croûtons, dicing the bread in fairly good-sized pieces (about ½ in. or 1·5 cm), and drying them out in a slow oven. This can be done in advance, and the croûtons frozen or kept in an airtight jar.
2. Wash the lettuce gently and dry well. Put the croûtons in a heavy frying pan and strain the garlic-flavoured olive oil over them. Heat until they are just warm, turning them over with a palette knife. Remove and put in a bowl.
3. Put the lemon juice in a cup. Put the eggs in a saucepan of cold water, bring it to the boil, cover, remove from the heat and let stand for two minutes. Grate the cheese into a small bowl. Set all this out on a tray with the Worcestershire sauce, the salt, croûtons, and a pepper grinder.

4. Arrange the lettuce leaves in a large bowl and pour on four tbsp of oil. Toss and scoop the leaves together with big wooden fork and spoon, turning them over and over on themselves so that they do not break. Sprinkle with a little salt, grind on some pepper, add two more spoonfuls of oil, and toss again. Pour on the lemon juice, six drops of Worcestershire sauce, and break in the eggs (which will still be quite runny). Toss again, lightly but thoroughly, and sprinkle on the cheese. Toss once more, throw in the croûtons, and give two final tosses.

5. Arrange the salad, leaf by leaf, with stems pointing outward, on plates with croûtons along the edge. It's hard to resist eating this glorious salad with your fingers, but a spoon helps scoop up the dressing and the croûtons.

This can be served as a first course for six, or as a light luncheon dish for two.

Tomato and Cucumber Aspic   *Serves 8–12, as a buffet dish*

28 fl. oz (793 ml) tomato juice

1 celery stalk, with leaves, roughly cut up

1 medium onion, diced

½ lemon, chopped

1 tsp dried basil

1 tsp caster sugar

1 tsp salt

Dash of hot pepper sauce

2 tbsp powdered gelatine

2 fl. oz (50 ml) cider vinegar

2 fl. oz (50 ml) boiling water

1 medium cucumber, peeled and diced

3 tbsp finely chopped onion

1 large ripe tomato, peeled and diced

The word 'aspic' in American cookery terms often means a dish of vegetables or meat set in a savoury gelatine mixture. Less often, it is used in the European sense of a glaze giving gloss and finish to chilled meat, fish, or vegetables. This recipe is for a typical and tasty Midwest 'Aspic', usually set in a decorative ring mould to show off its shimmering colour.

1. In a large saucepan, combine the tomato juice, celery, diced onion, lemon, basil, sugar, salt, and hot pepper sauce. Bring it to the boil, lower the heat, and simmer for twenty minutes. Strain the liquid. Dissolve the gelatine in the vinegar and boiling water, and stir into the tomato mixture. Chill until it is of the consistency of unbeaten egg white.

2. Stir in the diced cucumber, chopped onion, and diced tomato. Pour the mixture into a very lightly oiled decorative mould and chill it, at least four hours, until it is firmly set. To turn it out: wet a serving plate. Quickly dip the mould, almost up to its rim, in hot water, but be careful not to let the water spill over into the aspic. Put the plate over the mould and quickly invert it. The light film of water on the plate allows you to shake and slide the aspic into place without breaking it. Gently remove the mould. If this unmoulding process doesn't work perfectly, repeat the quick dip into hot water. The aspic should then instantly slide out on the plate.

Tuna Salad

Serves 4

Two 7½ oz (210 g) tins very good tuna

4 large stalks celery, coarsely diced

About 12 spring onions, coarsely chopped

About 6 oz (175 g) mayonnaise

Crisp salad greens (1 large cos lettuce for choice)

4 really ripe tomatoes

4 eggs, hard-boiled

I make no apologies for including this mundane, Cornbelt-America recipe. If it came from somewhere in Provence, it would have a more evocative name, but it couldn't taste better. Find the best white tuna you can, make the mayonnaise yourself, choose the ripest and most flavourful tomatoes, and resist the temptation to frill up this simple delight with anchovies, olives, or avocadoes.

1. Flake the tuna and mix it lightly with the celery and onion. Stir in enough mayonnaise to make it moist but not too rich. Arrange it on a large plate of lettuce, with tomatoes cut in eighths as a border around the tuna. Quarter the hard-boiled eggs and put them between the tomato wedges.
2. Serve with the lemon wedges, a further big bowl of a good, tart mayonnaise, and some thin crisp toast.

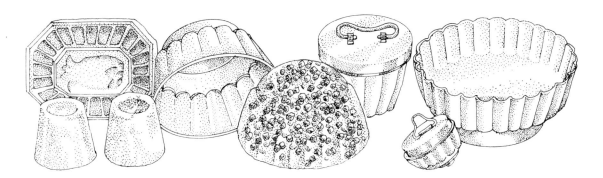

Milwaukee Potato Salad

Serves 6

8 large floury potatoes

4 oz (100 g) celery, very thinly sliced

3 medium onions, thinly sliced

3 tbsp parsley, very finely chopped

1 tsp celery seed

6 fl. oz (175 ml) cider vinegar

3 fl. oz (75 ml) water

½ tsp prepared mustard

4 rashers streaky bacon

3 extra tbsp good bacon dripping

Salt, freshly ground black pepper

Undoubtedly of German origin, this is a most delicious and unusual potato salad, quite unlike the much blander potato-and-mayonnaise dish. It's wonderful for picnics, or to pile high in the centre of a ring of tomato aspic.

1. Steam the potatoes unpeeled until just tender. Cool them slightly, peel, and cut in thin slices. Mix with the celery, onions, parsley, and celery seed. Heat the vinegar, water, and mustard, and pour over the warm potatoes. Season to taste.
2. Fry the bacon until very crisp, remove, drain on kitchen paper, and crumble. Heat the bacon drippings in the frying pan, and pour over the potato salad, mixing carefully. Then stir in the bacon bits. Let the salad stand at room temperature for three hours.

California Potato Salad with White Wine

Serves about 4

1½ lb (675 g) potatoes

3 fl. oz (75 ml) dry white wine

3 fl. oz (75 ml) good salad oil (olive, or olive and groundnut oils mixed)

Salt, freshly ground black pepper

This most delicious salad is traditionally served warm. Made with a dry white wine – the California whites with their crisp freshness are ideal – it's a revelation of delicate taste. A far cry from the delicatessen variety! The potatoes must be steamed in their jackets, not boiled.

1. Scrub the potatoes well and steam them until they are just tender, but by no means over-soft. Preheat the oven to 250°F (130°C), Gas 1.
2. Drain the potatoes, and when they are cool enough to handle, slip off the skins. Cut them in ¼ in. (·75 cm) slices, and put in a casserole. Sprinkle the potatoes with salt and pepper, mix the white wine and oil, and pour over the potatoes. Turn them over very lightly in order not to break the slices. Put the casserole in the oven, cover with a lid of aluminium foil, and let them stand just long enough to warm through (about ten minutes). Serve at once.

Egg Salad

Serves 4

6 hard-boiled eggs, size 2 or 3, halved

4 oz (100 g) mayonnaise

Juice of 1 lemon

1 tsp sea salt

Freshly ground black pepper

2 spring onions, finely chopped

1 large celery stalk, diced

1 tsp celery seed

This may be the place to point out that American and English conceptions of certain salads are greatly at variance. 'Ham Salad', to Americans, is a sharply seasoned mixture of chopped ham, celery, onion, mayonnaise, sometimes with the addition of small, sweet, gherkin-type pickles, in a sandwich or heaped into the centre of a scooped-out tomato. 'Egg Salad' is not a plate of hard-boiled eggs with tomato slices, bits of greenery, and salad cream, but a piquant mix of cut-up hard-boiled eggs, mayonnaise, spring onions, and seasonings which may include curry powder, chili season-ing, paprika, and so on. It can be extremely nasty (memories of soggy egg-salad sandwiches for school lunch must haunt many Americans), or very delicious indeed when freshly made, highly seasoned, and served with thin crisp biscuits or toasted home-made bread. I like this recipe.

Coarsely chop the eggs. Mix together the mayonnaise, salt, lemon juice, and pepper. Lightly mix the eggs, onion, and celery, and turn them all over in the mayonnaise. Sprinkle on the celery seed and mix gently. Chill, cover with plastic film, and serve within about four hours of making.

Western Perfection Salad

Serves 6

3 oz (75 g) packet lemon-flavoured
  gelatine

8 fl. oz (225 ml) boiling water

4 fl. oz (100 ml) cold water

2 tbsp wine or cider vinegar

1½ tsp salt

3 oz (75 g) carrots, grated

2 oz (50 g) white cabbage, grated

3 stalks celery, finely diced

Salad greens (cos or Webb's lettuce)

Brought to California by transplanted Midwesterners, most probably: a cool and shimmering moulded salad – not sweet, with vegetables that somehow maintain their crispness inside the golden dome. A yoghurt or soured cream dressing is a natural with any gelatine-based salad.

1. Dissolve the gelatine in boiling water, and stir in the cold water, vinegar, and salt. Chill until it is the consistency of unbeaten egg whites, then fold in the vegetables and pour into a decorative mould, or into an 8 × 8 × 2 in. (20 × 20 × 5 cm) tin. Chill until firm. Cut into six servings, and put on a bed of crisp, torn-up cos or Webb's lettuce.
2. Serve the salad with a bowl of soured cream dressing.

SOURED CREAM DRESSING

8 fl. oz (225 ml) soured cream

½ tsp salt

½ tsp dried dillweed

1 tsp onion, grated

Merely mix all the ingredients together and chill while the salad is setting.

Florida Grapefruit and Chicory Salad

Serves 4

1 large firm head of chicory

1 small bunch of watercress, washed,
  leaves only

1 grapefruit, peeled and sectioned

3 oz (75 g) cucumber, thinly sliced

3 oz (75 g) green pepper, peeled and
  thinly sliced

1 small mild onion, very thinly sliced

1 tsp sea salt

3 fl. oz (75 ml) good salad oil (olive, or
  olive and groundnut mixed)

1½ tbsp lemon juice

Optional: about a quarter-head of curly
  endive, and more cucumber,
  grapefruit segments, and thin onion
  rings if you like.

This is a salad for all seasons, since grapefruit from Israel and chicory from Belgium are so readily available. It's one of the American classics that plays the sharpness of citrus fruits against crisp salad greens and thinly sliced vegetables.

1. Cut the chicory into small pieces, mix with all the other ingredients and toss lightly together.
2. Arrange on plates and finish if you like with more of the fruits and vegetables, but serve quite quickly, as the chicory darkens if it stands.

Opposite Vegetables traditional and modern. Top Mrs Mannucci's Green Beans; Centre Boston Baked Beans; Bottom Scalloped Tomatoes

Overleaf Some ideas for a summer lunch. Clockwise from top left Caesar, Chef's Salads, California Sunshine Salad, Meatball Hero Sandwich, Club Sandwich

Waldorf Salad

Serves 4–6

6 large stalks of celery, diced

3 dessert apples, peeled and thinly sliced

2 ripe bananas, sliced

4 oz (100 g) walnuts, coarsely chopped

Mayonnaise

Salt, freshly ground black pepper

Crisp lettuce (cos or Chinese leaves)

This is one of the great American 'joke' salads: standby and cliché of the kind of English writer who writes, inevitably, of 'blue-rinsed matrons'! Waldorf salad is really rather pleasant, once you've adjusted to the idea of fruit, celery, and nuts in one dish, but be careful not to drown it in mayonnaise.

Mix the celery, apples, bananas, and walnuts and bind them with just enough mayonnaise to coat the mixture. Season and put on a bed of lettuce. Pass a bowl of mayonnaise with the salad.

Golden West Eggs

Serves 4 as a light luncheon dish

1 tsp olive oil, or olive and groundnut oil mixed

1 level tsp mild curry powder

4 fl. oz (100 ml) white wine

4 oz (100 g) mayonnaise

Salt, freshly ground black pepper

¼ pt (125 ml) double cream, whipped

8 eggs, size 2 or 3, hard-boiled

1 heaped tbsp chives, chopped

Small bunch of watercress, well washed

Paprika

1. Gently heat the oil in a small saucepan, stir in the curry powder, and cook on a very low heat for five minutes. Add the wine and simmer for two or three minutes more. Plunge the saucepan into a bowl of cold water and cool until it is tepid. Stir in the mayonnaise. Taste, and season with salt and pepper.

2. Gently cut and fold the mayonnaise mixture into the whipped cream, cover the bowl with plastic film, and chill well.

3. Cut the eggs in half, slip the yolks out, and with a wooden spoon, press them through a coarse sieve, onto a sheet of greaseproof paper. Slice the egg whites and lay them in a single layer on a serving dish, scatter the sieved yolks across them, and sprinkle on the chives. Garnish with sprigs of watercress. Dust with paprika and chill for at least an hour. Pass the sauce separately.

Spicy Lemon Dressing

Makes about 8 fl. oz (225 ml)

2 fl. oz (50 ml) lemon juice

1½ tsp salt

Dash of hot pepper sauce

2 small cloves garlic, crushed

6 fl. oz (150 ml) salad oil (olive for choice)

½ tsp each ground coriander, cumin, dry mustard, and paprika

1 tsp caster sugar

This recipe is the exception to the vinaigrette rule about sugar. Mix all ingredients, pour into a jar with a very secure lid, shake vigorously and refrigerate. Shake again before serving over vegetable salads.

French Dressing (or Vinaigrette)

This is the American term for a vinaigrette and can take many forms. It is also called, in some parts of the country, 'salad dressing', but as this is a term that occasionally means an old-fashioned boiled dressing like English salad cream, it can be very muddling.

MUSTARD VINAIGRETTE

Makes a generous 10 fl. oz (275 ml)

8 fl. oz (225 ml) good salad oil

1 tsp salt

1 tsp dry mustard

1 tbsp shallots, very finely chopped

Pinch of freshly ground black pepper

2 fl. oz (50 ml) red or white wine vinegar

Proportions vary according to taste, but a French dresssing is usually about four parts oil to one part cider or wine vinegar (malt or distilled vinegar is almost never used for salad dressings in America). Olive oil of course is the choice, but a mixture of equal parts of olive and groundnut (peanut) oil, or olive and soya, seems to do very well. Then it is salt and freshly ground black pepper to taste. Add a crushed clove of garlic, or about $\frac{1}{2}$ tsp dry mustard, $\frac{1}{2}$ tsp dried or fresh tarragon, chervil, or chives. And under no circumstances put in sugar!!

Mix the oil, salt, mustard, shallots, and pepper and let stand for two hours. Add vinegar and whisk briskly.

Hot French Dressing

Makes about 10 fl. oz (275 ml)

8 fl. oz (225 ml) French dressing

2 eggs, size 3, hard-boiled, chopped

1 tbsp parsley, very finely chopped

1 tbsp chives, chopped

1 level tsp dry mustard

$\frac{1}{2}$ tsp Worcestershire sauce

A little freshly ground black pepper

In a small saucepan, heat the French Dressing to boiling point. Add all the other ingredients and cook for one minute. Beat well and pour at once over whatever cooked vegetable you like – potato salad, asparagus, broccoli, or cauliflower. It also makes an excellent sauce for hot, thinly sliced tongue.

Italian Salad Dressing

Makes about 6 fl. oz (175 ml)

1 medium clove garlic

4 tbsp red wine vinegar

4 fl. oz (100 ml) olive oil (or olive and groundnut or soya oil, mixed)

$\frac{1}{2}$ tsp dry mustard

$\frac{1}{2}$ tsp salt

1. Cut the garlic clove in quarters. Mix the vinegar, oil, mustard, and salt in a jar with a tight top, add the garlic, screw down the top and shake hard. Store it, well closed, until you are ready to use the dressing.
2. Shake the dressing very well again, strain into a cup, and use with a simple lettuce salad, or with cold vegetables – delicious on broccoli, on cold white haricot beans, French-cut green beans, or sliced tomatoes.

Roquefort Dressing

Makes about 8 fl. oz (225 ml)

2 fl. oz (50 ml) white wine vinegar

¼ tsp salt

Freshly ground black pepper

4 fl. oz (100 ml) olive oil

2 tbsp double cream

2 oz (50 g) crumbled Roquefort cheese or any other good blue cheese

A few drops of lemon juice

This is a delight on crisp cos lettuce, Chinese leaves, or chicory, or with sliced tomatoes or hard-boiled eggs.

Mix the vinegar, salt, and pepper (add more salt later if you need it – this depends on the cheese), then stir in the oil and cream. Mix in the cheese and lemon juice and taste for seasoning.

Giovanni's Green Mayonnaise

Makes about 8 fl. oz (225 ml)

10 sprigs of watercress, leaves only

10 leaves of spinach

10 sprigs of fresh tarragon

1 very generous tsp lemon juice

7 oz (200 g) mayonnaise (home-made if possible)

A New York recipe from an excellent Italian restaurant, often served with a fish salad or as a dressing for cold, cooked mixed vegetables.

1. Wash the watercress, spinach, and tarragon leaves very well, and blanch them in boiling water for two minutes. Drain them thoroughly and refresh in cold water. Press them between two sieves, then purée in a blender or food processor, or pound in a mortar.
2. Mix the green leaves with the lemon juice and lightly stir all this with the mayonnaise.

Thousand Island Dressing

Makes a scant 12 oz (350 g)

4 oz (100 g) mayonnaise

2 oz (50 g) American chili sauce (see p. 144) or tomato chutney

1 tbsp celery, finely chopped

1 tbsp tinned pimiento, finely chopped

1 tbsp green pepper, seeded and chopped

2 fl. oz (50 ml) double cream, whipped

Why 'Thousand Island'? No one seems to know. There is a cluster of beautiful islands of that name, in the North-east near the Canadian border, and perhaps this recipe originated there. It is one of the two or three most popular American dressings, all over the country. This, and Russian Dressing, its variant, are delightful with hard-boiled eggs, any vegetable salad, or just served with crisp salad leaves. They make even the horrible iceberg lettuce edible.

Combine all the ingredients a few minutes before serving, as this dressing separates if it stands. One can buy bottled Thousand Island dressing everywhere in America, but it's a pale imitation fortified with weird-sounding preservatives.

Russian Dressing is exactly the same as above, but without the cream.

Poppy Seed Salad Dressing

Makes about 15 fl. oz (425 ml)

1 medium onion, peeled and finely chopped

2½ tsp poppy seeds

¾ tbsp caster sugar

½ tbsp sea salt

½ tbsp dry mustard

8 fl. oz (225 ml) good salad oil (olive and groundnut oil mixed is better for this recipe than pure olive oil)

6 fl. oz (175 ml) tarragon or cider vinegar

This seems to have a vaguely Hungarian-American background. It's very popular with simple fruit salads and as a dressing for plain, crisp lettuce.

1. Vigorously whisk together the onion, poppy seeds, sugar, salt, and mustard, and 2 tbsp of the oil. Then gradually whisk in the remaining oil, and lastly add the vinegar and mix until the sugar is completely dissolved.
2. Store in a tightly lidded glass jar, and shake well before using.

Green Goddess Dressing

Makes about a scant pint (550 ml)

½ pt (275 ml) mayonnaise

4 sprigs parsley, very finely chopped

2 spring onions, finely chopped

2 tbsp lemon juice or tarragon vinegar

Half a small clove of garlic, crushed with ½ tsp salt

¼ pt (125 ml) soured cream

1. Mix the mayonnaise, parsley, onions, lemon juice, and garlic well, then lightly stir in the soured cream. If you have a blender or food processor, put the mayonnaise in the container or bowl, add the parsley, onions, garlic, and lemon juice and blend with two or three on/off actions. Add the soured cream and blend again for one second.
2. Store in a tightly lidded jar in the refrigerator. Serve with salad greens or hard-boiled eggs.

Old-fashioned Boiled Dressing and Pacific Coleslaw

Serves 6

For the dressing

2 oz (50 g) butter or margarine

1 tbsp flour

4 fl. oz (100 ml) water

2 eggs, size 3

5 oz (125 g) caster sugar

1 tsp dry mustard

4 fl. oz (100 ml) cider vinegar (this dressing must *not* be made with the raw acid of malt or white vinegar)

Boiled dressing is the American version of salad cream, but made without the colourings and preservatives. It's sharpish, but with a sweet overtone. I suppose it is basically a Midwestern American recipe, but it has spread across the country. It is rather a nuisance to make, but those who love it would rather have it than the blander mayonnaise any day. Serve it with 'Pacific Coleslaw', which is merely raw, finely shredded cabbage dressed with boiled dressing.

1. In the top of a double boiler, over boiling water, melt the butter and stir in the flour. Gradually stir in the water, and cook, stirring, until it is smooth.

Salt to taste

For the coleslaw

About 2 lb (900 g) head of cabbage

2. Whisk the eggs with sugar and mustard in a 1 pt (550 ml) basin, and in a steady stream pour the hot sauce from the saucepan into the basin, stirring hard with a wooden spoon. (Well, I did say it was tricky to make, didn't I?) Pour the mixture back into the double boiler, and cook over simmering water until it is smooth, thick, and golden. Take the top of the double boiler away from the heat, stir in the vinegar, add about half a teaspoon of salt, and taste. Set the pan in a basin of cold water, while you prepare the coleslaw.

3. Finely shred the cabbage and soak in salted water for half an hour. Drain well and mix with the dressing.

Oregon Barbecue Sauce

Makes about $\frac{3}{4}$ pt (425 ml)

8 oz (225 g) home-made tomato sauce (see p. 147)

8 fl. oz (225 ml) cold water

1 small clove garlic, crushed with $\frac{1}{2}$ tsp salt

$1\frac{1}{4}$ tsp prepared mustard

$\frac{1}{2}$ tsp paprika

$1\frac{1}{2}$ tsp Worcestershire sauce

Juice of half a lemon

2 tbsp cider vinegar

1 small onion, very finely chopped

Hot pepper sauce to taste

This is a basting sauce for cooking almost any meat over charcoal – especially good with spitted lamb, and absolutely sensational for pork.

Mix all the ingredients except the hot pepper sauce in an enamel-lined saucepan, bring to the boil, cover, and simmer on a low heat for about thirty minutes, stirring from time to time. Add as much or as little hot pepper sauce as you can stand. Keep in a tightly-covered jar in the refrigerator if not used at once.

Citrus Barbecue Sauce

Serves 4

5 tbsp lemon juice

4 fl. oz (100 ml) orange juice

2 fl. oz (50 ml) tomato ketchup

1 tsp grated horseradish in vinegar

1 clove garlic, crushed with 1 tsp salt

1 tbsp light soft brown sugar

1 tsp dry mustard

$\frac{1}{2}$ tsp paprika

1 tsp Worcestershire sauce

Dash of hot pepper sauce

This recipe makes enough for about 4 lb (1·8 kg) of sheet spareribs.

1. For the sauce, mix all the ingredients and bring to the boil. Simmer for two minutes.

2. To roast the spareribs, preheat the oven to 425°F (220°C), Gas 7. Put the ribs in a roasting tin, brown for about forty-five minutes, then pour off the fat. Brush the ribs with barbecue sauce. Lower the heat to 350°F (180°C), Gas 4, and roast the spareribs on a rack over the roasting tin for one hour, basting often with the sauce.

Mississippi Barbecue Sauce

Makes about 1 pt (600 ml)

2 tbsp lard

1 medium onion, finely chopped

1 large clove garlic, crushed

28 oz (793 g) tin Italian peeled
    tomatoes, drained

6 oz (175 g) tomato purée

2 tsp black treacle

1 tsp golden syrup

1 large stalk celery with leaves,
    chopped

1 small green pepper, seeded and
    chopped

3 fl. oz (75 ml) cider vinegar

2 tsp dry mustard

1 tsp mixed spice

1½ tsp salt

2 thick slices lemon

2 tsp (or to taste) hot pepper sauce

For basting spareribs, chicken, or hamburgers – too strong for lamb or fish.

1. Heat the lard in a heavy saucepan and sauté the onion and garlic until soft but not brown. Add the remaining ingredients (start with about half a tsp of pepper sauce) and bring to the boil. Lower the heat and simmer for half an hour.
2. Taste, and add more hot pepper sauce if you like. Cool to lukewarm and sieve, or mix in a blender or food processor.

American Chili Sauce

Makes about 4 lb (1·8 kg)

3 lb (1·35 kg) ripe tomatoes

2 lb (900 g) mild onions

1 green pepper, seeded

¾ pt (425 ml) cider vinegar

1 tbsp salt

2 tsp ground cloves

2 tsp ground allspice

½ tsp cayenne

1 tsp ground cinnamon

8 oz (225 g) light brown sugar

A most misleading name for a mild, sweet, spicy, thick sauce that has no chilis in it, and is not hot or fierce in any way. I include it because it is an ingredient in so many American recipes. Bottled chili sauce is available everywhere in the country, and is most lavishly used on hamburgers, hot dogs, cold meats, and so on. Chili sauce is rather like a more flavoursome tomato chutney. A tablespoon of it, incidentally, does wonders in any cheese mixture such as welsh rarebit or a mild cheese fondue.

1. Peel the tomatoes by dropping them into boiling water for one minute, then run them under the cold tap, and slip the skins off. Chop them coarsely. Chop the onions and green pepper. Put all the ingredients except the sugar in a large enamel-lined saucepan (not aluminium), and bring to the boil. Simmer for about two hours, stirring from time to time.
2. Add the sugar and stir until it is dissolved. Raise the heat to a gentle boil, and cook about thirty minutes longer, stirring often. It should thicken and reduce somewhat to a sort of chutney consistency. Pour it into hot sterilised jars, and seal and store as for any chutney.

If the tomatoes are over-ripe, the chili sauce may not thicken properly even after the boiling period. In that case, cheat a bit by stirring in one tablespoon of cornflour stirred into about one teaspoon of water.

Southwestern Chili-Pepper Sauce

2 oz (50 g) chili seasoning (see Appendix)

a little cold water

1½ pt (825 ml) boiling water

1–1½ oz (25–35 g) lard

1 tsp salt

1 large clove garlic, crushed

Frighteningly hot, the Southwestern chili-pepper mixture is the base for many other sauces. It's worth making in quantity if you contemplate a run on Far West food. You must have proper chili seasoning – a blend of chili peppers, cumin, garlic, and salt, not merely the red-hot Indian chili powder (see page 249).

Blend the cold water and chili seasoning to a paste. Stir the salt and lard into boiling water in a large saucepan, and add the chili mixture. Simmer for about twenty minutes, then add the garlic. You now have about 1¼ pt (675 ml approx.) of a rather thin chili-pepper sauce, to use on its own or as a base for Red Chili Sauce.

RED CHILI SAUCE

Makes a scant 35 oz (1 litre)

2 tbsp melted lard

1 small onion, finely chopped

2 cloves garlic, crushed

1 lb (450 g) tomatoes, peeled, or tinned Italian peeled tomatoes

¾ pt (425 ml) Chili-Pepper Sauce

1 tsp oregano

1 tsp salt, or to taste

Use this for Tamale Pie, hamburgers, or with Tacos.

1. Heat the lard in a heavy frying pan, and sauté the onion and garlic until golden but not brown. Add the peeled or tinned, drained tomatoes, and simmer for fifteen minutes. Stir in the Chili-Pepper Sauce and oregano and simmer for five minutes.
2. Season with salt, and some freshly ground black pepper if you like (although it will hardly register with all this wealth of flavour). Refrigerate, tightly covered, until needed.

Drawn Butter

Makes about 15 oz (425 g)

3 oz (75 g) butter (*not* margarine)

3 level tbsp plain flour

½ level tsp salt

Good pinch of freshly ground black pepper

12 fl. oz (350 ml) boiling water *or* hot fish stock

1 tsp lemon juice

In restaurants, 'drawn butter' usually means merely unsalted butter melted and served hot, with lemon juice and sometimes a dash of Tabasco. However, there is a real sauce that goes by that name too, and very good it is with poached fish, steamed prawns, or any plainly cooked fish.

1. Melt 1½ tbsp butter, stir in the flour, salt, and pepper and blend until smooth. Gradually add the liquid, stirring well, bring to boil, lower the heat, and simmer for five minutes.
2. Cut the remaining butter into small pieces, and add it, alternately with the lemon juice, stirring constantly.

Cucumber and Soured Cream Sauce

Makes about 12 oz (350 g)

8 oz (225 g) soured cream (or plain natural yoghurt)

8 in. (20 cm) piece of cucumber, unpeeled, diced finely

½ tsp salt

1 small clove garlic, crushed *or* 1 tsp very finely chopped onion

½ tsp dried dillweed

This sauce from California is not unlike the Greek tzatziki. Although it is usually served with seafood salads, it is equally delicious as a dip with Potato Biscuits (see p. 22) or any firm, crisp savoury biscuits.

Stir everything together, and chill well. Finish with a grinding of black pepper if you like.

Dill Sauce

For seafood, makes a scant 8 oz (225 g)

6 fl. oz (175 ml) olive oil

3 tbsp lemon juice

Pinch of dry mustard

2 tsp dried dillweed, or 1 tbsp fresh chopped dill

Salt to taste

Optional: small clove garlic, sliced

Combine all the ingredients and pour into a jar with a tight cover; chill overnight. Strain, removing the garlic if used. Delicious with cold shrimp, crabmeat, or crayfish.

Chinese Plum Sauce (Duck Sauce)

6 oz (175 g) apricot or plum jam

1 tbsp soy sauce

1 clove garlic, finely chopped

Good pinch of ginger

This sauce, and the fiery, thin mustard sauce below, are almost always served in small bowls with American Cantonese food, wherever you find it. The spicier Peking and Szechuan dishes which are now becoming popular do not need these additions.

Mix all the ingredients together, either in a blender or food processor, or force the jam through the fine plate of a food mill and mix with the other ingredients. Stored tightly lidded in the refrigerator it keeps well.

Chinese Dragon Mustard. Mix dry mustard powder to a thin paste with lager. For a slightly less hot result, cream the mustard with chicken stock. Chinese mustard is 'runny', not the creamy consistency of the more familiar British and American prepared mustards.

Home-made Tomato Sauce

Makes about 2 pts (1·125 litres)

2 tbsp olive oil (or olive and soya oil mixed)

3 sprigs of parsley, finely chopped

1 large celery stalk, coarsely chopped

1 large clove garlic, crushed

2½ lb (1·125 kg) ripe tomatoes, peeled and chopped

10 oz (275 g) tomato purée

1 tsp salt

½ tsp freshly ground pepper

1 large bayleaf, broken up

1 tsp dried basil

1 tsp dried oregano

Good dash of hot pepper sauce (or five drops of Tabasco)

This incredibly versatile tomato sauce is actually an Italian-American recipe given to me by the daughter of a family famous for pasta, sauces, and soups. Oddly enough, if one leaves out the garlic the recipe is identical to a traditional sauce from Indiana (where beefsteak tomatoes grow huge, deep red in colour, sweet, and rich in flavour). If you have access to really ripe Marmande or other of the highly flavoured European tomatoes, use them in making the sauce: otherwise, the best Italian tinned peeled plum tomatoes you can find should be your choice. Use the sauce for any pasta recipe, for pizza, with vegetables, in soups, and as an ingredient in other sauces in this book. Leftover sauce keeps well for about ten days in a tightly-covered jar in the refrigerator; or it may be frozen.

1. Heat the oil in a large saucepan, add the parsley and celery and cook, stirring, until the celery is pale gold. Stir in the garlic, tomatoes, tomato purée, salt, and pepper. Simmer for forty-five minutes.
2. Add the bayleaf, basil and oregano and cook on a low heat about fifteen minutes more. Remove the bits of bayleaf if you can, and cool the sauce completely before refrigerating it.

Creole Sauce

Makes about 1½ pt (825 ml)

2 oz (50 g) butter or margarine

1 medium onion, finely chopped

1 medium clove garlic, crushed with 1 tsp salt

5 oz (125 g) mushrooms, wiped and thinly sliced

1 medium green pepper, seeded and thinly sliced

1 lb or 450 g (drained weight) tinned Italian peeled tomatoes

8 fl. oz (225 ml) tinned, condensed tomato soup

Bouquet garni

¼ tsp paprika

Salt, freshly ground black pepper

Dash of hot pepper sauce

This is a tremendously useful sauce to have on hand – it freezes quite well for about three months – to use for baking fish fillets, to fill an omelette, on pork chops, chicken, or rabbit. Note that it makes use of one of America's standard convenience foods – tinned, condensed soup.

1. Heat the butter in a heavy saucepan and sauté the onion, garlic, mushrooms, and green pepper until just tender. Stir in the tomatoes, soup, and bouquet garni. Season and simmer for twenty minutes; add the paprika.
2. Taste when it has cooled slightly, add a dash of hot pepper sauce if you like, freshly ground black pepper, or more salt. Serve hot, or cool well and freeze, allowing 1 in. (2·5 cm) headroom in the container for expansion.

Raisin Sauce

For ham or tongue, makes about 14 fl. oz (400 ml)

2 oz (50 g) raisins or sultanas, coarsely chopped or left whole

¼ pt (125 ml) dry cider

1 tsp lemon juice

Pinch of ground cloves

Scant 1 oz (25 g) butter

2 tbsp plain flour

¼ pt (125 ml) ham or tongue stock

A truly all-American sauce that seems to appear everywhere (except perhaps in the Southwest). Everyone's grandmother had a recipe in a hand-written notebook. One of the ingredients is cider: American cider is sweet and non-alcoholic, but English dry cider does very well in this kind of sweet-sour cooking.

1. Put the hot stock in a small saucepan and add the raisins, cider, lemon juice, and cloves. Bring to just below boiling point.
2. Work together the butter and flour on a plate, and drop by nut-sized pieces into the simmering liquid, stirring well until the sauce is thickened and smooth. Serve in a warmed sauce-boat.

Mexican Salsa Fría

Makes about 35 fl. oz (1 litre)

28 oz (793 g) tinned Italian peeled tomatoes

1 large onion, very finely chopped

3 dry, hot red chili peppers, seeded and finely chopped

1 tsp oregano, or more, to taste

4 tbsp wine vinegar *or* lemon juice

4 fl. oz (100 ml) good salad oil

1 tsp ground coriander

1 large clove garlic, crushed with 1 tsp salt

This sauce from the American Southwest is misleadingly named 'cold' sauce – it is blazing hot. To make it less fiery, use only one or two chilis. In any case, handle these very carefully – wear rubber gloves and don't touch skin or eyes as the chilis can burn. For hamburgers or any cold or hot meat.

Drain the tomatoes well and chop them as finely as you can. Mix with all the other ingredients, and taste for seasoning. It will keep for about a week, in a tightly-covered jar in the refrigerator. If you have a blender or food processor, simply whirl everything together.

White Sauce

Makes about 10 oz (275 g)

1 oz (25 g) butter or good margarine

2 tbsp flour

8 fl. oz (225 ml) cold milk

Pinch of salt, freshly ground black pepper

Freshly grated nutmeg

Sometimes called Cream Sauce or Béchamel, this isn't a true béchamel, of course. But it's the one usually meant in American cookbooks where that term is used. More often it is simply called 'white sauce'. Nothing could be easier to make, and it lends itself to some pleasant additions which are equally simple.

Put the flour, butter, and milk in a heavy-based saucepan, and bring to the boil, stirring continuously with a wooden spoon. Boil for one minute, stirring, lower the heat and simmer about two minutes, still stirring, until it is smooth and thick. That's all. Do not try to do it with hot milk, as this produces instant lumps. Season to taste with salt, pepper, and nutmeg.

Simple Dill Sauce. Stir in 1 tbsp fresh dill fronds, finely chopped or 2 level tsp dried dillweed – very good with poached fish.

Easy Curry Sauce. Add about 1 tsp mild curry powder, and work up from there if you like it stronger. This is not of course for real curries but for basic dishes like curried eggs.

Sweet-sour Mustard Sauce

Makes about 9 oz (250 g)

2 tsp dry mustard

$\frac{1}{4}$ tsp salt

1 tsp caster sugar

2 tbsp flour

6 fl. oz (175 ml) water

2 tbsp cider vinegar

2 egg yolks, size 3

1 oz (25 g) butter, melted

This is one of the sauces usually found among the Seven Sweets and Seven Sours of Pennsylvania Dutch cooking. It appears in many other parts of the country as well, notably in Chicago and Milwaukee with their large populations of German origin. Try it for ham, gammon, frankfurters, or cold roast pork. It will keep at least a week, in a tightly lidded jar in the refrigerator.

1. In the top of a double boiler, over simmering water, combine the mustard, salt, sugar, and flour. Stir in the water and vinegar, and cook, stirring, until it is thick and creamy.
2. Lightly whisk the egg yolks with the butter and stir into the sauce. As soon as it is thick, take the top part of the double boiler out at once, so that the sauce does not curdle.

Breads

The Good-Natured Hot Roll Dough

American 'hot rolls' are a quick form of yeast bread, rich in egg, milk, and sugar, shaped into a variety of delightful shapes: butterfly, fan-tan, cloverleaf, crescents, bowknots, finger rolls, figure-eights, and the best known of all, Parker House Rolls. They are not to be confused with the other American quick bread called Hot Biscuits which is leavened with baking powder instead of yeast. They are quick to make, spectacular to serve, and the flattering exclamations they produce do wonders for the battered ego of the cook. As the world is unfair, the person who can whisk up a batch of golden, rich, puffy hot rolls – crisp on the outside, soft and delicate on the inside – gets a disproportionate amount of praise.

All this is by the way of telling you how to make the Good-Natured Hot Roll Dough which evolved almost by accident while I was testing and adapting my American bread recipes to British flours, British sugar, and a dependable but totally unmodern gas cooker, circa 1937.

One batch of this rich yeast dough was literally forgotten in a cold larder for more than twenty-four hours. It was kneaded, pummelled, pinched off into bits for weighing, re-kneaded, and beaten up with heavily-floured hands. At one point someone forgot to cover it with plastic film, and it stood placidly rising uncovered in a corner of a hot kitchen. My cat tried to scoop up some on her paw and had to be thrown out of the kitchen (again). The dough was handled so much that it began to look not creamy white but just faintly grey – this didn't matter, as by now we thought of it only as something to be weighed and measured, not cooked. After about five hours, I decided to shape and bake it into Parker House rolls and Cloverleaf rolls, no matter how handled the dough now looked. Happy, and by now predictable, ending – twelve minutes in the very hot oven, and out came perfect, gilded, high, light 'American hot rolls'.

The recipe follows. And for those who prefer not to refrigerate a yeast dough, but to make a quick hot roll mixture and bake it straight away, I give the more conventional recipe. The results seem to be so alike as to make no difference. British sugar, used in the same quantity called for by the American recipe, made hot rolls that were oversweet, so I cut the sugar amount by half. You may like yours sweeter, so increase the amount of sugar by up to one tablespoon in either recipe if you prefer.

THE HOT ROLL RECIPE (chilled dough)

Makes about 3 lb (1·5 kg)

12 fl. oz (350 ml) milk (or milk and water in equal quantities)

4 oz (100 g) butter or margarine

4 tbsp caster sugar

2 tsp salt

4 level tsp dried yeast

4 fl. oz (100 ml) hand-hot water

1 egg, size 1 or 2, or 2 eggs, size 3 or 4 (depending on how rich you like the dough)

1½ lb (675 g) *or more* plain white flour (not strong bread flour)

Optional: 1 egg beaten with 1 tbsp water

Note: the dough should be refrigerated or put in a cold larder for at least four hours, or for as long as three days.

1. Heat the milk in a saucepan, add the butter, sugar, and salt. Remove it from the heat and let it stand until the butter melts, by which time the mixture should be lukewarm. Stir the dried yeast into the 4 fl. oz (100 ml) of hand-hot water, and let it stand in a warm place until it froths up.

2. Beat the yeast mixture and the egg or eggs into the warm milk. Put 1 lb (450 g) of the flour in a big bowl and stir in the yeast and milk liquid. Beat well, with an electric mixer, or a wooden spoon. Then begin to add more flour to this batter, until you have a soft dough: it will feel warm and alive, but not as firm as bread dough. Add flour cautiously until the dough no longer feels sticky and stringy.

3. Turn it out on a lightly-floured board. Put another mound of flour in the corner of the board, about 2 oz (50 g), to use if the dough feels sticky as you knead it. Knead until you have produced a satiny, springy, cohesive ball of dough. Oil a large bowl and turn the dough ball over and over in it until it glistens. Cover tightly with plastic film and chill.

4. When you are ready to shape the rolls, take off as much or as little as you need, and chill the remaining dough for the next batch.

Parker House Rolls. The basic recipe makes 24 rolls.
Roll the dough out on a floured surface to about ¼ in. (0·5 cm) thickness. With a plain-edged 3 in. (7·5 cm) cutter, cut out rounds. Brush the upper sides with melted butter or margarine, and make a crease – not a cut – down the centre with the dull side of a table knife. Fold over on the crease and pinch the edges of the rolls together. With your fingers, neaten the shape if it has become a little distorted in the handling. Put them on a lightly-oiled baking sheet, spaced slightly apart, cover with plastic film, and let them rise in a warm, but not hot, place until they double in bulk. In the meantime, preheat the oven to 425°F (220°C), Gas 7. If you want a luxurious, gilded finish, brush them with the egg and water; or bake them without gilding. Bake on the centre shelf of the oven for twelve to fifteen minutes.

Cloverleaf Rolls. For about 18–24 rolls.
Pinch off pieces of about ½ oz (15 g) each, or if it's easier for you to measure, make little balls about 1¼ in. (3 cm) in diameter. Make smooth balls and press three into a lightly-oiled deep patty tin (individual size), or fairy cake tins. Cover lightly with plastic film and let them rise until double in bulk. Don't make the balls too large for your tins, or they will

pop up and out, and look very odd. Bake for about ten minutes as in the instructions for Parker House Rolls.

Fan-Tans. Roll out the basic dough to about $\frac{1}{4}$ in. (0·75 cm) thickness. Brush it with melted butter. Cut the dough into strips about 1 in. (2·5 cm) wide. Pile six strips together, and cut them crosswise into $1\frac{1}{2}$ in. (4 cm) pieces. Grease deep patty tins, or glass custard cups, and fill with the bundles of dough strips set on end. Let them rise and bake exactly as for Parker House rolls. When baked, these rolls separate into six soft buttery pieces, each with a crisp top and bottom.

Conventional Hot Roll Recipe

$\frac{3}{4}$ pt (425 ml) milk

2 oz (50 g) butter or margarine

$1\frac{1}{2}$ tbsp caster sugar

2 tsp salt

4 level tsp dried yeast

2 fl. oz (50 ml) hand-hot water

20–24 oz (550–675 g) plain white flour (not strong bread flour)

1 egg, size 3

A little melted butter

Optional: 1 egg, size 3 or 4, mixed with a little water

1. Heat the milk in a saucepan, stir in the butter, sugar, and salt and let it stand off the heat until the butter melts. Whisk the yeast into the hand-hot water and let it stand in a warm place until it is frothy.
2. Beat the yeast and the egg into the milk mixture. Put about 1 lb (450 g) or $1\frac{1}{4}$ lb (550 g) of the flour in a big bowl and beat in the yeast and milk mixture. Beat hard, with an electric mixer if you have one, or with a big wooden spoon. Keep adding the flour gradually, until you can no longer beat the dough easily – then begin to mix and knead it in the bowl by hand. When the dough begins to leave the side of the bowl clean, turn it out on a floured board and knead until it feels soft and satiny. Add more flour if necessary. Wash out and grease the bowl, and return the dough to it.
3. Cover with plastic film, let the dough rise until it is double in bulk. Punch it down, and form into rolls as in the Good-Natured Hot Roll recipe. Glaze with egg and water if you want to, and bake at 425°F (220°C), Gas 7.

Buttermilk Biscuits

8 oz (225 g) plain flour

1 tsp salt

1 tsp baking powder

$\frac{1}{2}$ tsp bicarbonate of soda

2 oz (50 g) butter, lard, margarine, or white fat

6 fl. oz (175 ml) buttermilk or soured milk (approximately)

This recipe makes even airier and flakier hot biscuits than the classic recipe overleaf.

1. To sour fresh milk, stir $\frac{1}{2}$ tsp lemon juice into 8 fl. oz (225 ml) milk. A little less than this will sour the quantity of milk needed for these biscuits.
2. Mix and bake as in American Hot Biscuits, see overleaf.

American Hot Biscuits

Makes about 16 2 in. (5 cm) biscuits

8 oz (225 g) flour, plain or self-raising

1 tsp salt

2 tsp caster sugar

2½ tsp baking powder

2–2½ oz (50–60 g) butter, lard, white fat or margarine

About ¼ pt (125 ml) milk

From Maine to Georgia, and right across the country, everyone makes hot biscuits. True, they often come out of a box of prepared biscuit-mix these days, or even from a dear little tube from which they magically pop out and expand. But this is the all-American recipe. They are a little like a scone, but lighter, fluffier, more crumbly. They are a 'must' with fried chicken, or served on their own with butter and jam, jelly, or preserves

Preheat oven to 425°F (220°C), Gas 7.
1. Sift the flour, salt, sugar, and baking powder into a bowl. Cut the fat in until it feels like fine breadcrumbs. Stir in enough milk to make a soft but not sticky dough.
2. Turn out the dough on a lightly-floured board and knead it gently, only fifteen or twenty times. Pat out, do not roll, to about ½ in. (1·5 cm) thickness, and cut with a plain-edged 2 in. (5 cm) cutter. Put 1 in. (2·5 cm) apart on a lightly greased baking sheet and bake for twelve to fifteen minutes, until risen and golden.

Blueberry Muffins

Makes 24

8 oz (225 g) plain flour

3 tsp baking powder

3 tbsp caster sugar

¼ tsp salt

1 egg, size 3

6 fl. oz (175 ml) milk

4 oz (100 g) butter or margarine, melted

7 oz (200 g) blueberries

Blueberries are an American joy – they grow wild in many parts of the country, often on forest land that has been burned over, and are also cultivated in places as far apart as New Jersey and Oregon. I have used tinned Polish bilberries successfully in American blueberry recipes. Blueberries are being grown in Dorset now (see Appendix), but whortle-berries or bilberries, of the same family, may be used in this recipe or for Blueberry Pie (see p. 179).

Preheat oven to 400°F (200°C), Gas 6.
1. Sift the flour, then sift it again with the baking powder, sugar, and salt. Whisk the egg and milk together, mix with the dry ingredients, stir in the melted butter, and stir just until the ingredients are evenly moistened. *Do not beat, or the muffins will be grainy and full of holes.* Lightly fold in the blueberries.
2. Butter and flour two deep 12-cup patty tins. Fill each cup two-thirds full of batter. Bake for about twenty-five minutes, until they are brown and puffy. Serve hot, with butter.

Opposite Some famous American breads. Top Parker House Rolls; Centre California Sourdough Bread; Bottom Waffles (left); American Hot Biscuits (right)

American 'English Muffins'

Makes about 12

1 lb (450 g) strong white bread flour

1 tsp salt

2 tsp dried yeast

½ pt (275 ml) milk and water, mixed

1 tsp caster sugar

1 egg, size 3

1 oz (25 g) butter or margarine, melted

To English people, they aren't muffins, and they aren't English. No one seems to know how they collected this name. They are almost the most popular breakfast bread all across the United States. They are a little like a crumpet, but not 'holey', a bit like a Yorkshire pikelet but not quite. English muffins are always pulled apart with a fork, not cut with a knife, in order to preserve their crumbly texture – and should be toasted and buttered at once.

1. Sift the flour and salt into a bowl, and make a well in the centre. Heat the water and milk mixture to blood heat, stir in the yeast, and let it stand in a warm place about ten minutes until it develops a good thick layer of foam. Pour the yeast mixture into the flour. Lightly whisk the egg with the melted butter, and pour into the flour. Mix everything together very well, turn the dough out on a floured board and knead until it is firm and springy.

2. Oil the bowl, return the dough to it, and cover with oiled plastic film. Let the dough rise in a warm place until it is double in bulk. Turn it out on a floured board and knead it lightly, then pat it out to about ½ in. (1·5 cm) thickness and cut in rounds about 2½ in. (6·5 cm) in diameter. Put them on two well-floured baking sheets and dust the tops with flour, cover with inverted baking tins and let the muffins rise in a warm place until they are puffy and light.

3. Heat a griddle or large heavy frying pan and wipe it lightly with a piece of kitchen paper dipped in a little oil. Put in as many muffins as the pan will hold, lower the heat, and cook them gently for about six to seven minutes on each side. Remove to a rack. Then with a sharp knife cut round the middles to a depth about ½ in. (1·5 cm), as this makes it easier to pull them apart with a fork. Serve hot with lashings of butter, or store in plastic film in the refrigerator, where they will keep for three or four days. Or you can freeze them, and toast from frozen under a grill (but not in the average electric toaster).

Boston Brown Bread

Makes 2 round loaves

1 oz (25 g) white fat or margarine

1½ tbsp caster sugar

1 egg, size 3

5 oz (125 g) black treacle

Opposite A variety of luscious pies.
Top Blueberry; Centre Pecan; Bottom Lemon Chiffon

This is not a true bread: it's a dark, moist, sweet, steamed loaf, cylindrical in shape, and traditionally served with Boston Baked Beans (see p. 107). It's equally delicious spread with sweet unsalted butter or cream cheese, to go with mid-morning coffee or a cup of tea.

5 oz (125 g) golden syrup

11 oz (300 g) wholewheat flour

3 oz (75 g) fine cornmeal

1 tsp salt

1½ tsp baking powder

1½ tsp bicarbonate of soda

½ pt (275 ml) buttermilk or soured milk

4 oz (100 g) sultanas or raisins

1. Cream the fat and sugar well, and beat in the egg, treacle, and golden syrup until well blended. Beat in all the other ingredients.
2. Thickly grease two round 1 lb (450 g) coffee tins or round earthenware moulds of the same dimensions. Fill them a little more than half-full of batter. Cover with greased aluminium foil, do not tie down. Stand them in a deep saucepan on a rack, and add enough boiling water to come halfway up the sides of the tins. Steam for two and a half hours, topping up the boiling water if needed.
3. Turn out of tins immediately and cool on a cake rack.

Banana Bread

Makes 1 loaf

4 oz (100 g) butter or margarine

6 oz (175 g) caster sugar

3 medium bananas, as ripe as possible

2 eggs, size 3

4 oz (100 g) plain flour

4 oz (100 g) 81%–85% wholemeal flour

1 tsp bicarbonate of soda

½ tsp salt

5 tbsp very hot water

2 oz (50 g) walnuts, coarsely chopped

Preheat oven to 325°F (165°C), Gas 3.
1. Cream the butter and sugar together, mash the bananas well, and stir in. Whisk the eggs and add slowly to the mixture. Sift the dry ingredients together and add alternately with tbsps of hot water.
2. Stir in the walnuts. Butter a bread tin or oblong casserole, about 9 × 5 in. (23 × 13 cm), pour in the batter and bake for about one hour and ten minutes. This is a lovely moist tea bread, but you *must* have well-ripened bananas.

Breakfast Pancakes
(Griddle Cakes or Flapjacks)

Makes about 12

6 oz (175 g) plain flour

2½ tsp baking powder

½ tsp salt

1 egg, size 3

3 tbsp vegetable oil

½ pt (275 ml) milk, or half milk and half water

One of the most characteristic American breakfast dishes – and quite unlike the thin European pancakes. They are usually served with maple syrup or corn syrup, crisp bacon or sausages, and lots of butter.

1. Sift the flour, baking powder, and salt. Whisk the egg, oil, and milk together and beat well into the dry ingredients. Let it stand half an hour; if it has thickened, thin with a little milk or water to a pouring consistency.
2. Heat a heavy griddle (girdle), or a well-seasoned heavy frying pan so hot that cold water drops dance across the surface, instead of sputtering. Dip a piece of kitchen paper in oil and lightly grease the surface. Pour on pools of batter 4 in. (10 cm) in diameter, and cook until the surface bubbles and begins to look dry. Turn and cook the other side.

Buttermilk Griddle Cakes

1 egg, size 3

6 fl. oz (175 ml) soured milk or buttermilk

6 oz (175 g) plain flour

$\frac{3}{4}$ tsp bicarbonate of soda

1 rounded tsp caster sugar

$\frac{1}{4}$ tsp salt

2 oz (50 g) margarine or oil, melted

These are lighter, fluffier and more tender than the Breakfast Pancakes.

1. Beat the egg and buttermilk together. Sift the dry ingredients and stir them into the egg mixture, then whisk in the melted margarine. Add a little more milk or water if the mixture is very thick.
2. Cook as for Breakfast Pancakes.

Cornbread

Makes 1 loaf

7 oz (200 g) coarse yellow cornmeal

3 oz (75 g) flour (plain white or light brown)

4 tsp baking powder

1 tsp salt

3 tsp caster sugar

2 eggs, size 3

$\frac{1}{2}$ pt (275 ml) milk

$1\frac{1}{2}$ oz (35 g) melted margarine, or 2 tbsp oil

Cornmeal, of course, is made from maize. It has been a standby of American cooks since Colonial days and is used in recipes as diverse as cornbread and muffins and the Italian-derived polenta. This recipe comes from Georgia but one would find variations of it in every state.

Preheat oven to 400°F (200°C), Gas 6.
1. Grease a round or square baking tin about 8 × 1 in. (20 × 2·5 cm) and put it in the oven to heat. Sift all the dry ingredients, add the eggs, milk, and margarine or oil, and beat until well blended. The batter will be thin.
2. Bake in the prepared tin for about thirty to thirty-five minutes until it is well-risen and brown. Serve with cold butter, and plenty of it. It can be cut in slices or wedges, toasted under the grill if you like.

Corn Muffins

Makes about 15 2 in. (5 cm) muffins

7 oz (200 g) plain flour

3 tsp baking powder

2 tbsp caster sugar

$\frac{1}{2}$ tsp salt

3 oz (75 g) fine cornmeal

1 egg, size 3

6 fl. oz (175 ml) milk

4 oz (100 g) butter or margarine, melted

This recipe can be used to make cornbread, in a 9 in. (23 cm) square tin, but crisp-crusted muffins are simply irresistible. Use deep patty tins, or fairy cake tins, or small individual ovenglass moulds.

Preheat oven to 400°F (200°C), Gas 6.
1. Grease the tins or moulds well and put them in the oven to heat. Sift the dry ingredients. Beat the egg and milk together, and combine with the dry ingredients, mixing lightly – do not overbeat. Stir in the melted butter.
2. Fill the tins or moulds two-thirds full and bake for about twenty-five minutes until golden-brown and well risen.

Cracklin' Cornbread

Makes 8–10 cakes

6 oz (175 g) fine cornmeal (preferably white, if you can find it)

3 oz (75 g) sifted plain flour

2 tsp baking powder

½ tsp bicarbonate of soda

½ tsp salt

8 fl. oz (225 ml) soured milk or buttermilk

4 oz (100 g) diced cracklings

'Cracklin's' are the thin crisp skin of pork, bacon, duck, or goose, after the fat has been thoroughly rendered ('tried out' in American parlance) during cooking. If you can resist eating them sprinkled with salt, here's a lovely Southern corn-cake recipe to try.

Preheat oven to 400°F (200°C), Gas 6.

1. Sift the dry ingredients together and mix with the cracklings. Add milk and stir until smooth. Shape into small flat round or oval cakes.

2. Bake on a greased baking sheet for half an hour, and serve with fried chicken or Baked Chicken with Herbs (see p. 62).

Cheese Bread

Makes 2 loaves

2 level tsp dried yeast

1 tbsp caster sugar

¾ pt (450 ml) water (approximately)

20–24 oz (550–675 g) strong bread flour

1 tbsp salt

½ tsp hot pepper sauce

4 oz (100 g) softened butter or margarine

1 oz (25 g) Parmesan cheese, grated

3 oz (75 g) Jarlsberg, Gruyère, or Cheddar cheese, grated

1. Mix the yeast and sugar and dissolve in four tbsp of the water, hand-hot. Let stand until it is frothy. In a large bowl, mix 20 oz (550 g) of the flour with the salt, make a well in the centre, and mix in the yeast liquid, the hot pepper sauce, butter, and almost all of the remaining water, reserving a few tbsps. Mix well.

2. Turn out on a heavily-floured board, and put the remaining flour in a bowl at the side. Knead the dough until it feels springy, 'live', and has a slight sheen. Add more flour if it is needed, or more water. Shape into a ball and put in a well-greased bowl, turning it round and round. Cover and let it rise until it has doubled in bulk, which may take about two hours.

3. Turn the dough out on a lightly-floured board, and work in the grated cheese. Divide the dough into two parts and let it rest, covered with oiled plastic film for about ten minutes. Shape each piece into a loaf. Well grease two loaf tins (about $7\frac{1}{4} \times 3\frac{1}{2} \times 2\frac{1}{4}$ in. or $18 \times 9 \times 5$ cm) and press the dough into them. Cover with oiled plastic film and let rise until the dough reaches the top of the tins.

4. Preheat the oven to 375°F (190°C), Gas 5, and bake in the centre of the oven about half an hour. Turn the loaves out, and rap them on the bottom with your knuckles. If they sound hollow they are baked, but can be put back in the oven for five minutes' more baking directly on the oven shelf to crisp up the crust.

Cool completely on a rack, before slicing.

Crullers

Makes about 36

1 oz (25 g) butter or margarine

3 oz (75 g) caster sugar

1 egg, size 3

8 oz (225 g) plain flour

½ tbsp baking powder

¼ tsp grated nutmeg

¼ tsp salt

4 fl. oz (100 ml) milk

Oil for deep frying

Icing sugar for dusting the crullers

This is a sort of doughnut, but instead of being rolled and cut, the dough is shaped into a small ball and fried, or dropped by heaped spoonfuls into the hot fat. They seem to have a vaguely Scandinavian or German ancestry. Sometimes the dough is pinched off into small balls, which are then rolled between the palms to a sort of thin cigar shape, and two of them quickly twisted together and deep-fried.

1. Cream the butter and sugar until they are light and fluffy. Whisk the egg, and gradually beat it into the butter-sugar mixture. Sift the dry ingredients together twice, and add them to the batter by spoonfuls, alternately with spoonfuls of the milk. Cover the bowl with plastic film and chill the dough for about an hour.
2. Heat the oil in a deep-fryer to 375°F (190°C).
3. Drop the cruller dough on to a floured board by heaped tablespoonfuls, and quickly roll them into balls about 1 in. (2·5 cm) in diameter. Deep-fry them until they are crisp and brown, a few at a time. Or, if it is more convenient, drop the dough off the spoon directly into the hot oil – the result will be what a friend calls Crazy Crullers, as they fry up in a variety of shapes. Drain them on kitchen paper, and sprinkle with icing sugar when they have cooled.

I should think crullers would freeze well (conventional doughnuts actually taste better when retrieved from the deep-freezer, thawed, then heated in the oven), but as I haven't tried this I have no word of advice.

Michigan Oatmeal Bread

Makes 1 loaf

4 oz (100 g) sifted plain flour

2 tbsp caster sugar

2 tsp baking powder

½ tsp bicarbonate of soda

¾ tsp salt

3 oz (75 g) porridge oats

2 oz (50 g) butter or margarine

6 fl. oz (175 ml) soured milk or buttermilk

This is more like a not-very-sweet coffee cake than a true bread.

Preheat oven to 400°F (200°C), Gas 6.
1. Sift the flour, sugar, baking powder, bicarbonate, and salt. Add the oats, cut or rub in the butter, and add milk, stirring until smooth.
2. Pour the batter into a greased 8 in. (20 cm) square cake tin and bake for half an hour. Cut in squares while warm and serve with butter.

Egg Twist Bread

2 oz (50 g) margarine or butter

About ½ pt (275 ml) milk

2 tsp dried yeast

1 tsp caster sugar

1 egg, size 3

1 lb (450 g) strong white bread flour

A little butter or oil

Poppy seeds

A rich golden bread – in Jewish cookery called Challah – it keeps well, and even after four or five days makes wonderful toast. Be sure to slice it thinly, to enjoy the almost brioche-like flavour and texture.

1. Melt the margarine or butter and mix it with 4 tbsp milk, and cool to lukewarm. Mix the yeast and sugar, stir in the milk mixture, and whisk until it is well blended. Beat the remaining milk with the egg.
2. Put the flour in a bowl, make a well in the centre, pour in the yeast liquid, then add the milk and egg mixture gradually and work it all together with your hands until you have a soft but not sticky dough.
3. Turn the dough into a greased bowl and roll it over once or twice until it is shiny. Cover with oiled plastic film and let it rise about forty minutes in a warm place. Tip the dough out on a floured board and knead well until it feels springy and 'live' under your hands. Divide it into three equal pieces and shape each into a long rope. Plait the ropes together and press the ends firmly to seal the loaf. Brush the top with a little butter or oil and sprinkle with poppy seeds. Preheat the oven to 425°F (220°C), Gas 7.
4. Put the loaf on a lightly-oiled baking sheet and drape it loosely with oiled plastic film. Let it prove in a warm place for fifteen minutes. Bake for thirty-five minutes, until the loaf is a glossy golden colour and sounds hollow when rapped firmly on the underside with your knuckles. Cool completely on a wire rack before slicing.

This recipe can also be used to make a dozen plaited rolls, proved as in Step 4, and baked about fifteen minutes at the same oven heat.

Anadama Bread

There are as many stories about the origin of the name of 'Anadama' as there are recipes. One version is that a Maine woman named Anna was a very good baker who often made this rich golden bread; her husband came home one day to find that she had forgotten to bake, and cried out 'Anna, damn her bread!' No two people agree on either the tale or the recipe. The only point of agreement is that it is always made with cornmeal and molasses.

1. Dissolve the yeast and the sugar in 2 fl. oz (50 ml) of the warm water, and let it stand in a warm place to froth up. Mix

2 tsp dried yeast

1 tsp caster sugar

6 fl. oz (175 ml) hand-hot water

1 oz (25 g) margarine

2 tsp salt

3 oz (75 g) golden syrup mixed with 3 oz (75 g) black treacle

2 oz (50 g) yellow cornmeal

1 lb (450 g) plain flour, plus a few extra tablespoonfuls

the remaining water, margarine, salt, golden syrup, and treacle in a saucepan and heat to lukewarm. Remove from the heat and stir in the yeast liquid.

2. Pour the mixture into a large bowl and stir in the cornmeal. Add the flour, about 3 oz (75 g) at a time, and beat it hard with a wooden spoon or electric mixer. When all the flour is in, and it has formed a strong sticky dough, turn it out on a heavily-floured board, and sprinkle some of the extra flour over the surface. Knead the dough until it is smooth, easy to handle, and leaves the board clean. Shape it into a ball, put it in a greased bowl, and turn it over once or twice. Cover the bowl with plastic film and let it rise in a warm place until it doubles in bulk – this will probably take four hours.

2. Turn out the dough on a lightly-floured board, knead for a minute or two, and divide it in two. Shape each piece into a loaf. Grease two bread tins, about $6 \times 3\frac{1}{2} \times 2\frac{1}{2}$ in. ($15 \times 9 \times 6\cdot5$ cm), press the dough down very well, cover with oiled plastic film and let the loaves rise until they reach the top of the tin – at least an hour, perhaps an hour and a half. Preheat the oven to 425°F (220°C), Gas 7, and bake for ten minutes, then reduce the heat to 350°F (180°C), Gas 4, and bake about thirty-five to forty minutes more. Turn the loaves out of the tins, and return them to the oven for about five minutes, until a sharp rap on the bottom makes a hollow sound.

3. Cool on a rack, and let the loaves stand, if you can, for twenty-four hours before slicing and buttering thickly with unsalted butter.

Hamburger Buns

Makes about 15–20

1 lb (450 g) strong bread flour

$\frac{1}{2}$ tsp salt

$\frac{1}{2}$ pt (275 ml) milk

2 level tsp dried yeast

1 tbsp caster sugar

2 oz (50 g) butter or margarine, softened

A little extra milk

1. Sift the flour and salt together. Warm the milk to 105°F (41°C), stir in the yeast and sugar until they dissolve, then let stand until it froths up. Mix the softened butter, yeast liquid, and flour into a soft dough. Turn into a greased bowl, cover with a cloth dipped in boiling water and wrung out, and let stand in a warm place for about an hour until double in bulk.

2. Turn out on a floured board, divide into fifteen to twenty equal parts, knead each lightly and shape into a ball. Flatten them slightly, put them on greased and floured baking sheets, let them rise for about fifteen minutes. Preheat the oven to 425°F (230°C), Gas 7.

3. Brush the tops of the buns with milk and bake about twenty minutes. While they are still hot, rub them with a piece of kitchen paper dipped in margarine, to give the slightly hard glossy look of real American hamburger buns.

Split the buns when the hamburgers are ready, and if you like, toast the cut side under the grill for a minute or two (they burn easily, so watch them closely).

Hush Puppies

Makes about 15

8 oz (225 g) cornmeal

2 oz (50 g) plain flour

2 level tsp baking powder

½ tsp salt

6 fl. oz (175 ml) milk

1 egg, size 3

1 small onion, grated or very finely chopped

Oil for frying

The legend is that fishermen or hunters along the Carolina coasts would fry their catch in cornmeal, and to quiet the hungry dogs who encircled the fire, would hastily mix up a batch of cornmeal, milk, and flour; fry it in the same fat; and toss the resulting cakes out into the darkness, saying 'Hush, puppies!' Like most legends this one has some gaps in logic in it, but it sounds good. The dogs probably 'hushed' because the hot cakes burnt their mouths!

1. Sift together the cornmeal, flour, baking powder, and salt. Whisk the egg and milk together, stir in the onion, and blend with the dry ingredients.
2. In a deep-frying saucepan heat the oil to 360°F (185°C), and drop in the batter by spoonfuls. Fry until crisp and golden. Drain on kitchen paper.

To be truly Southern, one should fry the Hush Puppies in hot fat after fish has been fried.

Johnny Cakes

Serves about 4–6

5 oz (125 g) medium cornmeal

½ tsp salt

½ pt (275 ml) boiling water

Scant 1 oz (25 g) butter or margarine

½ pt (275 ml), or more, milk

Nothing in American cookery stirs up so much controversy as 'Johnnycake', or 'Johnny Cakes', or, to give it the original name, 'Journeycake'. In parts of the South, it is a sort of cornmeal bread baked in a cake tin. In New England, it is more like a cornmeal griddle cake, but thicker and softer. It was originally made to be carried in a saddlebag, before the days of superhighways and fast food. Nowadays, it is usually served at breakfast, with maple syrup and plenty of butter. This recipe is from Rhode Island.

1. In the top of a double boiler, over boiling water, mix the cornmeal and salt, and pour on fiercely boiling water slowly, stirring. Cook, stirring often, until it is a thick mass, about ten minutes. Add the butter, and slowly stir in the milk until the mixture is thin enough to drop slowly from the spoon when you lift it out of the pan. Add a little more milk, and stir, if it seems too thick.
2. Grease a heavy griddle or frying pan and heat it until a drop of cold water bounces across the surface. Drop the batter by tablespoonfuls, lower the heat, and cook for about ten minutes. Turn the cakes over and cook the other side. The Johnny Cakes should have a smooth, browned, glossy surface and a soft moist interior. Keep them warm until all are cooked, and serve for breakfast – or with bacon and eggs as a light supper.

Muffins

Makes about 12 3 in. (8 cm) muffins

8 oz (225 g) plain flour

2½ tsp baking powder

2 tbsp caster sugar

½ tsp salt

8 fl. oz (225 ml) milk

1 egg, size 3

2 oz (50 g) margarine or butter, melted and cooled

American muffins are totally different from those that go by the same name in Britain. They are crumbly, high-domed, baked in deep patty tins, or what Americans call muffin cups – which are metal, or glass, ovenproof, and shaped a little like an individual cocotte dish.

Preheat oven to 400°F (200°C), Gas 6.

1. Grease a deep 12-cup patty tin, or twelve individual tins. Sift the flour, baking powder, sugar, and salt together. Whisk the milk, egg, and butter together and stir, *do not beat,* into the dry ingredients. Stir gently just until the flour is moistened. The batter should be slightly lumpy and should drop lightly from the spoon. Overbeaten muffin batter is smooth, elastic, and makes muffins that are a mass of holes.

2. Spoon the batter into the tins, filling each about two-thirds full, and bake for about twenty-five minutes. Serve hot, with very cold butter.

Date Muffins. Toss 3 oz (75 g) chopped, pitted dates with the flour and stir into the batter.

Corn Muffins. Use the Cornbread recipe on p. 159.

North Carolina Hoe Cakes

Makes about 20

¾ pt (450 ml) boiling water

6 oz (175 g) yellow cornmeal

1 tsp salt

Bacon drippings

A legacy of the hard times in the South during and after the Civil War; it is said that these cornmeal cakes were literally baked on the blade of a wide hoe, in the ashes of the hearth fire. They must be rushed to the table, they will not stand, and cannot be reheated. Traditionally, they were served with 'light molasses' – the nearest British equivalent would be golden syrup or Tate & Lyle's Amber Syrup if you can find it – not black treacle or molasses.

1. Pour boiling water over the cornmeal, stir in the salt, and mix well. Let it cool until you can handle it, and shape into cakes about 3 × ½ in. (8 × 1·5 cm) thick.

2. Heat a heavy griddle (girdle) very hot, until drops of cold water flicked on the surface bounce and dance. Dip a folded piece of kitchen paper in bacon drippings and grease the griddle well. Bake the cakes on one side about three minutes, turn once only. Or, heat the bacon drippings in a heavy frying pan to a depth of about ¼ in. (0·75 cm), and drop the cornmeal cakes into the spitting-hot fat and cook until golden and crisp.

Philadelphia Sticky Buns
(also known as Cinnamon Buns)

Makes about 18

Parker House Roll dough (see p. 152)

About 2 tbsp melted butter or
    margarine

8 oz (225 g) light brown sugar

1 tbsp cinnamon

Good pinch of freshly grated nutmeg

3–4 oz (75–100 g) sultanas or raisins

1. Make the roll dough, through to Step 3. Turn it out on a well-floured board, divide in half, and pat each half into an oblong about 10 in. (25 cm) long and about $\frac{1}{4}$ in. (0·75 cm) thick. Brush with melted butter.
2. Sift the sugar, cinnamon, and nutmeg together, sprinkle half of it on the dough, and cover with half the raisins or sultanas. Roll tightly as for a Swiss Roll and cut into nine equal pieces. Repeat with the second half of the dough. Thickly butter two sandwich tins, about 8 in. (20 cm) square or round, and pack the rolls tightly together. Brush the tops with melted butter. Cover with oiled plastic film, and let them rise in a warm place about an hour until double in bulk.
3. Preheat the oven to 350°F (180°C), Gas 4. Bake for about thirty minutes, until golden and glossy.

They may be glazed with Confectioners' Sugar Glaze (see p. 238), but to be truthful this is a Midwestern frill added to the classic Philadelphia recipe.

French Market Doughnuts

Makes about 36

14 oz (400 g) plain flour

8 fl. oz (225 ml) milk

1$\frac{1}{2}$ tbsp caster sugar

$\frac{3}{4}$ tsp salt

$\frac{1}{2}$ tsp freshly grated nutmeg

2 tsp dried yeast

2 tbsp warm water

2 tbsp vegetable oil

1 egg, size 3

Oil for deep-frying

Icing sugar

These are raised doughnuts, quite different from the traditional doughnut-with-the-hole which is made of a cake-like batter. They came to the United States with Dutch and German settlers, some of whom took the recipe to New Orleans. They may be cut in rounds or squares. To make jelly doughnuts: put a teaspoonful of jelly or jam on half the rounds, cover with a second round and press the edges together, then fry.

1. Sift the flour. Scald the milk and stir in the sugar, salt, and nutmeg, cool to lukewarm. Dissolve the yeast in the warm water. Pour the milk mixture into a large bowl, and whisk in the yeast liquid, the oil, and the egg. Gradually beat in the flour.
2. Cover the bowl with greased plastic film, and let it rise in a warm place until double in bulk. Scrape out the mixture on to a well-floured board and knead five or six times – it will be a soft dough. Roll out half the dough to $\frac{1}{2}$ in. (1·5 cm) thickness, and cut in rounds or squares with a floured cutter. Repeat with the other half. Put the doughnuts on baking sheets, cover with oiled plastic film draped over jam

jars so that the surface does not touch the dough, and let rise for about half an hour.

3. Heat the oil in a deep-fryer to 375°F (190°C), and fry a few at a time until golden brown. Drain on kitchen paper. Toss in a brown-paper bag with icing sugar until well coated, and serve hot.

Sour Milk Doughnuts

Makes about 50

16–18 oz (450–500 g) plain flour

1½ tsp bicarbonate of soda

1½ tsp cream of tartar

1½ tsp salt

½ tsp mixed spice

3 eggs, size 3

Scant 6 oz (175 g) caster sugar

3 tbsp white fat or margarine, melted

8 fl. oz (225 ml) milk, soured with ½ tsp lemon juice

Oil for deep frying

No one really knows how or where doughnuts began – it is possible that the idea of a 'fried cake' came with the earliest colonists, or with later Dutch or German settlers. However, the legend in New England is that the doughnut with the hole owes its existence to a little boy named Hanson Gregory, in Camden, Maine. He complained to his mother that the centre of fried cakes was never completely cooked. So she pushed a hole through the centre before she fried the next batch, and that's how doughnuts were born.

1. Sift the dry ingredients together and mix well. Whisk the eggs with the sugar until thick and foamy. Stir in the melted fat and mix well, then stir in the soured milk, and lastly beat in the flour mixture until everything is blended. Chill in the refrigerator for half an hour.

2. Heat the oil in a deep-fryer to 375°F (190°C). The temperature must be kept high and steady so that the doughnut batter does not absorb fat.

3. Scrape the dough on to a well-floured board and pat it out to ¼ in. (0·75 cm) thickness. With a floured doughnut cutter, about 3 in. (8 cm) in diameter, cut out rounds. Either re-roll the little 'hole' portions and re-cut, or fry them as they are.

4. Fry a few at a time until brown, turning once only. Drain on several folds of kitchen paper, and dredge with icing sugar, or a mixture of caster sugar and cinnamon.

Orange and Lemon Bread

Makes 1 loaf

6 oz (175 g) plain flour

1 tsp baking powder

Good pinch of salt

4 oz (100 g) unsalted butter

6 oz (175 g) caster sugar

2 eggs, size 3

4 fl. oz (100 ml) milk

Grated rind of one lemon and one
orange

Juice of half a large lemon and an equal
quantity of orange juice

2 tbsp caster sugar

A sweet tea bread, from Corpus Christi, Texas, meant to be sliced thinly – and very good when toasted.

Preheat oven to 325°F (170°C), Gas 3.
1. Butter a loaf tin, $8\frac{7}{8} \times 4\frac{7}{8} \times 2\frac{5}{8}$ in. (22·5 × 12·5 × 6·5 cm), and line the bottom with greased greaseproof paper. Sift the flour, baking powder, and salt. Cream the butter with the sugar, and gradually beat in the eggs. Stir the milk into the butter and sugar mixture, about two tbsps at a time, alternating with four tbsps of the dry ingredients.
2. Mix in the orange and lemon rind, and pour the batter into the prepared tin. Bake for about forty-five minutes, until a thin skewer inserted in the centre of the cake comes out clean. In the last five minutes of baking, mix the fruit juice and two tbsps of sugar in a saucepan, and stir over a moderate heat until the sugar dissolves.
3. Take the bread from the oven, brush the top with the fruit juice mixture, and let it cool in the tin before turning it out.

Flour Tortillas

Makes about 16

4 oz (100 g) white cooking fat or lard

20 oz (550 g) 81%–85% light brown
flour

1 tsp salt

8 fl. oz (225 ml) hot water

Flour for dusting the pastry board

Tortillas are now available in packets and tins in various shops in Britain, and although I have never tried them I am sure they are good. Tortilla experts tell me that in New Mexico, Arizona, and Texas, only a tortilla made with masa harina, *the specially ground and prepared corn (maize) meal, is worthy of the name. This meal, under the Quaker Oats name, is beginning to appear in certain London shops. I haven't used it, so can't provide an adaptation of a recipe for the British reader. However, this recipe for flour tortillas came from a Southwestern cookbook published by a 'ladies' aid' society somewhere in New Mexico – it is astonishingly easy to make, tastes marvellous, and makes the perfect pusher, scooper and edible spoon to go with any of the chili recipes. Use these tortillas, too, as a base for Tacos (see p. 91).*

1. Rub the fat into the flour and salt until it feels like coarse breadcrumbs, or mix it even more quickly and evenly in a food processor. Slowly add the hot water, and mix into a firm dough. Grease a large bowl, put in the dough ball, turn it over and over, cover and let it stand about twenty minutes.
2. Divide the dough into sixteen parts (the easy way is to shape it into a sort of log, cut that in half, cut each half into halves, and so on). Roll each piece between your palms into a flattish ball, then pat the ball on the floured board, and with

a floured rolling pin roll it out to a 6 in. (15 cm) circle. Lay the uncooked tortillas on a big sheet of greaseproof paper, until they are all rolled out.

3. Heat a heavy griddle (girdle) or a big, heavy frying pan, rub it lightly with a piece of kitchen paper dipped in lard or bacon drippings, and heat it until a drop of cold water flicked over the surface dances around like quicksilver instead of sputtering away. Fry the tortillas one by one, pressing down with a big palette knife, turning them only once, until the surface is dry-looking, and light brown splotches appear. Stack them, and keep them warm and soft in a tea towel until you are ready to use them.

Tortillas freeze well, separated with greaseproof paper, and over-wrapped with heavy freezer film or foil – or so I am told by my Western friends who all seem to have deep freezers the size of my kitchen!

Raisin Bran Bread

Makes 1 loaf

9 oz (250 g) plain or self-raising flour

3 oz (75 g) porridge oats

4 oz (100 g) light brown sugar

1 oz (25 g) bran

4 tsp baking powder

1½ tsp cinnamon

1 tsp salt

½ pt (300 ml) milk

2 eggs, size 3

4 fl. oz (100 ml) vegetable oil

6–8 oz (175–225 g) sultanas or raisins

For the crunch topping

1 oz (25 g) porridge oats

1½ oz (25–35 g) light brown sugar

1 tbsp butter or margarine, melted

A great American favourite, for breakfast or tea. The cooled loaf can be sliced, re-assembled, wrapped securely and frozen, and a single frozen slice can then be detached for toasting without thawing the loaf.

Preheat oven to 325°F (170°C), Gas 3.

1. Combine the topping ingredients and set aside.

2. Grease a round or square cake tin, about 7 × 7 in. (18 × 18 cm). In a large bowl, combine the dry ingredients. Mix the milk, eggs, and oil together and stir into the first mixture, until it is moistened. Do not beat. Stir in the raisins and scrape into the prepared tin.

3. Sprinkle the crunch topping mixture evenly over the batter. Bake about an hour and ten minutes, until a skewer inserted in the centre of the loaf comes out clean. Cool it in the tin for ten minutes, then turn out on a wire rack.

This bread can also be made in a 2 lb (900 g) bread tin.

Nancy Lingle's Spoon Bread

Serves 4

4 oz (100 g) yellow cornmeal

1½ tsp bicarbonate of soda

1½ tsp salt

1½ pts (825 ml) buttermilk

Who is Nancy Lingle? My copy of this recipe says 'couldn't be simpler and divine'. Spoon bread, it must be noted, isn't really bread in the traditional sense, it is served as a side dish in place of potatoes, rice, or hominy grits in the South. Always lots of butter on the top.

Preheat oven to 350°F (180°C), Gas 4.
Mix the cornmeal, bicarbonate, salt, and buttermilk, pour into a buttered square cake tin or shallow casserole, and bake for about an hour and ten minutes until a knife put into the centre comes out clean.

Popovers

Makes about 8

4 oz (100 g) sifted plain flour

2 eggs, size 3

½ level tsp salt

8 fl. oz (225 ml) milk

1 tbsp good vegetable oil (soya, groundnut, corn – but *not* olive, nor the blended oil sold for frying)

Everyone thinks they're incredibly difficult to make and need special tins. Nonsense. You can make them in ovenproof glass or earthenware cups, just as long as the cups are deeper than they are wide. But you must have the oven very, very hot; put the cups in on a baking sheet to get hot, then grease them just seconds before they are filled.

Preheat oven to 425°F (220°C), Gas 7.
1. Set ovenglass or earthenware cups on a baking tray and put them on the top shelf of the oven. Put all the ingredients together and whisk until very smooth; it's very easy to do in a blender or food processor.
2. With oven gloves, slide out the baking tray, dip a piece of kitchen paper in oil or melted butter and swiftly grease the cups. Fill the cups a little less than half full of the batter, and bake for about thirty minutes *without opening the oven*: it's the steam in the batter that expands and pops them up.
3. They should be tall, toppling to one side, and hollow inside. If you prefer them drier, pierce each with a sharp knife and return to a turned-off oven for five minutes. Serve with jam or marmalade.

Sopaipillas

Makes about 36

1 lb (450 g) plain flour

2 level tsp salt

4 level tsp baking powder

2 oz (50 g) lard

A little iced water

Good frying oil, or (preferably) plenty of lard for frying

These Southwestern fried bread puffs – sometimes known as Navajo bread – are airy, hollow, and almost impossible to stop eating. 'Anglos' butter them, real South-westerners don't. Have them hot and fresh with chili; or roll in cinnamon and sugar and serve with coffee.

1. Sift the flour, salt, and baking powder and rub in the lard until the mixture feels like cornmeal. Handle lightly, raising your hands above the bowl and sifting the mixture through

your fingers to make it airy. Add just enough water to hold the dough together.

2. Cover the bowl, let stand in the refrigerator for ten or fifteen minutes. Roll out on a lightly-floured board ⅛ in. (0·4 cm) thick, and cut with a sharp knife into 1½ in. (4 cm) squares. Heat the oil or lard to 385°F (195°C) in a large deep-fryer, and fry two or three minutes on each side, until crisp and brown. Drain and serve at once.

Waffles

These quick, light, crisp patterned cakes are a very ancient form of bread. They came to America with Scandinavian or German families – the name goes back to a medieval German word meaning 'weave' or 'honeycomb', both of which are good descriptions of the classic indented waffle pattern. American waffle irons, usually round, are about half again as large as the ones available here. And the typical American waffle is usually either unsweetened, or with very little sugar in the mix; it is often used as a base for savoury mixtures such as creamed chicken or ham, as well as for the more publicised serving of waffles with maple syrup, bacon, or sausages. Waffles freeze well, and can be reheated in a few minutes under a grill, or in fact in some electric toasters.

Follow the directions for your own waffle iron meticulously. Some have non-stick surfaces, some have indicator lights which go out when the waffle is completely baked.

The first of these recipes is for the plain, unsweetened American waffle with a more bread-like texture than the European version, which is sweeter, crisper, and made with whisked egg whites – as in the second recipe. I can't be specific about how many waffles these recipes will make, as this depends on the capacity of your waffle iron.

CLASSIC WAFFLES

2 eggs, size 3

12 fl. oz (350 ml) milk

8 oz (225 g) plain flour

¾ tsp salt

2½ tsp baking powder

4 tbsp butter or margarine, melted

1. Whisk the eggs well and beat them into the milk. Sift the flour with the salt and baking powder and beat the mixture into the milk. Then stir in the melted margarine, do not beat the batter again.

2. Cook on a preheated waffle iron as the manufacturers' directions indicate. Serve with golden syrup, jam, honey butter (see p. 174), or maple-flavoured syrup. Or use as a Sunday-supper sort of dish, with chicken à la king or any other creamed savoury mixture.

Note: For sweetened waffles, add a scant 2 oz (50 g) of caster sugar to the batter.

CRISP 'GAUFRE' WAFFLES

7 oz (200 g) plain flour

2 tsp baking powder

½ tsp salt

1 tbsp sugar (omit this if you plan to use the waffles with a savoury mixture)

3 eggs, size 3, separated

5–6 tbsp vegetable oil, melted butter or margarine

12 fl. oz (350 ml) milk

1. Sift the flour with the baking powder, salt, and sugar if used. Beat the egg yolks well, then whisk in the oil and milk.
2. Put the dry ingredients in a good-sized bowl, make a well in the centre, and pour in the liquid. Mix the batter with a few strong, quick strokes of a wooden spoon, or a very brief whirl with a hand or electric whisk, but do not overbeat.
3. Whisk the egg whites stiffly, and lightly cut and fold them into the batter. Bake the waffles according to the manufacturers' directions. If, when you try to lift the top of the waffle iron there is some resistance, the waffle is not done, and you must cook it for about another minute. If you pull a waffle iron sharply apart, the waffle will tear.

Sourdough Bread

For the starter

2 fl. oz (50 ml) milk

4 fl. oz (100 ml) cold water

2 tsp vegetable oil

2 level tsp dried yeast

2 fl. oz (50 ml) hand-hot water

2 tsp caster sugar

1½ tsp salt

About 9–10 oz (250–275 g) strong bread flour

James Beard, who knows everything about bread of all nations, as well as all about American cookery, has been quoted as saying that he thinks sourdough bread is much over-rated, and very difficult to make at home. I have been rather inclined to agree with him – having had sourdough starter 'die' in my kitchen. However, this simple and fairly quick sourdough recipe makes a very good loaf, with the characteristic open texture and agreeably sour flavour to the bread. The method of making the actual dough is one evolved from the classic Grant loaf, which does not have to be kneaded. I have made it with great success with strong white bread flour, and with brown flour – the 81%–85% type – which gives a result that is probably close to the wholemeal bread pioneer women in the American West would have made.

1. Mix the milk, cold water, and oil in a saucepan, bring it to the boil, then cool to lukewarm. Stir the dried yeast into the 2 fl oz (50 ml) of hand-hot water and whisk with a fork until it is frothy. Stir the sugar and salt into the milk mixture, then add the yeast liquid and blend well.
2. Stir the liquid into the flour just enough to blend, but do not beat. Cover with plastic film and let it stand in a warm place for about twelve to eighteen hours, until it is puffy and has a somewhat beery smell. This recipe will make enough starter for about six loaves; store the unused portion in a tightly covered bowl in the refrigerator, for about a week to ten days, or freeze it for up to a month. Bring any chilled starter back to room temperature before adding it to the bread dough.

For the dough

4 fl. oz (100 ml) milk

8 fl. oz (225 ml) cold water

1½ tsp vegetable oil

2 level tsp dried yeast

2 fl oz (50 ml) hand-hot water

4½ tsp caster sugar (or light brown sugar, if you are using brown flour)

2½ tsp salt

About 20 oz (550 g) strong bread flour, or light brown flour

2 rounded tsp Sourdough Starter

Optional: 1 egg white beaten with 1 tbsp cold water

1. Mix the milk, water and oil in a saucepan, bring it to the boil, then cool it to lukewarm. Mix the yeast with the 2 fl oz (50 ml) warm water and stir it until it is frothy. Add the yeast liquid, the sugar and salt to the milk mixture.

2. Put the flour in a large bowl and make a well in the centre. Pour in the milk and yeast liquid, then add the starter and mix it all well with your hands or a big wooden spoon. The dough will be soft, not as firm as a conventional bread dough. Oil another bowl and turn the dough ball over and over in it until the surface glistens. Cover, and let it stand in a warm place until it has doubled in bulk.

3. Turn the dough out on a floured board, and have some extra flour in a bowl at hand. (The amount you need depends on the type of flour you are using.) Turn it over several times on the board, and add more flour if the dough is sticky and unmanageable. Divide it into two parts, and make each into an oval, flattened shape. Fold each piece in half, pat it down again, then shape it into a round, oval, or long tapered loaf as you please.

4. Put the loaves on lightly-greased baking sheets, and slash the tops once or twice with a sharp knife. Let them rise, covered with oiled plastic film, until double in bulk. Preheat the oven to 425°F (220°C), Gas 7. Bake about fifteen minutes, then reduce the temperature to 350°F (180°C), Gas 4, and bake for another fifteen minutes. Brush the tops with the egg and water mixture, and bake another five minutes until the loaf sounds hollow when rapped with your knuckles. Cool on racks in front of an open window, for a crisp crust.

Shaped into a tapered loaf about 15 in. (38·5 cm) by 1¼ in. (3 cm) high, this sourdough recipe makes a very good 'French' baton loaf.

Whipped Butter

Makes about 8 oz (225 g)

6 oz (150 g) unsalted butter

2 fl. oz (150 ml) double cream

In many American menus or cookbooks, you will see references to whipped butter, which can be bought in supermarkets and delicatessens. It's easy to make at home.

Use unsalted butter if you like it (and can find it). Let it stand at room temperature until it is soft but not 'oiled'. Whisk about 2 oz (50 g) of double cream and stir it into the butter lightly, blending well but not beating the air out of the cream. It is airy and light, on waffles or hot toast.

Perhaps this is the place to remind you that 'sweet butter' to Americans is unsalted butter, and that a stick of butter is 4 oz (100 g).

Tomato Marmalade or Preserve

Makes about 2½ pts (1·5 litres)

2 lemons

1 orange

28 oz (793 g) tin Italian peeled tomatoes, or their equivalent in fresh tomatoes, peeled

2¼ lb (1 kg) caster sugar

¼ tsp salt

Three 1 in. (2·5 cm) pieces of ginger root

½ tsp ground allspice

A recipe from the Midwest where beefsteak tomatoes grow so huge, rich, and sweet in flavour that they put all others to shame. This tangy-sweet preserve goes beautifully with hot biscuits or toast, or as a sweet accompaniment to cold ham or tongue. If you can find the tasty Marmande tomatoes or anything like them, do try it – otherwise use tinned Italian tomatoes, as Moneymakers and their ilk are too tasteless.

1. Peel the lemons and orange, removing all the white pith. Cut the peel in thin strips, blanch in boiling water for ten minutes, and drain. Cut the orange and lemon flesh into segments, remove the seeds, and as much of the membranes as you can.
2. Put the orange, lemons, peel, tomatoes, sugar, salt, and ginger in a large enamel-lined saucepan. Mix well, bring to the boil, and cook rapidly, uncovered, for about forty minutes or until thick.
3. Pour the hot marmalade into five ½ pt (275 ml) hot, sterilised jars, and seal at once. Store in a dark place.

Honey Butter

Makes about 4 oz (100 g)

3 oz (75 g) runny honey

1 oz (25 g) soft butter

2 tbsp double cream

This lovely sweetened whipped butter is (or used to be) served at breakfast in the Brown Palace Hotel in Denver, Colorado – a rococo edifice that recreates the splendid days of silver and gold mining in the West. It makes about 5 oz (125 g), enough for two or three people, and should be served with pancakes, waffles, scones, or toast.

Beat everything together until the mixture is light and airy. It is best used at once, but can be stored for a few days under tightly-stretched plastic film in the refrigerator.

Pies and Desserts

American Pies and American Pastry

American dessert pies tend to be rather bigger than the average English sweet pie or tart. Most recipes in standard cookbooks are calculated for a 9 in. (23 cm) tin – a single-crust pie uses about 7½–8 oz (210–225 g) of pastry for a pie that will make six to eight generous servings. The recipe for American Pie Pastry (see p. 177) gives you enough pastry for two single-crust pies or one double-crust pie.

If, however, you want to make smaller or larger pies, these notes about pastry quantities may be of some use: an 8 in. (20 cm) tin requires about 6 oz (175 g) of pastry, for a finished pie of six or seven average-sized servings, while a 10 in. (25 cm) tin takes about 12 oz (350 g) of pastry for eight to ten average-sized servings.

It seems presumptuous for an American to describe to English readers techniques for making pastry. Everyone I know on this side of the Atlantic seems to be born with cool hands, a natural knack of rubbing or cutting fat into flour, and a talent for knowing the precise amount of cold water needed to make a delectably flaky pie pastry. However, a few notes on the peculiarities of American pie-making may not go amiss. The words 'pie-crust' and 'pie-shell' are used interchangeably to denote pastry – unbaked or baked.

Unbaked pie-shells are almost always used for fruit pies, savoury meat and vegetable mixtures, and double-crust pies. To keep the bottom crust from going soggy in the baking, brush it with a little unbeaten egg white, or melted butter or margarine. When baking a single-crust pie, try to use a tin with a rather wide edge, to prevent juicy fillings from bubbling out and over as the pie bakes. For a single crust, use half the recipe on page 177. To cut out the correct size, invert the tin on the rolled-out pastry and cut a round 2 in. (5 cm) wider than the pie-tin. From the outer edge, cut a 1 in. (2·5 cm) strip. Without pulling or stretching, line the tin with the pastry round, dampen the top edge with cold water, and press on the extra strip, pinching and fluting it all around to make a decorative and useful standing edge. Fill and bake as your chosen recipe directs.

For double-crust pies, roll out the pastry – the full recipe this time – cut out one round as above, but don't cut out the sealing strip. Cut another round 1 in. (2·5 cm) wider than the inverted tin. Prick the larger round here and there with a fork, cut a few decorative gashes in it. Line the tin with the smaller round, add the cooled filling, and place the larger round over it. Turn the extra rim of the top pastry under the edge of the bottom pastry, pressing the two edges firmly together. Bake as set forth in your chosen recipe.

Baked pie-shells are always used for single-crust pies

with a cream, custard, or chiffon filling. They are baked blind exactly as in English cookery. Line the tin with the rolled-out pastry, prick all over, and fit in a lightly-oiled round of greaseproof paper or foil. Weight it down with a handful of beans or rice (keep these 'baker's friends' in their own clearly-labelled container for use every time you bake a pie-shell). Preheat the oven to 450°F (230°C), Gas 8, and bake for about twelve to fifteen minutes until golden brown. Cool well, before filling and finishing the pie as specified in whatever recipe you are using.

American Pie Pastry

8 oz (225 g) plain flour

Pinch of salt

1 tsp caster sugar (optional – for sweet pies only)

5 oz (125 g) chilled lard or white cooking fat

1 oz (25 g) chilled butter or good block margarine

About 4 tbsp very cold water

This recipe makes enough pastry for two single-crust, 9 in. (23 cm) pie-shells, or one double-crust pie of the same size. It is one of the most popular American pie pastries, used for either sweet or savoury pies – a teaspoon of caster sugar may be added to the flour and salt for a sweet pastry, if you like. It is slightly richer than the classic English shortcrust. This pastry can be used as soon as it is made, or chilled and 'rested' if that suits you better. It freezes exceedingly well. For any American pie, of course, your own recipe for shortcrust pastry may be used.

1. Sift the flour and salt into a basin. Mix in the sugar if using. Cut the two fats into small pieces and lightly mix them together. Rub half the fat into the flour, lifting the mixture up in your fingers and letting it fall back into the basin, until the mixture feels like fine breadcrumbs. Cut in the remaining fat with a knife or pastry blender to make lumps the size of small peas.

2. Sprinkle the mixture evenly with cold water, a little at a time, and blend it gently with your fingers until you can gather it lightly into a cohesive ball. Depending on the flour, you may need about a teaspoon more cold water – but add this almost literally drop by drop so that the dough doesn't suddenly go heavy and damp.

3. Cut the dough into two even-sized pieces, each weighing about 7½ oz (about 210 g). Pat each piece gently into a flattened round, and either roll out at once to ⅛ in. (0·5 cm) thickness, or wrap the pieces separately in plastic film and chill until you are ready to make a pie. If using chilled dough, let it come back to room temperature before rolling it out.

If the dough tears a bit as you roll it, patch it carefully with pieces of dough cut from the edges and slightly damped – don't re-roll the pastry, as this makes it tough. As you roll, keep rounding the edges with your hand.

Apple Pie

A 9 in. (23 cm) double-crust pie, serves 6–8

Unbaked American pie pastry (see p. 177)

3–4 oz (75–100 g) caster sugar (depending on the flavour of the apples)

1 tbsp cornflour

Generous pinch of salt

$\frac{1}{4}$ tsp cinnamon

A little freshly grated nutmeg

5 medium-sized tart apples, peeled and thinly sliced

1 tbsp lemon juice (if apples are not really tart)

Scant 1 oz (25 g) butter

Preheat oven to 450°F (230°C), Gas 8.

1. Roll out the two pieces of pastry on a lightly-floured board, and cut to fit your tin – making the top round an inch larger than the tin. Line the tin with the smaller of the two rounds, and brush with a little of the butter. Combine the sugar, cornflour, salt, and spices (adding lemon juice if necessary), and stir the mixture gently into the apples. Turn them over until they are well coated. Put the apples in layers in the pie-shell, and cut the butter evenly over them.

2. Prepare the top portion of pastry by pricking, and slashing a decorative pattern. Set it on top of the pie and press the edges together. Bake for ten minutes, than reduce the heat to 350°F (180°C), Gas 4, and bake another thirty-five to fifty minutes.

For a frosty look, brush the top crust lightly with milk before baking and scatter on some caster sugar.

Apricot Fried Pies

6 oz (175 g) dried apricots, washed

Light brown sugar for cooking apricots, to taste

8 oz (225 g) plain flour, sifted

1 tsp baking powder

$\frac{1}{2}$ tsp salt

4 oz (100 g) white cooking fat

6–7 tbsp iced water

Good-quality vegetable oil for deep-frying

This recipe hails from Alabama, and will make about twelve little pies.

1. Simmer the apricots in enough water to cover for about half an hour until they are tender, then add sugar (about 2 tbsp) and cook on for another ten minutes until the apricots and sugar and water are all cooked together into a soft but not mushy blend. Cool.

2. Sift flour with baking powder and salt, and cut in the fat until it resembles very small peas. Sprinkle on water, pressing the pastry together with a fork, and handle as little as possible. Divide into two parts, and roll out each to about $\frac{1}{16}$ in. (0·25 cm) thickness on a floured board.

3. Lay a 6 in. (15 cm) diameter plate lightly on the pastry and cut circles with a very sharp knife. Put them aside on greaseproof paper. Put a spoonful of the apricots on each, in the centre, moisten the pastry edges with iced water, fold in half and crimp the edges securely.

4. Heat the oil in a deep frying saucepan to 375°F (190°C), and fry the pies, about five minutes, turning once. Drain well on kitchen paper, serve warm or at room temperature. They will keep well in an airtight tin for a few days. Don't chill, the pastry goes limp.

Dutch Apple Pie

Serves 6

Half recipe for American pie pastry (see p. 177), unbaked

A little softened butter

3 large tart apples, peeled and roughly chopped

2 tbsp flour

1 tbsp cider vinegar

1 egg, size 2 or 3

8 fl. oz (225 ml) single cream

4 oz (100 g) caster sugar

$\frac{3}{4}$ tsp mixed spice

No one seems to know why this is called 'Dutch', but that is the traditional name. In some parts of the country, the same recipe is called Cream Apple Pie, Normandy Pie, or Marlborough Pie. It's meant to be made in a deep tin – 9 in. (23 cm) × 2 in. (5 cm) deep as the filling is very juicy. An oblong baking tin of that depth may be used it you have no round tin deep enough.

Preheat oven to 450°F (230°C), Gas 8.

1. Roll out the pastry and line the tin or baking dish. Brush the bottom with the softened butter. Sprinkle the apples with the flour and cider vinegar. Beat the egg with the cream, sugar, and mixed spice and stir into the apples. Fill the pie shell.

2. Bake for twenty to twenty-five minutes, until the edges of the custard filling begin to brown. Then reduce the heat to 350°F (180°C), Gas 4, cover the edges of the pastry with aluminium foil, and bake another thirty to forty minutes, until the filling is firm and glossy. Serve warm, not hot.

Blueberry Pie

Serves 6

Unbaked American pie pastry (see p. 177)

1 lb (450 g) blueberries

6 oz (175 g) caster sugar

1 oz (25 g) plain flour

$\frac{1}{4}$ tsp salt

$\frac{1}{2}$ tsp ground cinnamon

$\frac{1}{2}$ tsp grated lemon rind

1 tbsp lemon juice

1 oz (25 g) butter

Blueberries – or their European cousins, bilberries or whortleberries – make the most luscious blue-purple pie. Be sure the berries are a ripe blue with a hazy bloom on the skins, and discard any with a reddish or greenish tinge. Tinned Polish bilberries make a very good pie, but open them carefully over a bowl – their juice causes an indelible stain on anything – even supposedly impervious Formica – that it touches!

Preheat oven to 450°F (230°C), Gas 8.

1. Roll out the two pieces of pastry and cut one to fit a 9 in. (23 cm) tin. Cut the other 1 in. larger than the tin. Line the pie tin with the smaller piece and brush it with a little of the butter. Fill it with blueberries.

2. Combine the sugar, flour, salt, cinnamon, lemon rind, and juice and mix well. Distribute this over the blueberries and cut the remaining butter in flakes over the top. Prick the top pastry crust and cut a few decorative slits, fit it over the filling, and pinch the edges to seal.

2. Bake for twenty minutes, then lower the heat to 400°F (200°C), Gas 6, for another twenty minutes, then lower it again to 350°F (180°C), Gas 4, for a final twenty minutes. Serve the pie warm, with pouring cream.

Chess Pie

Serves about 8

Half recipe for American pie pastry (see p. 177), unbaked

2 eggs, size 3

1½ tbsp plain flour

Pinch of salt

3 oz (75 g) light brown sugar

8 fl. oz (225 ml) single cream

3 oz (75 g) sultanas

3 oz (75 g) dates, chopped

4 oz (100 g) walnuts, chopped

1 tsp vanilla essence or light rum

This is a recipe whose provenance is shared equally between Virginia and Massachusetts. James Beard, who knows everything about the history of American cooking, says that it came originally from England – and suggests that instead of being made in a large pie tin, its traditional form was as individual tarts.

Preheat oven to 350°F (180°C), Gas 4.
1. Roll out the pastry and cut to fit a 9 in. (23 cm) tin. Separate one egg and use a little of the white to brush the bottom of the pastry. Mix the yolk and remaining white with the other egg and beat well. Mix the flour, salt, sugar, and cream and beat into the eggs. Stir in the sultanas, dates, walnuts, and vanilla or rum, and pour into the pie-shell.
2. Bake about an hour, or a little less, until a knife thrust into the centre comes out clean. Serve warm or cold, not hot.

Cherry Pie (George Washington Pie)

Serves 6–8

Unbaked American pie pastry (see p. 177)

28 oz (775 g) tin of tart pie cherries

6 oz (175 g) caster sugar

4 tbsp flour

A few drops of almond essence

1 oz (25 g) butter or good margarine

'I did it with my little hatchet,' said the noble child George Washington, caught by his papa standing beside a felled cherry tree. Whether or not you believe the cherished American legend, you will enjoy this lattice-top tart traditionally served on February 22, the birthday of the Father of his Country.

Preheat oven to 425°F (220°C), Gas 7.
1. Roll out half the pastry and cut into a round to fit a rather deep 9 in. (23 cm) tin. Roll out the other half and cut into strips to make the lattice. (Any unused strips can be sprinkled with salt or sesame seeds, and baked to make rich savoury sticks to serve with drinks.) Brush the bottom of the pastry shell with a little of the butter.
2. Drain the juice from the cherries into an enamel-lined saucepan, stir in the sugar and flour, bring to the boil, and cook on a low heat, stirring constantly, until it thickens.
3. Add the cherries, bring to the boil again, then plunge the saucepan into a basin of cold water. When it is almost cool, stir in the almond essence and remaining butter, and pour the mixture into the pie-shell. Interlace the strips to make a lattice and lay it on top of the filling.
4. Bake for fifteen minutes, then reduce the heat to 350°F (180°C), Gas 4, and bake another fifteen minutes until the pastry is browned. Cool well – cherry pie is never served hot.

Pumpkin Pie

Serves 6–8

Half recipe for American pie pastry (see p. 177), unbaked

2 eggs, size 3

8 fl. oz (225 ml) milk

14 oz (400 g) cooked or tinned pumpkin

5 oz (125 g) caster sugar or light brown sugar

$\frac{1}{4}$ tsp salt

$\frac{1}{4}$ tsp ground ginger

$\frac{1}{4}$ tsp freshly grated nutmeg

$\frac{1}{4}$ tsp cinnamon

1 tbsp butter or margarine, melted

An old verse from American colonial times runs,

'For pottage and puddings and custards and pies
Our pumpkins and parsnips are common supplies.
We have pumpkins at morning and pumpkins at noon,
If it were not for pumpkins, we should be undoon.'

These great golden fruits are true natives of the New World. They were grown in Central America, and by the American Indians, long before the first settlers arrived from England. Pumpkin was boiled, baked, made into soup, even dried to make meal which then went into breads and puddings. Pumpkin pie was so associated with Thanksgiving Day that it is said that once, in the seventeenth century, when a Connecticut town could not get molasses to make the traditional pie, the holiday had to be postponed.

This recipe comes from 'downstate' Indiana, near the Kentucky border, where pumpkins grow large and sweet, and are often planted between rows of sweetcorn.

Preheat oven to 400°F (200°C), Gas 6.
1. Line a 9 in. (23 cm) pie tin with the pastry, brush the bottom with a little of the butter, and make a standing fluted edge. Whisk the eggs slightly. Combine the milk with the pumpkin (strained if it is freshly cooked, not necessary with tinned pumpkins), and beat well. Beat in all the other ingredients. Pour into the pie- shell.
2. Bake for forty-five minutes, until a knife-blade inserted in the centre comes out clean.

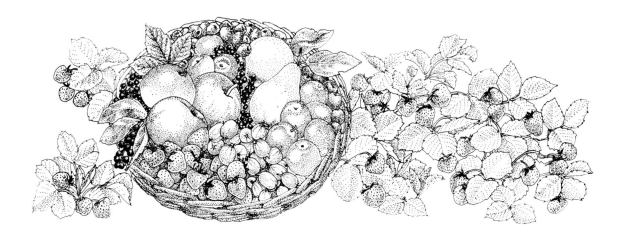

Pecan Pie

Serves 6

Half recipe for American pie pastry (see p. 177), unbaked

3 eggs, size 3

9 oz (250 g) light brown sugar

2 oz (50 g) caster sugar

1 tsp vanilla essence

Good pinch of salt

3 tbsp butter or margarine, melted

4 oz (100 g) pecans (or walnuts), coarsely chopped

The very mention of pecan pie makes expatriate Americans misty with nostalgia. This classic American recipe came from the South, where pecan-nut trees grow in great profusion – they are one of the native American wild trees, and spread all across the country from their Georgia home wherever a wandering Southerner went. Pecans can sometimes be found in British health-food shops; when they are not available, I use walnuts, with very good results. Pecan pie is sometimes known as Dentist's Delight, it's so sweet it makes your teeth ache.

Preheat oven to 350°F (180°C), Gas 4.

1. Line a 9 in. (23 cm) tin with the pastry. Separate one of the eggs, and brush the pastry with a little of the unbeaten egg white. Whisk all three eggs until they are light and frothy, then beat in the brown and white sugars a little at a time. Add the vanilla essence, salt, and melted butter, and beat well.

2. Scatter half the pieces of nuts over the pastry, pour in the egg mixture, and distribute the rest of the nuts evenly across the top. Bake for forty minutes, then reduce the heat to 300°F (150°C), Gas 2, and bake a further twenty minutes. The centre of the pie should be set but not firm. Cool at room temperature, then chill before serving.

Shoofly Pie

Serves 6–8

Half recipe for American pie pastry (see p. 177), unbaked

3 oz (75 g) black treacle

4 oz (100 g) golden syrup

8 fl. oz (225 ml) cold water

7 oz (200 g) plain or self-raising flour

4 oz (100 g) light brown sugar

¾ tsp bicarbonate of soda

6 oz (150 g) cold butter or very good margarine

A recipe from the Pennsylvania Dutch country, this is sometimes called Crumb Pie, or Gravel Pie, because of the texture of the crumb mixture in the filling. The method I give here is the best-known one – with layers of treacle mixture and crumbs – but it can be made with the treacle mixture as the base and a thick layer of crumbs spread evenly across the top. This recipe will fill a standard pie tin, a fluted flan ring set on a baking sheet, or two smaller pie tins.

Preheat oven to 375°F (190°C), Gas 5.

1. Roll out the pastry and cut to fit a 9 in. (23 cm) tin or flan ring. Soften a little of the butter and brush over the pastry. Mix the black treacle, golden syrup, and water in a small saucepan, bring to the boil, lower the heat, and simmer for about two minutes.

2. Sift the flour, sugar, and bicarbonate into a large bowl. Cut off 1 oz (25 g) of the butter and set it aside, cut the remaining butter into the flour mixture and rub it in until it feels like coarse crumbs.

3. Pour one-third of the treacle mixture into the pastry shell, sprinkle on one-third of the flour mixture, add another layer of treacle mixture, and continue, finishing with a layer of crumbs. Dot the reserved butter over the top and bake for fifty minutes. Serve warm or cold, not hot.

Vinegar Pie

Serves 6–8

Half recipe for American pie pastry (see p. 177), unbaked

1 tbsp plain flour

1½ tsp mixed spice

4 egg yolks, size 3

2 egg whites, size 3

6 oz (175 g) caster or light brown sugar

8 oz (225 g) soured cream

3 tbsp butter or good margarine, melted

3 tbsp cider vinegar

4 oz (100 g) walnuts, coarsely chopped

6 oz (175 g) sultanas or raisins

Optional: double cream

This is a recipe from the Southwest – the story goes that it was invented by a ranch cook in the days before apple trees had been planted on those immense plains, to bring a hint of fruit flavour (from the cider vinegar) to the hungry cowhands. That's as may be, but certainly chuckwagon vinegar pie out on the range was never as rich and luscious as this one!

Preheat oven to 450°F (230°C), Gas 8.

1. Roll out the pastry and cut to fit a 9 in. (23 cm) pie tin. Brush the bottom with a little of the unbeaten egg white. Sift the flour with the mixed spice. Beat the egg yolks until pale and fluffy. Whisk the remaining egg whites to stiff peaks, then carefully cut in the sugar. Cut and fold the egg yolks into the egg white mixture.

2. Add the flour alternately with spoonfuls of the soured cream to the egg mixture – be careful not to flatten out the air. Stir together the butter, vinegar, nuts, and sultanas, and carefully fold into the first mixture.

3. Gently scrape this filling into the pie-shell, and bake for ten minutes. Lower the heat to 400°F (200°C), Gas 6, and bake another five minutes. Lower heat again to 350°F (180°C), Gas 4, and bake about fifteen minutes more, until the filling begins to set. The centre will still shiver a bit, but don't worry, as the pie goes on cooking for several minutes after it has been taken from the oven.

4. Cool before serving – make it even richer and more extravagant with rosettes of stiffly-whisked double cream.

Butterscotch Pie

Serves 6

9 in. (23 cm) baked pie-shell (American
　pie pastry, p. 177)

5 oz (125 g) dark brown sugar

2 oz (50 g) plain flour

½ tsp salt

¾ pt (425 ml) rich milk

2 egg yolks, size 2 or 3

1 oz (25 g) butter or good margarine

½ tsp vanilla essence

Optional: meringue topping (p. 187)

The colour and flavour of this American pie depends on the kind of dark brown sugar you use. One very good supermarket group sells a rich caramel-coloured one as dark brown. Another equally reputable chain labels a paler sugar – about the colour of a cane chair – 'dark soft brown'. To me 'butterscotch' is a rich, fairly deep colour and taste, so I use the darker one. I've never made it with Muscovado or 'molasses' sugar, but it might be worth trying.

1. In the top of a double boiler, mix the sugar, flour, and salt. Stir in the milk and mix it as smoothly as you can. Set it over boiling water in the base of the double boiler, and cook, stirring often, until it begins to thicken. Take it off the heat.
2. Lightly whisk the egg yolks, slowly stir about 3 tbsp of the hot mixture into them, then pour this into the remaining sauce. Cook (still over boiling water), stirring constantly, until the mixture is smooth and thickened. Beat in the butter and vanilla, remove from the heat, and cool. Pour into the baked pie-shell. If you are topping it with meringue, bake in a preheated oven, 400°F (200°C), Gas 6, until it is gilded.

Lemon Chiffon Pie

Serves 6–8

9 in. (23 cm) baked pie-shell (American
　pie pastry, p. 177)

1 level tbsp gelatine

2 fl. oz (50 ml) cold water

4 eggs, size 3, separated

6 oz (175 g) caster sugar

Good pinch of salt

4 fl. oz (100 ml) lemon juice

Grated rind of one lemon

Optional: whipped cream

A particularly American form of sweet course which, for want of a better description, one might call a flavoured gelatine-meringue mixture, poured into a baked pie-shell, and chilled. In some cases, a whipped cream topping is the final touch. They are very pretty, and more delicate in taste than rich cream pies. The Lemon Chiffon Pie recipe gives you the basic ingredients and technique, the others are variations.

1. Soak the gelatine in the cold water, in a cup, for five minutes. Set the cup in a pan of hot water, bring water to the boil, and stir the gelatine until it is dissolved. Beat the egg yolks well, add half the sugar, the salt, lemon juice, and grated rind. In the top of a double boiler, over simmering water, cook this mixture until it is a smooth custard that will coat the back of the spoon. Stir frequently as it cooks. Mix in the gelatine and set the top of the double boiler in a basin of cold water. Cool the custard until it is lukewarm, stirring from time to time.
2. In a large bowl, whisk the egg whites to the soft peak stage, and whisk in the remaining sugar by teaspoonfuls. When the meringue mixture is stiff and beginning to lose its gloss, scrape the custard over the top and gently cut and fold together. Pour into the baked pie-shell and chill well.

Coffee Chiffon Pie. Soak the gelatine in cold coffee instead of water. Beat the egg yolks as above with half the sugar and the salt, then stir in 4 fl. oz (100 ml) hot coffee. Cook the custard as above. This version of a chiffon pie really *does* call for a whipped cream topping.

Apricot Chiffon Pie. Instead of lemon juice and rind, use 6 oz (175 g) of cooked apricot pulp (made from simmered, dried apricots). Beat this into the egg yolk mixture in the top of the double boiler, and cook for five minutes, stirring. Then add the soaked gelatine, and finish as in Step 2 above.

Pumpkin Chiffon Pie. Use 6 oz (175 g) cooked, strained pumpkin mixed with $\frac{1}{2}$ tsp cinnamon and $\frac{1}{4}$ tsp grated nutmeg, instead of lemon. Soak the gelatine in 4 fl oz (100 ml) cold milk instead of water, and then heat until it dissolves. Proceed as in Steps 1 and 2 above.

Nesselrode Pie

Serves 6–8

9 in. (23 cm) baked pie-shell (American pie pastry, p. 177), baked in a 2 in. (5 cm) deep tin

2 tsp rum

3 tbsp cut mixed peel

$\frac{3}{4}$ tbsp gelatine

4 tbsp boiling water

$\frac{3}{4}$ pt (425 ml) milk

$\frac{1}{2}$ tsp salt

5 oz (125 g) caster sugar

·3 eggs, size 3, separated

8 fl. oz (225 ml) double cream

This incredibly rich, high, and bright pie is a lineal descendant of Nesselrode pudding, and was allegedly created by a Swiss restaurateur for Diamond Jim Brady, the high-rolling New York gambler and real-estate speculator of the 'Nineties. He, it is said, liked the pie to be even more luxurious than this recipe – with a glossy thatching of marrons glacés. He died young, not as one might suppose of over-eating, but by lead poisoning – a bullet from the gun of a jealous husband.

1. Mix the rum with the peel in a cup and set aside. Put the gelatine in a cup and pour on the boiling water, stir until it is completely dissolved. In the top of a double boiler, over simmering water, mix the milk, salt, and $2\frac{1}{2}$ tbsp of the sugar. Heat, and stir in the dissolved gelatine liquid.
2. Whisk the egg yolks well in a 2 pt (1·125 litre) basin, gradually pour on the hot milk mixture and whisk again, then tip all this back into the top of the double boiler. Cook, stirring, until the custard mixture thickens enough to coat the back of the spoon. Set the top of the double boiler into a basin of cold water and cool. Stir in the rum and peel.
3. Whisk the egg whites to soft peaks, and gradually beat in the remaining sugar. Gently fold in the custard. Whisk the cream stiff and carefully cut that in. Pour into the deep baked pie-shell, and chill. Lily-gilding: a scatter of preserved orange-peel slivers over the top, or a shaving of plain dark chocolate.

Key Lime Pie

Serves 6 or more

9 in. (23 cm) baked pie-shell (American pie pastry, p. 177)

3 egg yolks, size 3

14 oz (400 g) tin of sweetened condensed milk

5 fl. oz (125 ml) fresh lime juice or bottled (unsweetened)

Grated rind of one lime

2 scant drops of green food colouring

Meringue topping (see p. 187)

My Aunt Hattie was a truly terrible cook – a noble joint of beef would be cooked until it was grey inside and out, and her chicken gravy could have been used as wallpaper paste. The only thing she could do well was Key Lime Pie (and even then, the pastry had to be made by someone else). Living as she did in backwoods Florida, she could not depend on a supply of fresh milk. The only way to preserve food was in an icebox, with dripping sawdusty lumps of ice in a compartment at the top. This recipe seems to me to make a pie very much like hers. It is adapted from a smudgy handwritten 'receipt' book from the Florida Cracker country. As the Kenya limes in our market are smaller and sharper in flavour than the true Key lime, and the juice is a paler golden-green, I have slightly changed the original proportions, and added a little green food colouring to give it the characteristic pale jewel-colour. To decide whether you like the sweet, sharp, and very distinctive lime flavour, you may want to make a half recipe in a 6 in. (15 cm) baked pie-shell.

1. Chill the condensed milk. Whisk the egg yolks well, then beat in the milk, the lime juice, and rind, whisking until the mixture thickens. Dip a skewer into the bottle of food colouring and gently shake a drop or two into lime custard (don't let it touch your hands, unless you like green finger nails). Stir the mixture gently and pour it into the baked pie-shell. Cool well. Preheat the oven to 400°F (200°C), Gas 6, while you prepare the meringue.
2. Spread the meringue evenly over the lime custard, so that the meringue is sealed to the crust. Bake for about twelve to fifteen minutes, until the meringue peaks are gilded.

Vanilla Cream Pie

Serves about 6

9 in. (23 cm) baked pie-shell (American pie pastry, p. 177)

6 oz (175 g) caster sugar

2 oz (50 g) plain flour

½ tsp salt

¾ pt (425 ml) scalded milk

3 egg yolks, size 3

1 oz (25 g) butter or margarine

There is a whole genre of American desserts, the Cream Pies. Velvety and rich, they are topped off with a meringue and baked until lightly golden-brown. This is the basic recipe with some of its delicious variations. The pastry for a cream pie is always completely baked before the filling is added.

1. In the top of a double boiler, over simmering water, mix 4 oz (100 g) of the sugar with the flour and the salt, and gradually stir in the hot milk. Cook the mixture, covered, about ten minutes, stirring often, until it is smooth and thick.

1 tsp vanilla essence

Meringue topping (see below)

2. Whisk the egg yolks lightly and blend in 2 tbsp of the hot custard, then stir this back into the rest of the mixture. Cook, stirring constantly, until it is thick and creamy – about two minutes should do. Add the butter and vanilla, and set the top of the double boiler in a basin of cold water. Let it stand, stirring from time to time, until the custard is lukewarm. Prepare the meringue. Preheat oven to 400°F (200°C), Gas 6.
3. Pour the custard into the baked pie-shell and spread on the meringue. Bake for about twelve to fifteen minutes, and chill before serving.

Butterscotch Cream Pie. Instead of the caster sugar in the custard as specified in the Vanilla Cream Pie recipe, use 4 oz (100 g) of light brown sugar, and increase the butter to a very generous 1½ oz (35 g).

Chocolate Cream Pie. Grate 2 oz (50 g) plain dark chocolate, melt it in the hot milk, and proceed as in basic recipe.

Coconut Cream Pie. As above through Step 2, then stir 2 oz (50 g) desiccated coconut into the custard filling, before pouring it into the pie-shell. Scatter 1 level tbsp coconut over the meringue before baking.

Meringue Topping

For a 9 in. (23 cm) pie

This standard meringue mixture is made exactly as an English 'soft' meringue. Meringue toppings for pies or cakes to be baked must be spread over the entire surface, so that the meringue is 'attached' to the baked pie crust or the edge of the cake tin. So made, it will not shrink in the baking. To keep from 'weeping', bake it not more than about twelve to fifteen minutes, and let it cool at room temperature so that it will not form horrid little beads. Usually a meringue topping is baked at about 400–425°F (200–220°C), Gas 6–7, so that it stays soft and fluffy although the peaks are golden brown.

A new recipe which is called Never-Fail Meringue Topping uses a cornflour mixture for stability, and is useful to know although it has not quite the classic meringue texture.

STANDARD MERINGUE

3 egg whites, size 3

¼ tsp cream of tartar

Pinch of salt

About 6 tbsp caster sugar

Whisk the egg whites until they are foamy, add the cream of tartar and salt, and beat again until the egg whites are in soft peaks. Gradually whisk in the sugar, a tablespoon at a time, until the meringue is stiff and glossy. Spread it on the prepared pie.

NEVER-FAIL MERINGUE

1 tbsp cornflour

2 tbsp cold water

4 fl. oz (100 ml) boiling water

3 egg whites, size 3

Pinch of salt

6 tbsp caster sugar

Optional: ½ tsp vanilla essence

For this you will need an electric mixer, unless you can whisk very fast by hand.

1. Blend cornflour and cold water to a smooth paste in a small saucepan. Add the boiling water and cook, stirring, until the mixture thickens and clears. Set the pan in a basin of cold water and cool the mixture completely.

2. Whisk the egg whites until they are foamy, and add the salt. Gradually whisk in the sugar, a tablespoon at a time, until the meringue is stiff: do this on the highest speed of your mixer. Turn mixer to low speed and add the vanilla, then gradually beat in the cooled cornflour mixture. Turn the mixer to high again, and beat the meringue well. Spread on the prepared pie and bake.

Ambrosia

Serves 4–6

3 ripe bananas

3 oranges, peeled and cut in sections

1 oz (25 g) or more, desiccated coconut

An 'instant' pudding, this very old American recipe is fresh and flavourful, much nicer than it sounds.

Peel and slice the bananas thinly. Cut the orange sections in half, saving any juice. Mix the banana and orange pieces, put them into a bowl, strew the coconut over the top. Pour the juice over the coconut, and chill.

Apple Pandowdy

Serves 4–5

5 oz (125 g) butter or margarine

2 oz (50 g) caster sugar

1 egg, size 3 or 4

5 oz (125 g) plain flour

1½ tsp baking powder

¼ tsp salt

4 fl. oz (100 ml) milk

2 medium to large tart apples, peeled

3 oz (75 g) light brown sugar

½ tsp ground cinnamon

To serve:

¼ pt (125 ml) double or whipping cream

½ tsp icing sugar

½ tsp vanilla essence

What extraordinary names turn up in old American cookbooks! Apple Pandowdy, Blueberry Slump, Huckleberry Buckle. They are all closely related fruit or berry puddings, using the fruits of the season.

Preheat oven to 350°F (180°C), Gas 4.

1. Cream the butter and sugar together. Beat the egg well and whisk it into the butter mixture. Sift the flour, baking powder, and salt together twice, and add to the above mixture, alternately with the milk, beating well after each addition.

2. Slice the apples thinly, and spread them evenly in a buttered shallow baking dish – a deepish quiche dish is perfect. Mix the brown sugar and cinnamon and sprinkle over the apples. Pour on the batter and spread it evenly.

3. Bake for forty-five to fifty minutes, remove from the oven, and let stand for ten minutes. Turn out on a fairly deep round plate. Serve with cream whisked with icing sugar, and vanilla.

Cheese Blintzes

Serves 4

For the batter:

4 oz (100 g) plain flour

2 eggs, size 3

4 fl. oz (100 ml) milk

4 fl. oz (100 ml) water

2 tsp good oil (*not* olive oil)

A little extra oil for frying

For the filling

8 oz (225 g) curd cheese

1 egg, size 2 or 3

Caster sugar to taste, about 1 tsp

Grated rind of half a lemon

A lovely, rich, but delicate affair, basically Russian-Jewish in background, often served at the feast of Shavuoth in May or June which features milk, cheese, and honey as symbolic festival foods. It makes a most delicious dessert.

1. Mix the batter ingredients extremely well, pour into a jug, cover, and let stand in a cold place for at least half an hour. When ready to fry, it should be no thicker than single cream: thin with a little water if it has thickened too much.
2. Heat a 6 in. (15 cm) frying pan very hot, until a few drops of cold water dance and bounce across its surface. Wipe it with a piece of kitchen paper dipped in a very little oil. Pour in enough batter to coat the sides and base of the pan, tilting the pan so that it spreads evenly. It should 'seize' at once, and the edges of the pancake will curl away from the pan. Do not fry the blintz on the other side, but slip it out of the pan onto a sheet of greaseproof paper, *cooked side up*. Keep oiling the pan lightly and fry the rest of the blintzes – this recipe makes about twelve blintzes.
3. Combine the curd cheese with the rest of the ingredients for the filling, blending well. Put 1 tbsp of filling on each pancake, and turn in the sides, then the ends, to make little envelopes.
4. Heat about 1 tbsp of oil in a large frying pan, and quickly fry the blintzes on all sides.

Serve with a bowl of cold soured cream, and either caster sugar or icing sugar as you like.

Chocolate Pudding

Serves 4–6

18 fl. oz (500 ml) milk

2 oz (50 g) plain dark chocolate

2 oz (50 g) caster sugar

3 tbsp cornflour

$\frac{1}{4}$ tsp salt

$\frac{1}{2}$ tsp vanilla essence

Single or double cream

So many smooth-textured puddings come out of packets nowadays that it is rare to find anyone making a 'proper' choc one, but anyway, here it is.

1. In the top portion of a double boiler set over direct heat, scald $\frac{3}{4}$ pt (450 ml) of the milk with the chocolate broken up in it. Stir until blended. Mix the sugar, cornflour, and salt and gradually stir in the remaining milk to make a smooth paste.
2. Put the top part of the double boiler over boiling water in the bottom part, stir the sugar and cornflour mixture into the milk, and cook for fifteen minutes, stirring, until the mixture thickens. Lower the heat so that the water is barely moving, and cook for another five minutes. Add the vanilla. Pour into a bowl and chill. Serve with unwhipped cream.

Vanilla Refrigerator Cake

Serves 6

6 oz (175 g) unsalted butter

7 oz (200 g) icing sugar

6 eggs, size 3, separated

1 tsp vanilla essence

Sponge fingers, or strips of spongecake

Cream the butter until light, add the sugar and cream again. Add the egg yolks one at a time, beating well, and stir in the vanilla. Whisk the egg whites stiff and fold the two mixtures together. Finish as in Step 2 of Chocolate Refrigerator Cake.

Lemon Refrigerator Cake. As for the vanilla cake, but omit the vanilla. Add the juice and rind of one lemon to the butter and egg batter before cutting in the egg whites.

Danish Almond Torte

Serves about 6

5 egg whites, size 3

¼ tsp cream of tartar

1½ tsp vanilla essence

1 tbsp cider vinegar

8 drops almond essence

2 tsp cold water

8 oz (225 g) caster sugar

½ pt (275 ml) double or whipping cream, flavoured with ½ tsp vanilla essence

Like its cousin the Seafoam Torte (see p. 196), this meringue-like torte travelled to America from somewhere in Northern Europe – it is a favourite delicacy of Danish and Swedish families in the upper Midwestern states of Minnesota and the Dakotas.

Preheat oven to 250°F (120°C), Gas 1.
1. Have the egg whites at room temperature. Whisk them lightly with the cream of tartar, then beat until they stand in stiff peaks. Mix the vanilla essence, vinegar, water, and almond essence. Slowly whisk 6 tbsp of the sugar into the egg whites, then add the liquid, whisking after each addition. Finally, fold in the remaining sugar.
2. Make two 9 in. (23 cm) circles on a sheet of greaseproof paper, and lay paper on a large baking sheet. Spoon the meringue mixture evenly onto the circles, spreading it with a palette knife. Bake for about half an hour, then raise the temperature to 300°F (150°C), Gas 2, and bake for another half an hour until lightly browned. Cool on a cake rack, remove the paper, and spread the flavoured whipped cream between the layers and over the top.

Blueberry Slump

Serves 4

1 lb (450 g) blueberries or bilberries

2 oz (50 g) caster sugar

Dough for American Hot Biscuits (see p. 154)

Double cream

1. Wash and pick over the blueberries or bilberries, removing any unripe ones that are red or green. Sprinkle with the sugar and cook in a heavy saucepan on a low flame until the berries are slightly soft and a thin syrup has formed. Strain off the berries and return the sauce to the pan.
2. Bring to the boil, drop in squares of biscuit dough rolled out to about ½ in. (2·5 cm) thick, cover tightly, and cook on a moderate heat for twenty minutes. Pour the blueberries over these dumplings and serve with unwhipped double cream.

Chocolate Refrigerator Cake

Serves 6

4 oz (100 g) plain dark dessert
chocolate

3 oz (75 g) caster sugar

¼ tsp salt

2 fl. oz (50 ml) hot water

4 eggs, size 3, separated

1 tsp vanilla essence

8 fl. oz (225 ml) double cream, whipped

24 sponge fingers, halved

1. Melt the chocolate in a double boiler over hot water; add the sugar, salt, and water and blend well. Remove from the heat, and, one at a time, stir in the egg yolks, whisking well after each addition. Put the pan back over simmering water and cook, stirring, for two minutes. Add the vanilla essence and cool slightly.
2. Whisk the egg whites until stiff in a large bowl. Turn the chocolate mixture onto the egg whites and lightly cut and fold together. Cool. Fold in the whipped cream. Line a bread tin with greaseproof paper, then with the halved sponge fingers, laid in rows across the base of the tin and stood on end at sides and ends. Pour in the chocolate mixture to within half an inch of the top, and lay another row of halved sponge fingers over the top. Chill, covered with plastic film, overnight, and turn the 'cake' out carefully.

German Cheesecake

Serves 8–10

For the crust

8 oz (225 g) digestive biscuits

3 oz (75 g) butter or good margarine,
melted

For the filling

2 eggs, size 2, separated

3 oz (75 g) caster sugar

1½ tbsp lemon juice

½ tsp vanilla essence

Grated rind of half a lemon or half an
orange

1 lb (450 g) cream or curd cheese

For the topping

½ pt (275 g) soured cream

1 tbsp sugar

½ tsp vanilla essence

A recipe from a cook in the city of Milwaukee, Wisconsin, famous for its wonderful beer and its tradition of German cooking. This remarkable cheesecake is unlike any other recipe; it is flattish instead of being high and light, and has a creamy, tart topping. It is, in fact, very much like the most popular frozen American cheesecake. I've never tried freezing it, but there seems no reason why it shouldn't be successful. It must be served very well chilled.

Preheat oven to 300°F (150°C), Gas 2.
1. Oil the base of a 7½ in. (18 cm) loose-based sandwich cake tin. Crush the digestives, mix with butter, and press firmly in an even layer on the base. Bake for five minutes and cool.
2. For the filling, whisk the egg yolks, sugar, lemon juice, vanilla essence, and lemon rind very thoroughly, then whisk in the cheese and beat until blended. (In a blender or food processor, combine all these or as much as your machine will hold and blend until smooth, if necessary, adding cheese in two batches.) Whisk the egg whites in a large bowl and turn the cheese mixture in on top, lightly cut and fold together. Gently scrape onto the crumb crust, level the top with a palette knife and bake for forty-five minutes. Remove from the oven. The cake will fall slightly. Cool.
3. For the topping, whisk the soured cream, sugar, and vanilla essence together, and spread smoothly over the top of the cake. Chill very well. Run a sharp knife around the edge of the tin to loosen the cake, remove rim, and set the cake on a plate. Do *not* attempt to take the cake off the base.

Indian Pudding

Serves 6

1½ pts (850 ml) milk

1 oz (25 g) coarse yellow cornmeal

1 very heaped tbsp of black treacle and golden syrup

2½ tbsp light soft brown sugar

2 oz (50 g) butter or margarine

¾ tsp cinnamon

¾ tsp ginger

Optional: Cream, vanilla ice cream

Preheat oven to 300°F (150°C), Gas 2.

1. In the top of a double boiler, scald 1 pt (550 ml) milk. Mix the cornmeal with ¼ pt (150 ml) cold milk and stir into the hot milk. Put the top of the double boiler over the bottom portion (containing about ½ pt or 300 ml boiling water), and cook the cornmeal mixture for fifteen minutes, stirring from time to time. Add the treacle, golden syrup, sugar, and butter and cook five minutes more. Stir in the spices and pour into a well-buttered baking dish.

2. Pour the remaining ¼ pt (150 ml) milk over surface – do not stir – and bake for three hours. Remove the pudding from the oven and let it stand half an hour. Serve it warm with pouring or whipped cream, or vanilla ice cream. Indian pudding must not be served hot! It's very good cold, the next day, too.

Lindy's Cheesecake

Serves 6

For the pastry

2 oz (50 g) plain flour

1½ tbsp caster sugar

½ tsp grated lemon rind

1 egg yolk, size 3 or 4

2 oz (50 g) butter or good margarine

For the filling

1½ lb (675 g) cream or curd cheese

Generous 4 oz (100 g plus about 1 tsp extra) caster sugar

1½ tbsp plain flour

¾ tsp grated orange rind

¾ tsp grated lemon rind

Few drops of vanilla essence

3 eggs, size 2

1 egg yolk, size 2

1 fl. oz (25 ml) double cream

This recipe is alleged to be the veritable one for the famous cheesecake served in the New York restaurant which was the model for 'Mindy's' in Damon Runyon's stories about guys, dolls and horse-players in the 1920's and 30's. I wouldn't like to stake my all on its authenticity, but it is a superb confection, creamy and rich, and finished off with strawberrries under a shining glaze. You will need a 6 in. (15 cm) cake tin with removable base.

To make the pastry:

1. Mix the flour, sugar, and lemon rind in a basin and make a well in the centre. Add the egg yolk and butter and work it all together, quickly and lightly, until well blended. Pat the pastry out into a flat circle, wrap in plastic film and chill for an hour.

2. Preheat the oven to 400°F (200°C), Gas 6. Butter the loose base of the cake tin. Roll out three-quarters of the pastry dough to ⅛ in. (0·5 cm) thickness, and lay it over the cake tin base only. Trim the edges, bake for twenty minutes then remove and cool. Raise the oven heat to 550°F (290°C), Gas 9.

To mix the filling:

Combine the cheese, sugar, flour, grated orange and lemon rinds, and vanilla essence. Add the eggs and the egg yolk, one at a time, stirring lightly after each addition. Finally, stir in the cream.

For the strawberry topping

12 oz (350 g) ripe strawberries

2 fl. oz (50 ml) water

2 oz (50 g) caster sugar

1 scant tbsp cornflour

1 tsp butter, melted

To bake the cake:

Butter the *sides* of the cake tin and set it over the base (which holds the partially baked base of the cake). Roll out the remaining pastry and cut it to fit the inside of the cake tin wall, press it firmly to the sides. Fill the tin with the cheese mixture, and bake for twelve to fifteen minutes, then reduce the oven heat to 200°F (95°C), Gas 1, and bake for a further hour. Let it cool for two hours before glazing.

To glaze:

Wash the strawberries and crush half of them. Boil the crushed berries with the water, sugar, and cornflour for two minutes, stirring constantly. Beat in the melted butter and cool the mixture. Cut the remaining berries in half and lay them on top of the cheesecake. Pour the strawberry glaze evenly over the top and chill the cake well before cutting.

Ghirardelli Square
Chocolate Ice Cream

Serves 6

7 oz (200 g) plain dark dessert chocolate (Menier if you feel extravagant)

4 tbsp cold water

2 oz (50 g) caster sugar

3 egg yolks, size 3

¼ pt (125 ml) single cream

¼ pt (125 ml) double cream

In San Francisco's Ghirardelli Square, an old chocolate factory has been beautifully converted into a warren of shops, restaurants, fountains, paved walks, hanging plants, and gas lights. This recipe seems to be derived from an ice cream place in Rome – it's incredibly rich, suave, and distinctive. And it needs no stirring, as for some reason it doesn't form ice flakes as it freezes. But you will need a blender or food processor.

1. Grate the chocolate and put in a blender or food processor. Bring the water to the boil, stir in the sugar and dissolve it completely, return to boiling point, then turn down the heat and simmer about five minutes. Pour the syrup onto the chocolate, switch on, and blend until it is completely smooth.
2. Lightly whisk the egg yolks, add them to the mixture and blend very well. Whisk the two creams together in a large bowl until it stands in soft peaks. Scrape the chocolate blend over it and very gently fold together. Freeze in a covered container about three to four hours. Let stand for half an hour in the refrigerator before serving.

Resist the temptation to add rum or anything else, as apparently any addition destroys the chocolate-velvet texture.

Brownie Pudding

Serves 4

2 oz (50 g) plain or self-raising flour, sifted

1 tsp baking powder

½ tsp salt

3 oz (75 g) soft light brown sugar

1 tbsp cocoa powder

2 fl. oz (50 ml) milk

1 tbsp butter or margarine, melted

½ tsp vanilla essence

2 oz (50 g) walnuts or hazelnuts, coarsely chopped

For the sauce

4 oz (100 g) light brown sugar

2 tbsp cocoa powder

5 fl. oz (125 ml) boiling water

Preheat oven to 350°F (190°C), Gas 4.

1. Mix the sifted flour with the baking powder, salt, sugar, and cocoa powder, and sift again. Mix in the milk, butter, and vanilla until just smooth but do not overbeat. Stir in the nuts and pour the mixture into a buttered casserole.

2. For the sauce, mix the brown sugar and cocoa powder and sprinkle evenly over the pudding batter. Pour the 5 fl oz (125 ml) of boiling water all over the top. Bake for thirty to forty minutes. Serve warm or cold, not hot. This is a fudgy, chewy pudding, and must be inelegantly scraped out of the casserole and dolloped onto plates.

Strawberry Shortcake

Serves 6

6 oz (175 g) plain flour

2½ tsp baking powder

½ tsp salt

1 tbsp caster sugar

3 oz (75 g) white cooking fat

1 egg, size 3

2 fl. oz (50 ml) milk

About 2 tbsp melted butter

1 lb (450 g) strawberries, washed and sliced

Caster sugar to taste

Whipped cream, about ¼–½ pt (125–275 ml)

American shortcake is not a cake, and certainly it is not a shortbread: it's really a slightly sweetened hot-biscuit dough, baked in a big round, and layered with ripe fruit, sugar, and cream.

Preheat oven to 450°F (230°C), Gas 8.

1. Sift the dry ingredients together and cut or rub in the fat lightly. Mix the egg and milk and add it to the flour mixture, stirring with a fork until all the flour is moistened. You may need a teaspoon more milk. Very gently mix with your hands. Turn it out on a floured board and knead lightly ten times.

2. Pat, do not roll, the dough to ½ in. (1·5 cm) thickness. Cut the dough in two portions, and shape each with your hands into a circle. For individual shortcakes cut with a 4 in. (10 cm) cutter. Prick the dough all over with a fork and bake on an ungreased baking sheet eight to ten minutes.

3. Brush with melted butter and sandwich together quickly with strawberries, sugar, and cream, serve at once while still hot.

Fruit Cobbler

Serves 4

1 lb (450 g) fruit, washed, and sliced if
necessary

5 tbsp caster sugar

1 tbsp lemon juice

4 oz (100 g) margarine or butter

6 oz (175 g) self-raising flour, *or* 6 oz
(175 g) plain flour and 1½ tsp baking
powder

About 3 tbsp milk

Optional: single or double cream,
vanilla ice cream

*This is the sort of generic name for one of the easiest
American puddings, much easier and quicker to make than
a pie. Any fairly firm fruit, such as blackberries, boysen-
berries (called tayberries in England and Scotland), apples,
or peaches may be used. Light brown flour (81% or 85%
extraction type) makes a most delicious topping.*

Preheat oven to 400°F (200°C), Gas 6.

1. Mix the fruit with 3–4 tbsp caster sugar and lemon juice,
and put it in an ovenproof, fairly shallow casserole (about
2 in. or 5 cm deep). Rub the margarine or butter into the
flour, stir in the remaining sugar, and add just enough milk
to make a soft but not sloppy dough.

2. Drop by heaped tablespoonfuls on top of the fruit,
spacing the blobs of dough apart as they will spread in
cooking. Bake for thirty minutes, until the crust is risen and
browned, and serve with cream – or vanilla ice cream.

Lemon Whip

Serves 6

1 rounded tbsp gelatine

3 tbsp cold water

Juice of 2 large lemons

6 eggs, size 3, separated

8 oz (225 g) caster sugar

1. Sprinkle the gelatine over the cold water, let it soak for
five minutes. Heat the lemon juice to boiling and add the
soaked gelatine. Stir over a low heat, until the gelatine
dissolves, then plunge the pan into cold water for about five
minutes.

2. Whisk the egg yolks and sugar until light and foamy, in a
bowl set over but not in a pan of simmering water, until the
whisk when lifted leaves a slowly subsiding trail behind it.
Then gradually add the warm gelatine mixture, whisking as
you do so. Stand the basin in a pan of cold water, and stir it
occasionally as it cools and thickens.

3. Whisk the egg whites to stiff peaks in a large bowl, tip the
lemon mixture in and gently cut and fold through. Let it chill
for at least two hours. Serve with thin dry biscuits (cookies).

Refrigerator Cheesecake

Serves 8–10

8 oz (225 g) digestive biscuits

2 oz (50 g) butter or good margarine, melted

½ tsp cinnamon

½ tsp grated nutmeg

1½ tbsp gelatine

4 fl. oz (100 ml) boiling water

4 eggs, size 3

3 oz (75 g) caster sugar

¼ pt (125 ml) single cream

1 lb (450 g) cream or curd cheese

Grated rind and juice of one lemon

¼ pt (125 ml) double cream

For this you will need an 8–9 in. (20–23 cm) loose-based cake tin. It's very rich, so small portions are in order. And it freezes well.

1. Crush the digestives and mix with melted butter, cinnamon, and nutmeg. Oil the bottom and sides of the tin, and press the digestive crumb mixture evenly all around. If any crumbs are left over, save them for topping.
2. Dissolve the gelatine in boiling water. Separate the eggs, and whisk the yolks with the sugar in the top of a double boiler over simmering water until thick and light. Stir in the gelatine and single cream.
3. Beat the cream or curd cheese with a fork with the lemon rind and juice. Carefully blend into the egg yolk mixture. Whisk the egg whites until stiff in a large bowl and turn the cheese mixture in on top, cut and fold together lightly. Whisk the double cream until stiff and gently fold into the cream mixture. Pour into the tin and scatter the digestive crumbs over the top. Cover with plastic film and chill for four hours. Carefully remove from the tin.

Seafoam Torte

Serves about 6

5 egg whites, size 3

¼ tsp cream of tartar

2 tsp vanilla essence

2 tsp cider vinegar

2 tsp cold water

8 oz (225 g) caster sugar

Sliced strawberries or whole raspberries

¼ pt (125 ml) double cream

½ tsp vanilla essence

The ancestor of this airy, crisp, meringue-y torte is the Austrian Schaumtorte, brought to New York by immigrants before the First World War. Its Danish cousin (see p. 190) has a delicate flavour of almonds.

Preheat oven to 250°F (130°C), Gas ½.
1. Have the egg whites at room temperature. Whisk them very lightly, add the cream of tartar, and beat until they stand in stiff peaks. Mix the 2 tsp vanilla essence, vinegar, and water. Slowly add half the sugar, a spoonful at a time, alternately with half a spoonful of the liquid, whisking after each addition. Finally, fold in the remaining sugar.
2. Draw two 7 in. (18 cm) circles on a sheet of greaseproof paper and lay it on a large baking sheet. Spoon the mixture evenly into the circles, spreading it lightly with a palette knife. Bake for one and a half hours, remove the paper to a cake rack and cool. Sandwich the layers together with the berries. Whip the cream and ½ tsp vanilla essence, and spread it on top of the torte.

Real Vanilla Ice Cream

Makes about 1½ pts (900 ml)

Two 4 in. (10 cm) lengths vanilla beans, broken in pieces

6 oz (175 g) caster sugar

¾ pt (425 ml) milk

¾ pt (425 ml) double cream

8 egg yolks, size 3 or 4

This is a revelation in taste, as far from commercial ice cream (based as it is on 'non-dairy' fat and synthetic flavours, and bound together with nameless emulsifiers) as daylight from darkness.

1. Pulverise the vanilla beans with the sugar in a blender or food processor. Mix with the milk and cream and cook over a moderate heat, stirring until just below boiling point.
2. Beat the egg yolks until thick and pale, pour the milk mixture through a sieve onto the yolks, stirring all the while. Put into a heavy saucepan and cook, stirring constantly, until it thickens enough to coat the back of the spoon.
3. Put the custard in a metal bowl and plunge that in a basin of cold water with ice cubes in it. Cover with plastic film and let it cool, then chill for two hours. Freeze as you would any ice cream.

Burnt-Almond Ice Cream. Add 2 oz (50 g) caramel flavouring and 4 oz (100 g) toasted, coarsely chopped almonds, before freezing.

Caramel Ice Cream. Stir in 2 oz (50 g) caramel flavouring.

Caramella

Serves 4–5

4 oz (100 g) soft light brown sugar

¾ pt (425 ml) double cream

2 egg yolks, size 3

Southwestern fruit is of a legendary sweetness and size – honeydew melons, Casabas, Texas watermelons and grapefruit, apples and grapes, and golden peaches – so that most of the highly-flavoured meals of this region have a simple finish. One of the rare desert-country 'desserts' that isn't fruit is this airy 'burnt sugar' ice cream.

1. In a heavy saucepan melt the sugar very slowly, stirring, until it turns to a dark syrup. Very slowly, again, stir in the cream, blending in each tablespoonful before adding more. Take pan off the heat instantly as soon as the last drop of cream is in.
2. In a large bowl, whisk the egg yolks and beat in the hot cream mixture, whisking vigorously. Cool enough to pour into a freezer container, and freeze without stirring.

Since it has no stabilisers, egg white, or whipped cream, Caramella melts very fast, so don't let it linger in a hot kitchen.

Tennessee Boiled Custard

Serves 4–6

3 eggs, size 1

6 tbsp caster sugar

Pinch of salt

2 fl. oz (50 ml) cold milk

1 pt (550 ml) milk, scalded and kept hot

2 tsp whisky or rum

This soft custard flavoured with whisky or rum is traditionally served as a Christmas treat in the South, in tall stemmed glasses with something of a contrasting texture, such as coconut cake.

1. In the bottom of a double boiler, heat the water to a rolling boil, then lower the heat until it simmers gently. In the top portion, whisk together the eggs, sugar, salt, and the cold milk. Gradually stir in the hot scalded milk, and cook, stirring, until the custard coats the back of the stirring spoon.
2. Remove from the heat, strain, cool, and add whisky or rum. Chill in serving glasses.

An even richer custard can be made, using six egg yolks instead of whole eggs.

Pumpkin Soufflé

Serves 4–6

3 oz (75 g) light brown sugar

1 tsp cinnamon

$\frac{1}{2}$ tsp freshly grated nutmeg

$\frac{1}{4}$ tsp ground cloves

$\frac{1}{4}$ tsp ground ginger

$\frac{1}{4}$ tsp salt

10 oz (275 g) cooked, puréed pumpkin,
   or tinned pumpkin

8 fl. oz (225 ml) milk

2 eggs, size 2 or 3

Optional: whipped cream

This spicy pudding may be baked in a soufflé dish, in individual moulds – or as a soufflé pie.

Preheat oven to 350°F (180°C), Gas 4.
1. Mix the sugar, spices, and salt and blend with the pumpkin. Stir in the milk and mix well. Separate the eggs, beat the yolks well, and stir into the pumpkin mixture. Whisk the egg whites stiff and scrape the pumpkin mixture into the bowl on top of them, then gently cut and fold together.
2. Fill a 2 pt (1·125 litre) buttered soufflé dish two-thirds full, or use individual soufflé dishes. Set in a pan of hot water and bake for about forty minutes for the large soufflé, twenty-five to thirty minutes for the individual ones.

Pumpkin Soufflé Pie. Prepare a 9 in. (23 cm) unbaked pie-shell (see p. 177), pour in the filling. Preheat oven to 425°F (220°C), Gas 7, and bake for forty-five minutes. Cool, and top with whipped cream if you like. This pie will serve 6 generously.

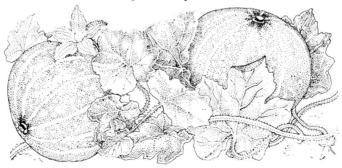

Cookies and Candies

Brown-edged Butter Cookies

Makes about 24

3 oz (75 g) plain flour

Good pinch of salt

4 oz (100 g) soft butter or margarine
plus 1 tbsp

2 oz (50 g) caster sugar

½ tsp vanilla essence, *or* 2 drops
almond essence

1 egg, size 3

One of the most popular packaged sweet biscuits in America is a delicate, thin, vanilla-scented cookie with lightly browned edges. This recipe comes close to it. The cookies keep well in an airtight tin, but they are fragile and crumbly.

Preheat oven to 350°F (180°C), Gas 4.
1. Sift the flour and salt together into a bowl and set aside. Cream the butter and sugar together until pale and fluffy, then stir in the vanilla. Whisk the egg lightly and gradually beat it into the butter and sugar mixture. Finally, sift in the flour mixture slowly, beating well as you do so.
2. Drop by teaspoonfuls on an ungreased baking sheet, spacing the cookies well apart, and bake for about ten minutes until the edges begin to brown. You may have to do this in two batches, or on two baking sheets: if the latter, after five minutes' baking time reverse the positions of the two sheets. While still warm, slide the cookies carefully on to a wire rack to cool.

Charleston Lemon and Oatmeal Bars

Makes about 20

6 oz (175 g) plain flour

1 tsp baking powder

½ tsp salt

15 oz (450 ml) tin of condensed milk

Grated rind of one lemon

4 fl. oz (100 ml) lemon juice

5 oz (125 g) butter or margarine

5 oz (125 g) light brown sugar

4 oz (100 g) porridge oats

A South Carolina recipe – crumbly, tart, sweet cookies. They won't travel so don't plan to take them on a picnic, but they are so good that they are usually finished off in one sitting anyway so the question rarely arises.

Preheat oven to 350°F (180°C), Gas 4.
1. Lightly butter a Swiss roll tin about 11 × 8 in. (28 × 20 cm). Sift the flour, baking powder, and salt. Mix the condensed milk and the lemon rind, and gradually stir in the lemon juice. Whisk lightly until the mixture thickens. Cream the butter until it is fluffy and whisk in the sugar. Gradually mix in the flour, baking powder, and salt, and blend until just mixed. Stir in the oatmeal to make a crumbly mixture.
2. Press half the oat mixture into the tin, cover with the lemon mixture, spreading it evenly with a palette knife. Cover with the remaining oat mixture. Bake for about thirty to thirty-five minutes. Let it cool in the pan, then chill for an hour.
3. Loosen the edges with a palette knife, and cut into twenty-four bars. Gently remove with the palette knife, and chill, covered.

Butterscotch Cookies

Makes about 36

5 oz (125 g) butter or margarine

5 oz (125 g) light brown sugar

1 oz (25 g) golden syrup

1 oz (25 g) black treacle

10 oz (275 g) plain flour

1 egg, size 3

1 tsp bicarbonate of soda

Good pinch of ground mace

These are said to keep well in an airtight tin, but my informant adds that they seldom have the chance. The original recipe calls for sorghum molasses, which is the light sweet syrup made from grain, not sugar cane; a mixture of half golden syrup and half black treacle gives almost the same result.

Preheat oven to 375°F (190°C), Gas 5.

1. Melt the butter over low heat in a heavy saucepan and stir in the sugar, golden syrup, and treacle. Cook on a low heat, stirring, until the sugar has dissolved, then increase the heat and bring to a rolling boil and remove at once from the cooker. Cool.

2. Stir half the flour into the sugar mixture. Beat the egg and stir it in too. Sift the remaining flour with bicarbonate and mace, and mix in, stirring, until it forms a soft dough. Drop it by spoonfuls, about 1 in. (2·5 cm) apart on an oiled baking sheet. Bake for about ten minutes until light brown. Cool on a wire rack. When they are cold, the cookies are crisp: to make them soft, store them with half an apple in an airtight tin.

Ginger Crisps

About 36 3 in. (8 cm) cookies

3 oz (75 g) butter or margarine

Scant 3 oz (75 g) light brown sugar

6 oz (175 g) mixture of golden syrup and black treacle

About 10 oz (275 g) plain flour

$\frac{3}{4}$ tbsp ground ginger

$\frac{1}{2}$ tsp bicarbonate of soda

1 egg, size 3, lightly beaten

Optional: grated rind of half an orange

The dough for this recipe feels and looks like brown mudpies, and it's tricky to roll out to an even, thin layer – but persist, and you will have wonderful, very crisp, spicy biscuits. They are unlike the typical American gingersnap which is chewy, with a crackled top. Stored in an airtight tin, they keep for at least a month.

1. In a good-sized saucepan, bring the butter, sugar, and black treacle mixture to the boil (it bubbles up fiercely, so needs plenty of room), lower the heat, and boil it about five minutes. Cool to lukewarm.

2. Sift the dry ingredients together, and stir them into the treacle and sugar mixture. Add the beaten egg and orange rind and stir well. The batter should be very thick and stiff – if not, add more flour. Let it cool completely. Preheat oven to 350°F (180°C), Gas 4.

3. On a heavily floured board, with a heavily floured pin, roll out the mixture as thinly as you can. Cut with a floured 2 in. (5 cm) plain cutter. Bake in batches on a lightly oiled 13 × 9 in. (33 × 23 cm) baking tin, about ten minutes. Cool on a wire rack.

Hermits

Makes about 30

4 oz (100 g) butter or margarine

9 oz (250 g) caster sugar

12 oz (350 g) flour

2 tsp mixed spice, *or* 1 tsp ground cinnamon mixed with ½ tsp each of ground clove and nutmeg

1 tsp salt

1 tsp bicarbonate of soda

2 eggs, size 3

8 fl. oz (225 ml) milk, soured with ½ tsp lemon juice

4 oz (100 g) mincemeat, *or* 2 oz (50 g) walnuts, chopped, and 2 oz (50 g) of sultanas either whole or chopped

Preheat oven to 325°F (165°C), Gas 3.

1. Cream the butter and sugar together. Sift the dry ingredients together. Whisk the eggs, and gradually beat them into the butter and sugar mixture. Add the dry ingredients by spoonfuls, alternately with spoonfuls of milk. Finally, stir in the mincemeat (or the nuts and sultanas). Do not overbeat.

2. Grease two baking sheets, and drop on the batter by spoonfuls – well spaced out – the Hermits spread a good deal. Bake about twenty minutes, until risen and brown. Unless you have a very large oven, you may have to do these in two batches, or reverse the position of the baking sheets in the oven halfway through the cooking time.

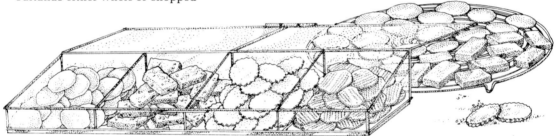

Hazelnut Kisses

Makes about 6 dozen

3 egg whites, size 3

Good pinch of salt

4 oz (100 g) caster sugar

4 oz (100 g) hazelnuts, toasted and ground

1 tsp grated lemon rind

¼ tsp ground cinnamon

To toast hazelnuts: spread them in a single layer in a shallow baking tin, or on a sheet of foil. Preheat the oven to 400°F (200°C), Gas 6, and brown, turning them every five minutes. Turn them out on kitchen paper to cool.

Preheat oven to 275°F (140°C), Gas 1½.

1. Have the egg whites at room temperature. Whisk them until they are foamy, add the salt, and whisk again until they begin to stand in soft peaks. Add the sugar by tablespoonfuls, whisking after each addition, and beat until the mixture is stiff and glossy.

2. Grind the hazelnuts finely in a blender or food processor. Mix them with the lemon rind and cinnamon and fold this mixture into the meringue lightly. Oil three baking sheets, about 13 × 9 in. (33 × 23 cm) and drop on the meringue by teaspoonfuls, spacing the 'kisses' as you would macaroons. Bake for twenty to twenty-five minutes, cool on a wire rack, and store in an airtight tin.

Mandelbrote

Serves about 6

4 oz (100 g) white cooking fat

6 oz (175 g) caster sugar

3 eggs, size 3

Juice and grated rind of half a lemon or orange

12 oz (350 g) plain flour

2 tsp baking powder

¾ tsp salt

2 oz (50 g) almonds (flaked or coarsely chopped)

This crisp, dry almond cake or cookie – it's hard to describe – is a traditional Jewish dish with an Austrian background, and is often served with tea. It keeps very well in an airtight tin.

Preheat oven to 350°F (180°C), Gas 4.
1. Cream the white fat and the sugar together, beat in the eggs, then add the grated rind and juice of the orange or lemon. Sift the flour with the baking powder and salt and gradually beat it into the first mixture, adding the almonds at the same time. Spread in a buttered shallow tin – an 8 in. (20 cm) sandwich tin for example – and bake for forty-five minutes to an hour until the cake is firm.
2. Cool, and cut it in ¾ in. (2 cm) thick slices. Lay them on a very lightly buttered baking sheet and bake for ten minutes on one side, turn the slices over, and bake for another five minutes.

Lebkuchen

Makes about 48

8 oz (225 g) runny honey

5 oz (125 g) light brown sugar

2 tbsp water

1 oz (25 g) butter or margarine

14 oz (400 g) plain flour

½ tsp bicarbonate of soda

½ tsp salt

¼ tsp powdered cloves

¼ tsp ground ginger

½ tsp ground cinnamon

4 oz (100 g) cut mixed peel

4 oz (100 g) flaked almonds

For the glaze

4 oz (100 g) icing sugar

3 tbsp boiling water

One of the festive glazed cookies which owes its existence to the medieval honey cakes made by the Bakers' Guilds in Central European cities: and a tradition among German-American families at Christmas. Lebkuchen can be formed into any fancy shape you like, cut into strips, or even dropped by spoonfuls on a baking sheet. It is a sweet, spicy cookie not unlike a thin gingerbread, and it improves with storage from two to six weeks in an airtight tin.

1. Heat the honey, sugar, water, and butter slowly until it comes to the boil, remove the pan from the heat and let it cool to lukewarm. Sift the flour with the bicarbonate, salt, and spices. Stir into the honey mixture until completely blended. Add the peel and almonds.
2. If you have the time, store the dough wrapped in plastic film for two or three days. Otherwise, roll it about ¼ in. (0·75 cm) thick, on a lightly floured board and cut with an ornate cutter, or cut into 3 × 1 in. (8 × 2·5 cm) strips. Put them on oiled baking sheets.
3. Preheat the oven to 300°F (150°C), Gas 2. Bake the cookies for about ten to fifteen minutes – you may need to do this in batches, depending on the capacity of your oven. They should be delicately browned and firm but not hard. Slide them off on a rack while they are warm.
4. Mix the icing sugar and boiling water and brush it over the cookies. Store between sheets of greaseproof paper in an air-tight container.

Granola Bars

Makes about 15

10 oz (275 g) porridge oats, toasted

6 oz (175 g) sultanas or raisins

4 oz (100 g) walnuts, chopped

3 oz (75 g) soft, light brown sugar

2 oz (50 g) honey *or* golden syrup

1 egg, size 3

½ tsp vanilla essence

½ level tsp salt

This is a high-protein, vitamin and mineral-rich 'candy bar', with a hearty texture. I am indebted to The Quaker Oats Company, USA, for the recipe.

Preheat oven to 350°F (180°C), Gas 4.

1. To toast the oats: spread them evenly on ungreased baking sheets, and bake for twenty to twenty-five minutes until a uniform light golden brown. (They may now be cooled, and stored, tightly lidded, in the refrigerator for as long as six months. They have many uses – for breading chicken, for adding to meat loaf, or in place of nuts or coconut in drop cookies. Their nut-like flavour is the secret of Granola Bars.)

2. Mix all the ingredients together, and press down firmly into a greased 15 × 12 in. (38·5 × 30 cm) Swiss roll tin. Bake at the above temperature for about twenty minutes. Cool in the tin, then cut into bars. They keep well in an airtight tin.

Jumbles

Makes about 36

6 oz (150 g) sifted self-raising flour

¼ tsp bicarbonate of soda

½ tsp salt

8 oz (225 g) soft margarine or white fat

3 oz (75 g) caster or soft, light brown sugar

1 egg, size 3

1 tsp vanilla essence

Preheat oven to 375°F (190°C), Gas 5.

1. Sift the dry ingredients. Mix the margarine or fat, sugar, egg, and vanilla very well, then stir in the dry ingredients. Lightly grease two baking sheets, and drop on the batter by rounded teaspoonfuls, about 2 in. (5 cm) apart. Bake for about eight to ten minutes until golden brown. The Jumbles will be soft.

2. Cool slightly on the baking sheets, then cool the Jumbles on a wire rack. Store in an airtight tin.

Molasses Cookies (Joe Froggers)

Makes 12 big cookies

4 oz (100 g) margarine

6 oz (175 g) caster or light brown sugar

½ tsp salt

3 fl. oz (75 ml) water

1 fl. oz (25 ml) light rum

1 tsp bicarbonate of soda

7 oz (200 g) black treacle

14 oz (400 g) plain flour

Joe Froggers are beloved New England cookies – large, chewy, and eaten warm with a steaming mug of coffee. The dough should be made the day before you plan to bake them, and chilled overnight – then it takes only about ten minutes to bake.

1. Cream the margarine and sugar, and mix in the salt. Blend the water and rum, dissolve the bicarbonate in the black treacle, and mix the two. Sift the dry ingredients together twice.

Opposite *Three typical American desserts. Top Strawberry Shortcake; Right Indian pudding; Left Boston Cream Pie*

$\frac{1}{2}$ tsp powdered ginger

$\frac{1}{2}$ tsp ground cloves

$\frac{1}{2}$ tsp grated nutmeg

Good pinch ground allspice

2. Add the liquid mixture alternately with the dry mixture to the creamed butter and sugar, beating well between each addition. The dough will be very sticky and you will need either a good, stout electric mixer, or a big wooden spoon. Chill the dough overnight, or put it in the deep freeze for fifteen minutes.

3. Preheat the oven to 375°F (190°C), Gas 5. Roll the dough out on a well-floured board to about $\frac{1}{2}$ in. (1·5 cm) thickness. Cut them out with a 5 in. (13 cm) cutter, or use a plate as a pattern, and cut neatly round it with a very sharp knife. Bake them on an ungreased baking sheet about ten to twelve minutes.

Peanut Butter Cookies

Makes about 48 1 in. (2·5 cm) cookies

4 oz (100 g) butter or good margarine

4 oz (100 g) peanut butter

6 oz (175 g) light brown sugar

1 egg, size 3

$\frac{1}{4}$ tsp salt

8 oz (225 g) 81% – 85% light brown flour

Optional: 2 oz (50 g) unsalted peanuts, chopped

Preheat oven to 375°F (190°C), Gas 5.

1. Cream the butter or margarine and the peanut butter together, then mix well with the brown sugar. Slowly add the egg. Sift the salt and flour, and stir it in to make a very stiff dough. You may need a little more or less of the flour, depending on what brand you use, so stir in about 7 oz (200 g) at first, then add more as necessary. Add the peanuts if you like them.

2. Pinch off pieces of dough and roll each into a ball, then flatten them out on a floured surface into 1 in. (2·5 cm) circles. Press them down with the floured base of a tumbler. For a professional finish, mark out a criss-cross pattern on the top with the tines of a table fork. Lightly grease two baking sheets, space out half the cookies at least an inch (2·5 cm) apart, and bake them for about ten to twelve minutes. Slide them off the baking sheets while they are warm, and bake the next two batches. Cool them on wire racks before storing in an airtight tin.

The dough can be frozen: roll it into 'logs' about 1 in. (2·5 cm) in diameter, wrap securely in heavy freezer film or foil. To bake without thawing: with a very sharp knife dipped in flour, cut off thin rounds of frozen dough, and bake at the above temperature on oiled baking sheets for about fifteen to eighteen minutes. I have to confess that I always have a problem about cutting really thin rounds of cookie dough that is frozen; I seem to have the wrong knife or the wrong technique. I resort to cutting the dough into cookies first, open-freezing them on baking trays, then slip off the frozen discs into a big plastic bag. Press the sides of the bag together so there is not much air inside, secure the top tightly, and with luck you will be able to decant whatever number of cookies you want to bake.

Opposite *Mouthwatering cookies and candies*. Clockwise from top left *Charleston Lemon Bars, Oatmeal Cookies, Benné Brittle, Penuche, Hermits*

Toll House Cookies

5 oz (125 g) plain flour

½ tsp baking powder

Pinch of salt

3 oz (75 g) butter or margarine

3 oz (75 g) caster sugar

3 oz (75 g) light brown sugar

1 egg, size 3 or 4

1½ tbsp milk

6 oz (175 g) chocolate bits

Some vegetable oil in a small cup

Optional: 2 oz (50 g) walnuts or
    almonds, chopped

This recipe came into my hands, like hundreds of others, by a piece of shameless cadging from one friend who seemed to know how to make authentic chocolate-chip cookies. They are very like the ones invented by a restaurant called The Toll House, in Massachusetts, many years ago. A cookie manufacturer bought the 'secret' recipe from the restaurant and now produces a very excellent commercial version. As far as I know, no comparable ones are sold in the United Kingdom. It uses the pricey but convenient chocolate bits sold in small packets. If you can't buy them, get a block of good plain dark chocolate (not milk chocolate), and with a sharp knife cut it up into small bits – don't shave it or grate it, as the texture of the finished Toll House Cookie depends on the little surprise of lumps of chocolate distributed through the dough.

Preheat oven to 375°F (190°C), Gas 5.

1. Sift the flour, baking powder, and salt together. Cream the butter until it is pale and fluffy, then cream it again with the sugars. Whisk the egg and milk together, and beat it slowly into the butter-sugar mixture. Stir in the sifted dry ingredients, then stir in the chocolate bits (and the nuts if you are using them).

2. Lightly oil two baking sheets. Dip two teaspoons in the cup of oil, scoop up a teaspoonful of cookie batter with one, and with the back of the second spoon slide the dough off on to the baking sheet. Take care to space the cookies at least 1 in. (2·5 cm) apart. Bake for eight to twelve minutes. If you can fit both baking sheets into your oven, move the top one down and the bottom one up halfway through the baking. Take the cookies off the baking sheets at once and cool on a wire rack. When completely cool, store in an airtight tin, or freezer.

Raisin Bars

Makes about 20 4 × 1 in. (10 × 2·5 cm) bars

6 oz (175 g) raisins or sultanas

6 oz (175 g) self-raising flour

2 tsp baking powder

½ tsp salt

2 eggs, size 3

6 oz (175 g) light brown or caster sugar

1 tbsp hot water

1 tsp vanilla essence

2 oz (50 g) walnuts, chopped

Preheat oven to 375°F (190°C), Gas 5.

1. Cover the raisins or sultanas with boiling water and let them stand ten minutes, then drain. Sift the dry ingredients together. Whisk the eggs, then gradually whisk in the sugar, and blend well. Stir in the hot water and vanilla and mix well. Beat in the dry ingredients and stir in the raisins and nuts.

2. Line a Swiss roll tin, about 11 × 8 in. (28 × 20 cm), or an oblong cake tin about 10 × 6 in. (25 × 15 cm), with greased greaseproof paper, and pour in the mixture. Bake it for half an hour until brown and firm. Cut into bars before removing from the tin, and carefully take out with a palette knife.

Oatmeal Raisin Cookies

Makes about 54 2 in. (5 cm) cookies

6 oz (175 g) butter or margarine

9 oz (250 g) light brown sugar

1 egg, size 3

2 fl. oz (50 ml) milk

4 oz (100 g) plain flour (white or light brown)

½ tsp salt

¼ tsp bicarbonate of soda

8 oz (225 g) porridge oats

4–6 oz (100–150 g) raisins or sultanas

Preheat oven to 375°F (190°C), Gas 5.

1. Beat the butter, sugar, egg, and milk together. Sift the flour with the salt and bicarbonate, and stir into the butter mixture. Add the oats and raisins, the amount according to your taste.

2. Butter two baking sheets rather thickly, and drop on the batter by heaped teaspoonfuls spaced at least 1 in. (2·5 cm) apart. Bake for ten to twelve minutes, until golden brown. Remove at once with a palette knife, and cool on a rack. Store in an airtight tin, or freeze.

Oatmeal, Nut and Date Cookies. Replace the raisins or sultanas with 2 oz (50 g) chopped walnuts and 2 oz (50 g) chopped dates.

Quick Oatmeal Cookies

Makes about 36 2 in. (5 cm) cookies

4 oz (100 g) butter or margarine

3 oz (75 g) light brown sugar

3 oz (75 g) caster sugar

1 egg, size 3

1 tbsp milk

½ tsp vanilla essence

4 oz (100 g) plain flour

½ tsp bicarbonate of soda

½ tsp baking powder

½ tsp salt

Good pinch of cinnamon

4 oz (100 g) porridge oats

Preheat oven to 350°F (180°C), Gas 4.

1. Cream the butter and both the sugars together. Whisk the egg, milk, and vanilla together and beat into the butter mixture. Sift the flour, bicarbonate, baking powder, salt, and cinnamon and stir into the first mixture. Beat until smooth. Then add the porridge oats and beat well again.

2. Grease two baking sheets and drop by spoonfuls about 2 in. (5 cm) apart, and bake until light brown (about ten minutes). Slide them off the baking sheets and cool on a rack.

Sugar Cookies

Makes about 50–60 small cookies

8 oz (225 g) sifted self-raising flour

1½ tsp baking powder

½ tsp salt

1 egg, size 3

4 oz (100 g) butter or margarine

6 oz (175 g) caster sugar

1 tsp vanilla essence

1 tbsp milk or single cream

1. Sift the dry ingredients. Beat the egg well. Cream the butter and sugar together, add the egg, vanilla essence, and milk and mix. Gradually add the dry ingredients. The dough should be quite stiff but cohesive; if it feels crumbly stir in a spot more milk. Chill for one hour.

2. Preheat the oven to 375°F (190°C), Gas 5. Roll the dough out on a floured board very thinly – about ⅛ in. (0·4 cm) thick, and cut with plain, fluted, or fancy small cutters. Place on ungreased baking sheets and bake for eight to ten minutes.

American Candies

Making candies at home was one of the joys of an American childhood in more leisurely times. On a rainy day, if the television breaks down, why not try this recipe or some of the others following?

Chocolate Fudge

Makes about 12 oz (350 g)

8 oz (225 g) caster sugar

2½ tbsp butter or margarine

3 tbsp milk

2 oz (50 g) plain dark chocolate

1. Grease a shallow tin about 7 in. (18 cm) square. Place all the ingredients in a heavy saucepan or in the top of a double boiler over very hot water. Stir and cook the mixture until the sugar and chocolate dissolve. Remove the top portion of the double boiler from its base and cook over a moderate heat until the mixture boils: continue to cook until it reaches 240°F (115°C) on a sugar thermometer, or until a few drops in a cup of very cold water form a soft ball. Take the pan off the heat at once.

2. Set the pan into a basin of cold water for a few minutes, or let it stand in a cool place. Then beat vigorously with a wooden spoon or electric mixer until it is thick, rather stiff, and beginning to lose its glossy look. Pour into the oiled tin and mark into squares with a sharp knife. Cool completely before cutting the squares.

Benné Brittle

Makes about 18 oz (500 g)

9 oz (250 g) caster sugar

2 tbsp water

3 oz (75 g) clear honey

1 tsp lemon juice

5 oz (125 g) sesame seeds (Benné seeds)

This is a sesame seed candy which comes from South Carolina.

1. Cook the sugar, water, honey, and lemon juice in a heavy saucepan over a low heat until dissolved. Cook without stirring until it will form a hard brittle thread when a few drops are put into a cup of very cold water. Remove from the heat and stir in the sesame seeds.

2. Pour a thin layer on an oiled baking sheet or pastry slab. Score it into squares before it hardens. With a palette knife, loosen it from the baking sheet while it is still slightly warm and, when cool, break it along the scored lines.

Butterscotch

Makes about 14 oz (400 g)

10 tbsp water

8 oz (225 g) soft brown sugar

2 tsp cider vinegar

Scant 5 oz (125 g) butter or margarine

1. Butter a shallow baking tin about 7 in. (18 cm) square. Mix the water, sugar, vinegar, and butter in a heavy saucepan and boil without stirring to 290°F (145°C), or until a few drops in a cup of very cold water make a brittle ball.

2. Add the vanilla and pour into the tin, and cool slightly. Mark into squares and break apart when cool.

Candied Grapefruit Peel

An all-American favourite, and a delightful winter gift. It is easy to make this tart-sweet confection out of the rinds of your breakfast grapefruit (or orange).

Cut away every bit of the bitter white pith from the peel, and cut it into thin strips about 3 in. (8 cm) long. In a saucepan, cover the peel with cold water, bring it to the boil, and simmer for five minutes. Drain well, and repeat this blanching operation twice more. Weigh the drained peel and measure out an equal weight of caster sugar. Put the peel and sugar in a saucepan, add 3 fl. oz (75 ml) of water for every 6 oz (175 g) of sugar. Bring to the boil, lower the heat, and simmer until the peel is glazed and rather translucent (about twenty minutes). Drain and roll in caster sugar. Store in an airtight tin.

Candied Orange Peel. As above, but blanch by simmering for twenty to thirty minutes without changing the water. Then drain, weigh, and proceed with the candying process.

Chocolate Candied Orange Peel. Melt plain dark dessert chocolate over hot water, dip in one end of each strip of candied peel, cool on greaseproof paper.

Molasses Candy

Makes 1¾ lb (775 g)

4 oz (100 g) golden syrup

4 oz (100 g) black treacle

3 oz (75 g) margarine

8 oz (225 g) caster sugar

8 fl. oz (225 ml) boiling water

This is a New England recipe whose history goes back to the sugar cane brought by Christopher Columbus to the West Indies. Molasses was called the lifeblood of American colonial trade. American molasses is lighter in colour, sweeter in taste, and not so thick as English treacle; in most recipes, a combination of half golden syrup and half treacle serves best.

1. Mix the golden syrup and treacle. Melt the margarine in a heavy saucepan and add the syrup mixture, sugar, and water. Stir until it comes to the boil, then cook without stirring to 236°F (118°C) on a sugar thermometer, or until a few drops form a soft ball when dropped into very cold water.
2. Turn it out on an oiled marble slab, or an oiled, cold baking sheet. When it is cool enough to handle, but still malleable, pull it with the tips of buttered fingers and thumbs until it is light-coloured and becoming too hard to pull. Cut into small pieces with oiled knife or scissors. Wrap in greaseproof paper.

Penuche

14 oz (400 g) dark brown sugar (try to get cane sugar, not beet sugar)

8 fl. oz (225 ml) evaporated milk, undiluted

Good pinch of salt

1–1½ oz (25–35 g) butter or margarine

4 oz (100 g) walnuts, coarsely chopped

1 tsp real vanilla essence

The name of this traditional American sweet comes from a word of Mexican-Spanish, panocha, which means something like raw sugar. It is a rich, intensely sweet, and utterly seductive candy – something like a walnut-studded butterscotch but of a different texture that almost melts in the mouth. Penuche is always slightly sticky to the touch, no matter how firm it looks, so don't offer it to anyone too well-brought-up to lick his or her fingertips. The name, by the way, is pronounced 'pehnoocheh' in the Southwest – although I have heard it rather affectedly said 'Pay -nyuchay' in a very proper Philadelphia house. Penuche is often made like fudge, cut into squares in its tin, and offered round on a plate. I think it's easier to make, and nicer to eat, when it is dropped by spoonfuls on a piece of greaseproof paper, then removed to a pretty dish when it is firm – or dropped into little fluted paper cases. Made this way, it can take the place of a sweet course for a family dinner, and the paper cases might even be the way to get around the sticky-fingers problem.

1. In a heavy saucepan cook the sugar, milk, salt, and butter to 240°F (118°C) on a sugar thermometer, or until a little bit dropped in very cold water forms a soft ball. Cool the mixture to lukewarm, beating with a spoon from time to time. Stir in the walnuts and vanilla, and beat again until it is smooth and has a creamy, not grainy, texture.

2. Drop by spoonfuls, well spaced, on a lightly oiled baking sheet or sheet of greaseproof paper, and chill until firm. Store, if necessary, lightly covered in a cool place, not in an airtight tin, as a very sugary sweet like this attracts moisture in a closed container. It doesn't affect the flavour, but the glossy surface goes dull and lifeless.

Cakes

Stollen

8 oz (225 g) plain flour
1 tsp salt
3 fl. oz (75 ml) milk
2 tsp dried yeast
2 oz (50 g) butter or good margarine, at room temperature
1 egg, size 2
2 oz (50 g) caster sugar
1 oz (25 g) flaked almonds
1 oz (25 g) sultanas
1 oz (25 g) raisins
1 oz (25 g) cut mixed peel
Grated rind of half a large lemon
1 tbsp butter or good margarine, softened

A traditional German-American sweet coffee cake bursting with sultanas, nuts, and raisins, Stollen is served at breakfast with the accompaniment of unsalted, very cold butter. It goes equally well with small cups of strong black coffee, but the rich fruity flavour is really too strong to make it suitable for tea. It's very much a holiday treat, for such feasts as a late Christmas morning breakfast after the presents have been opened.

1. Sift the flour and salt together. Warm the milk to blood heat, stir in the dried yeast and the butter, and stir until the yeast and butter dissolve. Whisk the egg and beat it into the yeast mixture. Stir in the sugar and whisk everything together until the sugar dissolves. Tip this into a large bowl and stir in the flour – plunge in your hands and work it all together very well. Turn the dough out on a well-floured board, and have some extra flour at hand to knead in if the dough seems sticky. Knead until it feels springy and satiny.
2. Grease a large bowl and turn the dough ball over once or twice until it glistens. Cover with a cloth wrung out of hot water, then wrap the bowl with a heavy towel and let the dough rise until it is double in bulk.
3. Punch down the dough, cover the bowl with plastic film, and let it rise about forty-five minutes. Mix in the almonds, sultanas, raisins, peel, and the lemon rind. Turn the dough out on a well-floured board and shape it into a long, flat oval. Spread the surface with half the softened butter, then fold it in half the long way, pressing it together firmly. Brush the top of the loaf with the rest of the butter and loosely cover with plastic film. Let it rise on a lightly greased baking sheet for about half an hour. Preheat the oven to 400°F (200°C), Gas 6.
4. Bake about forty minutes until it is golden-brown and firm. It may be glazed with a Confectioners' Sugar Glacé (see p. 238), or dusted with icing sugar while it is warm. Serve Stollen warm, not hot. Store it in a ventilated tin or bread bin. Reheat it for serving in a warm oven – about 325°F (165°C), Gas 3 – not in a hot one, which might burn the nuts and sultanas in the loaf.

American Brownies

At the latest count, there are eighteen brownie recipes in my own collection – and I am sure that it is only a fraction of the number of recipes extant across the United States. The source of each of my recipes swears by all that is sacred that his or hers is the one and only, the true, the essential brownie recipe. Here are my two favourites made with chocolate – one the classic fudge type, the other more like a marble cake – plus a recipe for butterscotch, or 'blonde', brownies.

FUDGE BROWNIES

Makes about 12 large or 36 small brownies

7 oz (200 g) margarine

6 very heaped tbsp cocoa powder

4 eggs, size 3

½ tsp salt

14 oz (400 g) caster or light brown sugar

1 tsp vanilla essence

4 oz (100 g) plain flour

4 oz (100 g) walnuts, coarsely chopped

Preheat oven to 350°F (180°C), Gas 4.

1. In the top of a double boiler, over simmering water, melt the margarine with the cocoa. Stir well, remove, and cool the mixture to lukewarm. Whisk the eggs and salt until they are foamy, and gradually beat in the sugar and vanilla until it makes a creamy batter.

2. Sift the flour. Stir the chocolate mixture into the batter very gently, and while it still looks rather 'marbleised', gradually fold in – do not mix – the flour. While some patches of flour are still to be seen, stir in the nuts. The reason for all this caution in setting down the directions is that brownie batter must not be overbeaten, or it loses its fudge-like texture.

3. Grease a tin about 9 × 13 in. (23 × 32 cm), for thin brownies. For thicker ones, use an 8 in. (20 cm) square tin. Line the base with greased greaseproof paper. Bake for about twenty-five minutes, and remove the brownies from the tin while they are still hot. Peel off the paper and cool them on a rack. Cut them into large or small squares.

CAKE BROWNIES

Makes 12 large or 36 small brownies

4 oz (100 g) margarine

1 tsp vanilla essence

7 oz (200 g) caster sugar

2 eggs, size 3

4 oz (100 g) flour

½ tsp salt

4 oz (100 g) walnuts, coarsely chopped

2 oz (50 g) plain dark chocolate

Preheat oven to 350°F (180°C), Gas 4.

1. Cream the margarine until it is light and fluffy, whisk in the sugar and vanilla. Beat the eggs lightly, then gradually beat them into the first mixture. Sift the flour and salt together, and gently fold in. Stir in the walnuts and divide the batter in two parts.

2. Melt the chocolate over simmering water and stir it into half the batter. Grease and flour a 9 in. (23 cm) square cake tin. Drop the batter by alternate spoonfuls into the tin, and run a knife-blade lightly through it to make a swirling marble pattern.

3. Bake for forty-five minutes, let the brownie cake cool in the tin for five minutes, then turn it out on a rack to cool. Cut it into squares.

BUTTERSCOTCH BROWNIES

Makes about 24 small bars

4 oz (100 g) butter or good margarine

1 tsp vanilla essence

1 tsp black treacle, mixed with 1 tsp golden syrup

7 oz (200 g) light brown sugar

2 eggs, size 3

4 oz (100 g) cake flour

2–3 oz (50–75 g) walnuts, coarsely chopped

Preheat oven to 350°F (180°C), Gas 4.

1. Cream the butter well, and beat in the vanilla essence, black treacle, and golden syrup. Add the sugar and beat well. Beat in the eggs one at a time, until the mixture is smooth.

2. Add the flour gradually, and mix until well blended but do not overbeat. Stir in the nuts. Butter and flour a 9 in. (23 cm) square baking tin. Pour in the batter and smooth the top with a palette knife. Bake it for thirty to thirty-five minutes, until a thin skewer pressed into the centre of the cake comes out clean.

3. Let the brownie cake cool in the tin, then loosen it gently with a palette knife. Cut in quarters and remove to a plate. Cut each quarter in half, then cut each of these halves into thirds to make bars.

They freeze beautifully, and keep well in an airtight tin. Wrapped individually in plastic film, these butterscotch brownie bars are much more delicious than commercial chocolate or toffee bars on a long motor trip.

American Pound Cake

Makes two loaf cakes, to serve about 8–10

1 lb (450 g) butter or good margarine, at room temperature

12 oz (350 g) caster sugar

10 eggs, size 3, at room temperature, separated

½ tsp salt

1 lb (450 g) plain flour (or 12 oz/350 g plain flour, sifted with 4 oz/100 g cornflour)

1 tsp vanilla essence

As the name would indicate, this traditional American cake is based on a formula of one pound of sugar, one pound of butter, one pound of eggs (shelled weight), a pound of flour, and flavouring. It has no chemical leavening such as baking powder or bicarbonate of soda, and no added liquid. It is a dense-textured, rich cake. This recipe departs slightly from the 'poundage' formula, because of the differences between American and English sugars and flours. Pound cake stores well, in an airtight tin; and my cake-making friends tell me it freezes well for as long as three months.

Preheat oven to 350°F (180°C), Gas 4.

1. Cream the butter until it is pale and fluffy, in a big bowl, and gradually beat in the sugar until the mixture is light-coloured. You will probably need an electric mixer for this operation, as it is a heavy mixture no matter how much the butter and sugar are creamed. In another large bowl, whisk the egg whites with the salt until they stand in stiff, glossy peaks.

2. In a smaller bowl beat the egg yolks, and gradually beat them into the sugar and butter mixture. Sift the flour onto this batter, a few tablespoonfuls at a time, mixing just

enough to blend the flour in but do not overbeat. Scoop two or three heaped tablespoons of the egg whites into the batter and mix for about thirty seconds, with your electric whisk, so as to 'slacken' the mixture.

3. Scoop the batter on top of the egg whites and gently cut and fold the two mixtures together. Grease and flour two loaf tins (about 9 × 5 × 3 in. or 23 × 13 × 8 cm), and line the bases with greased greaseproof paper. Divide the batter between the tins, and bake in the centre of the oven for about one and a quarter hours. Test the centre of the cake with a thin skewer after about an hour, if it comes out covered with batter bake the cake for another fifteen to thirty minutes. The centre of each loaf will rise and crack open attractively.

4. Let the cakes cool in their tins for five minutes, then turn out on a rack. Traditional pound cakes are never frosted, but may be dusted with icing sugar if you like – although this is adding sweetness to sweetness.

Apple Sauce Cake

Serves 4–6

8 oz (225 g) plain flour

1 tsp baking powder

1 tsp salt

1 tsp mixed spice (or $\frac{1}{4}$ tsp freshly grated nutmeg, $\frac{1}{4}$ tsp cinnamon, $\frac{1}{4}$ tsp powdered cloves)

3 oz (75 g) butter or good margarine, at room temperature

10 oz (275 g) caster sugar

1 egg, size 2, or 2 eggs, size 3 or 4

6 oz (175 g) cooked apple purée

4 oz (100 g) sultanas or raisins

Icing sugar

Apple purée gives this cake a delicious, moist crumbly texture, enriched with sultanas, and fragrant with spices. It is a very good keeping cake, lightly wrapped in plastic film, and does not need to be stored airtight. The more flavourful your apples, the better the taste – try a spoonful of the apple purée, and if it's bland, give it a teaspoon of lemon juice for sharpness. The purée must be dryish, not watery, which would spoil the finished cake.

Preheat oven to 350°F (180°C), Gas 4.

1. Sift together the flour, baking powder, salt and spices. Cream the butter and sugar together until pale and fluffy. Whisk the egg or eggs lightly, and gradually beat into the sugar mixture. Stir in the apple purée and mix well but do not overbeat.

2. Toss the sultanas in the flour mixture until they are well coated, so that they will not sink to the bottom of the cake. Lightly fold the flour and sultanas into the batter. Grease and flour an 8 in. (20 cm) round cake tin and fill it with the cake batter.

3. Bake for about forty-five minutes, until the top feels firm and springy when you press it with a fingertip. Let the cake cool in its tin for five minutes, then turn out on a rack and dust with icing sugar.

Chocolate Torte

Serves 6

2 oz (50 g) plain chocolate

2 tbsp water

2 oz (50 g) unsalted butter

1½ tbsp caster sugar

2 eggs, size 3, separated

1 oz (25 g) ground almonds

1 tsp rum or brandy

2 tbsp plain flour

Sour cherry jam (see Appendix)

Chocolate frosting (see p. 240)

Preheat oven to 350°F (180°C), Gas 4.

1. Melt the chocolate in the water in a small saucepan set on a very low heat. Stir it well, and add the butter. Remove the pan from the heat and stir until the butter is melted and blended with the chocolate. Stir in the sugar and let the mixture cool. Whisk the egg yolks, one at a time, into the chocolate mixture. Stir in the almonds, rum, and flour and mix well.

2. Whisk the egg whites to stiff peaks in a good-sized bowl, scrape the chocolate mixture in on top of them, and gently cut and fold it all together. Grease and flour two 6 in (15 cm) sandwich tins – or small flan tins with removable bases – and spoon the batter in, smoothing out the top with a palette knife.

3. Bake for about twenty-five minutes, until a thin skewer inserted in the centre of the *torte* comes out clean. Remove the *tortes* to cake rack to cool. Spread as much or as little cherry jam as you like on one of the layers, add the second layer, and spread the jam very thinly across the top. Frost the top and sides completely with Chocolate Frosting.

Coffee Cakes and Rings

This is rather a catch-all category: a great variety of sweet breads, to be served with morning coffee or as a snack. Some are quickly made, raised with baking powder. Others are rich, sweet yeast breads. They may be simply finished with a crumb topping or nut mixture, or more elaborately shaped into rings, braids (plaits), twists, or horseshoes. For best flavour, coffee cakes should be served warm. They freeze well, and can be reheated in a moderate oven, about 325°F (165°C), Gas 3.

QUICK COFFEE CAKE

Serves 4

6 oz (175 g) plain flour

2 tsp baking powder

2 oz (50 g) margarine

6 oz (175 g) caster sugar

1 egg, size 2 or 3

4 fl. oz (100 ml) milk

Pinch of salt

Preheat oven to 375°F (190°C), Gas 5.

1. Butter and flour an 8 in. (20 cm) square tin. Sift the flour and baking powder together, rub in the fat, and stir in the sugar. Whisk the egg and milk together, then beat it into the first mixture and beat well for three or four minutes.

2. Scrape the batter into the prepared tin and cover it with one of the toppings. Bake about thirty minutes. Cut into squares in the tin, and serve warm.

Streusel topping

1oz (25 g) walnuts or hazelnuts,
  chopped

2 oz (50 g) plain flour

3 oz (75 g) light brown sugar

2 oz (50 g) cold butter or margarine

Sugar and spice topping

2 tsp mixed spice

2 oz (50 g) light brown sugar

1 tbsp plain flour

2 oz (50 g) cold butter or margarine

For the streusel topping, mix the nuts with the flour and sugar, then cut in the butter until the mixture feels like coarse crumbs.

For the sugar and spice topping, mix the spice, sugar, and flour, and cut in the butter to make coarse crumbs.

GERMAN CRUMB COFFEE CAKE
Serves 4–6

10 fl. oz (275 ml) scalded milk

2 tsp dried yeast

3 oz (75 g) butter or margarine

1½ tbsp caster sugar

½ tsp salt

1 egg, size 2

15 oz (425 g) plain flour

3 oz (75 g) sultanas or raisins, coarsely
  chopped

1. Measure out 2 fl. oz (50 ml) of the milk and cool it to lukewarm. Whisk the yeast into the milk and let it stand in a warm place until it froths up. Stir the butter, sugar, and salt into the remaining hot milk until the butter melts. Mix in the egg, flour, and sultanas and beat until it is a smooth batter. Add the yeast mixture, and beat again.
2. Grease a bowl and scoop the dough into it. Cover with plastic film and let it stand in a warm place for about half an hour. Preheat the oven to 375°F (190°C), Gas 5.
3. Butter a 9 in. (23 cm) square cake tin and pour in the batter. Make the crumb topping (below) and spread it evenly over the batter. Bake about thirty-five to forty-five minutes until the topping is brown and bubbling, and a thin skewer put into the centre of the cake comes out clean. Cut in squares and serve warm.

Crumb Topping

3 tbsp plain flour

2 tbsp light brown or caster sugar

3 tbsp butter or margarine

For the topping, stir together the flour and sugar, and cut in the butter until it feels like coarse crumbs. (This topping can be frozen, in a plastic container, for about three months.)

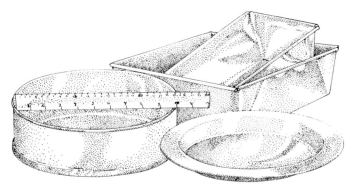

SWEDISH TEA RING

2 tsp dried yeast

2 fl. oz (50 ml) warm water

2 fl. oz (50 ml) warm milk

Generous 1 oz (25–35 g) caster sugar

½ tsp salt

1 egg, size 3

2 oz (50 g) butter or margarine

9–11 oz (250–300 g) plain flour (or 81%–85% light brown flour)

Filling

1 oz (25 g) butter or margarine, softened

3 oz (75 g) light brown sugar

1 tsp mixed spice, or cinnamon

2–3 oz (50–75 g) sultanas or raisins

Generous 2 oz (50–60 g) walnuts, coarsely chopped

Confectioners' Glaze

2 oz (50 g) icing sugar

1 tbsp milk

Although this is called a Tea Ring, it's usually served with mid-morning coffee, or as a Sunday or holiday breakfast 'bread' instead of toast. This amount of dough makes one very large ring, or two smaller ones. Unless you have a large baking sheet, or a big Swiss roll tin, the two smaller rings may be easier to handle. The dough is rich, sweet, and rather soft, and when it is rising it spreads and puffs alarmingly!

1. Whisk the yeast into the warm water in a cup. Pour it into a large bowl, add the milk, sugar, salt, egg, 2 oz (50 g) butter, and about half the flour. Beat until it forms a soft batter. Mix in enough of the remaining flour to make a soft but not sticky dough which can be easily handled.

2. Turn the dough out on a well-floured board, and have a bowl with a few tablespoons of extra flour standing near. Knead the dough until it is smooth, satiny, and elastic. Shape it into a ball, put it in a large well-greased bowl, turn it over once or twice and cover with plastic film. Let it rise in a warm place until the dough doubles in bulk. Punch it down and turn it out on a well-floured board. At this point, you may find that it feels sticky and clingy, so work in still more flour until the dough again has a satiny, elastic feeling. With a floured pin, roll it out into a rectangle about 15 × 9 in. (38 × 23 cm). Neaten the edges with your fingers. Turn the dough so that the wide side faces you.

3. For the filling, spread the dough evenly with the softened, but not melted, butter. Sprinkle on the brown sugar, the cinnamon, the raisins or sultanas, and the nuts, evening out the surface with a palette knife. Roll it up as tightly as you can, from the wide side. Pinch the edges together well. Put it sealed side down on a very lightly greased baking sheet, and join the ends to make a ring. (Here you may want to divide the roll in two, and make two rings.) With a sharp knife, dipped in flour, make even cuts all around the ring, about 1 in. (2·5 cm) apart, on the top surface.

4. Lightly cover with plastic film and let it rise in a warm, but not hot, place until the ring has doubled in bulk. Preheat the oven to 375°F (190°C), Gas 5. Bake for about twenty-five to thirty minutes. Cool to just barely warm, on a wire rack, and finish with this Confectioners' Glaze.

5. For the glaze, beat the sugar and milk together to a thin, creamy texture and brush over the top surface of the ring. It will seem to sink in, but as the cake cools and the glaze hardens it takes on a delicious, professional-looking frosty snow-sparkle.

This recipe looks incredibly complicated, but in fact it's very simple to make, and looks as though a very good pastry-shop had created it.

BOHEMIAN BRAID

Serves about 6

2 tsp dried yeast

8 fl. oz (225 ml) milk, scalded and cooled

Generous 1 oz (25–35 g) caster sugar

1 tsp salt

1 egg, size 3

14–15 oz (400-425 g) plain flour, or more as needed

2 oz (50 g) butter or margarine, melted and cooled to lukewarm

Filling

About 12 tbsp jam, preserves, or prune filling (see above)

The Czechoslovakian and Hungarian women who bake sweet yeast breads for their families often make this rather spectacular-looking plaited coffee cake. Because of its shape, it is sometimes called The Swaddled Russian Baby, but don't let that put you off. It can be filled with your favourite brand of very good jam, or the rich, thick, sweet prune filling called Povidl or Lekvar, depending on whether it is packed in jars with a Czech or Hungarian label.

1. Put the yeast in a large mixing bowl and stir in the milk, sugar, and salt. Mix well, cover, and let it stand in a warm place for five minutes. Add the egg and half the flour, and beat with a wooden spoon or electric whisk until it begins to feel smooth and elastic. Stir in the melted butter and beat again. Gradually add the remaining flour until the dough is soft but firm enough to be manageable.

2. Turn it out on a well-floured board, and have some extra flour at hand. Knead until the dough is satiny and 'live' feeling under your hands. Shape it into a ball, and put it in a well-greased bowl, turning it over once or twice. Cover with plastic film, and let it stand for about two hours until it is well risen. Punch it down, and let it rise again for about forty-five minutes until it is nearly double in bulk. Turn it out on a well-floured surface and roll it out to about 15 × 8 in. (38 × 20 cm).

3. With a knife, lightly score the surface the long way into three equal parts. Spread your chosen filling evenly down the centre panel. Using a very sharp knife, and working quickly, cut the two outer panels into horizontal strips about 1 in. (2·5 cm) wide, so that you have a panel of filling flanked by two tidy rows of fringe. Fold a strip at the top in across the filling, slanting it down a little, then fold in one from the right across it. Continue until all the strips are plaited across each other. Pinch the bottom end of the plait together so that the filling will not ooze out. Carefully lift it onto a lightly oiled baking sheet.

4. Cover lightly with an inverted baking tin, or plastic film, and let it rise until the plait doubles in bulk. Preheat the oven to 375°F (190°C), Gas 5. Bake the Bohemian Braid about twenty minutes, until it is lightly browned. Cool on a wire rack, and frost with the Confectioners' Glaze (see the previous recipe), or this thicker, harder, Confectioners' Sugar Icing.

Confectioners' Sugar Icing:

6 oz (175 g) icing sugar

2 tbsp hot water or milk

1 tsp vanilla or almond essence

Stir the sugar into the milk or water until it is a thick, spreadable mixture. Add the vanilla or almond essence. Use more milk or water for a thinner frosting.

American Sponge Cake

5 oz (125 g) plain flour, or 4 oz (100 g) flour sifted with 1 oz (100 g) of cornflour

6 oz (175 g) caster sugar

½ tsp salt

½ tsp baking powder

6 eggs, size 3, at room temperature, separated

4 tbsp cold water

1 tsp vanilla essence

½ tsp almond essence

1 tsp cream of tartar

3 oz (75 g) caster sugar

This delicate, slightly dry-textured sponge cake is completely different to the English fatless sponge or Genoese sponge. American sponge cakes are almost as light as an angel cake and are baked in the same type of ungreased funnel or tube tin. Sponge cakes should never be cut with a knife as this compresses the fragile crumb: mark off serving portions with a sharp knife-blade, then gently pull the cake apart with two forks held back to back. Sponge cake a day or two old is delicious pulled apart and lightly toasted under the grill, but it burns very easily.

The tin you use must be immaculately clean, without a trace of fat, and rinsed in very hot water so that no touch of detergent clings to it. I ruined a huge (and costly) sponge cake by trusting the washing of the tin to someone who believed the claim of the detergent advertisers that their product washes so clean that dishes need not be completely rinsed.

Preheat oven to 350°F (180°C), Gas 4.
1. Sift the flour, or the flour and cornflour mixture – which is a close approximation of the American 'cake flour' – with the 6 oz (150 g) of caster sugar, the salt, and the baking powder. Stir in the egg yolks, the water, the vanilla, and almond essences. *Do not beat* – merely give it a few good stirs.
2. Whisk the egg whites slowly for about one minute, add the cream of tartar, and beat more briskly until it forms a thick frothy mass. Then gradually beat in the 3 oz (75 g) of caster sugar, whisking until you have achieved a glossy meringue mixture that stands in stiff peaks.
3. Whisk the flour, egg yolk, and water mixture for about one minute, scoop up two heaped tbsps of the meringue and beat that in for not more than about thirty seconds, as what you are doing is merely lightening the flour batter. Scoop the batter onto the remaining egg whites, and carefully cut and fold the mixtures together. Slide it gently into the ungreased 10 in. (25 cm) tube or funnel tin, and bake about forty to fifty minutes. The surface of the cake should be golden and slightly dry-looking, and should spring back when you press it with your finger.
4. Invert the tin with the tube hanging on the neck of a large bottle (or on an upside-down funnel), and let it hang without disturbance until it is completely cold. Gently loosen the edges with a palette knife and the cake should drop neatly onto a plate.

Opposite *Chocolate delights.* Top *Brownies;* Right *Chocolate Refrigerator Cake;* Left *Devil's Food Cake*

Angel Food Cake

Serves about 10

3¾ oz (a little less than 100 g) plain flour, *or* 3 oz (75 g) plain flour sifted with 1 oz (25 g) cornflour

7 oz (200 g) caster sugar

8 fl. oz (225 ml) container of egg whites at room temperature, about ten size 3 eggs

1 tsp cream of tartar

¼ tsp salt

1 tsp vanilla essence

Angel cakes are tricky to make, as the batter must be blended with the greatest care, and the gentlest cutting and folding action. The batter, in fact, is a sort of sweet meringue mixture, with flour added. The texture of a baked angel food cake is light, dry, delicate. Those who like this kind of cake are rapturous about a perfectly made one; others feel that, like sourdough bread, it is a difficult trick to bring off and perhaps the resulting cake is somewhat over-rated. However, an angel food cake is spectacular to look at, and can make a cook's reputation. To be successful there are a few simple but essential rules.

1. Egg whites fluff up to the greatest volume if they are at room temperature, so take them out of the refrigerator or a cold larder at least an hour before beginning to make the cake. They must be whisked until they are stiff enough to hold a peak when you lift the beater blades, but must not be at all dry or grainy which makes a coarse-textured cake. On the other hand, *underbeaten* egg whites give the cake a texture like soft glove leather! A wire whisk in the classic unlined copper bowl, wielded with patience and skill, gives the greatest volume. Next comes the hand-operated rotary beater, and, I'm sorry to say, last is the useful electric mixer or whisk.

2. Angel food cakes must be baked in a scrupulously clean, *ungreased* tin. Rinse it in the hottest possible water, as even a trace of detergent can leave an invisible oily film and the cake will not rise. Usually the cake is baked in a special tin, variously called a tube, funnel, or angel mould – often with detachable sides. You can, however, use a loaf or square tin with perfect success.

3. The egg whites must be calculated by volume, not in numbers: you will need a glass that holds 8 fl. oz (225 ml).

4. Finally, when the cake comes out of the oven, the tin must be turned upside down and the centre tube or funnel suspended on the neck of a large bottle or on an inverted funnel, to allow the cake to hang until completely cold before it is gently removed. If using a loaf or square tin, invert it and prop up the corners with cups or jam jars.

Preheat oven to 350°F (180°C), Gas 4.

1. Have ready a very clean, completely dry, 10 in. (25 cm) tube or funnel tin, or whatever tin you like. Sift the flour four times with 3 oz (75 g) sugar and set it aside. Sift the remaining sugar four times into another bowl and set that aside too. Whisk the egg whites until they are a frothy mass,

Opposite Drinks from the 18th to the 20th century. Clockwise from top left Fishhouse Punch, Mint Julep, Old-fashioned, and Dry Martini

add the cream of tartar and salt, and whisk again until they stand in fairly stiff peaks – not as stiff as for a meringue.

2. Add two tbsp of the sugar to the egg whites, and whisk; repeat until all the sugar is beaten in, whisking gently after each addition. Finally stir in the vanilla essence. You now have a stiff but not dry meringue mixture.

3. Sift about one-quarter of the flour mixture over the egg whites, and cut and fold it in. Continue to do this, sifting, cutting, and folding, until everything is amalgamated into a huge fluffy mass.

4. Gently spoon the mixture into the tin, and bake for about fifty minutes to an hour until the surface is lightly golden and the centre springs back when you touch the surface near the tube or funnel.

Hang the cake in its tin upside down until it is cold. To serve: mark off portions with a sharp knife blade, but do not cut it, as this compresses the delicate texture. Pull it apart with two large forks held back to back. Any left-over angel food cake pieces may be lightly toasted under a grill, and there are those who think this is the best way to eat it.

Boston Cream Pie

Serves 4–6

2 oz (50 g) butter or good margarine

6 oz (175 g) caster sugar

1 egg, size 3

7 oz (200 g) plain flour

3 tsp baking powder

$\frac{1}{2}$ tsp salt

6 fl. oz (175 ml) milk

$\frac{1}{2}$ tsp vanilla essence or rum

Icing sugar

Despite the name, this is actually a cake. It is served in wedges, however, like a pie. The basic cake is a version of the simple and popular one-egg cake, but enriched and glamourised with a rich filling like a crème patissière. If you finish off Boston Cream Pie with a very thin chocolate frosting, it then becomes Parker House Chocolate Pie – this version was invented, it seems, by the same Boston hotel which gave its name to Parker House Rolls (see p. 152).

Preheat oven to 350°F (180°C), Gas 4.

1. Cream the butter with the sugar until it is pale and fluffy, then beat in the egg. Sift the flour, baking powder and salt. Mix the milk and vanilla or rum. Add the sifted dry ingredients, alternately with tablespoonfuls of the milk, to the butter mixture. Mix well, but do not overbeat.

2. Grease and flour two 8 in. (20 cm) round sandwich tins. Pour the batter into the tins, and rap them sharply on the table to settle the batter. Bake for about thirty minutes, until the centre of the cake springs back when you press it lightly with your finger. Let it cool in the tin five minutes, then turn out on a rack to cool completely, before spreading with the filling. Chill the cake well before serving. Cover the top of the cake with icing sugar.

BOSTON CREAM FILLING

2 eggs, size 3

3 oz (75 g) caster sugar

5 tbsp plain flour

Pinch of salt

¾ pt (425 ml) scalded milk

½ tsp vanilla essence

½ oz (15 g) butter

Whisk the eggs lightly, then beat in the sugar, flour, salt, and milk. Cook in the top part of a double boiler over simmering water, stirring frequently, until the mixture is thick and smooth. Stand the pan in a basin of cold water, and stir occasionally to prevent a skin forming. When it is lukewarm, add the vanilla and the butter, and beat well. Spread between the two layers of the cake.

Martha Washington Pie

Serves 4–6

One-Egg cake recipe (p. 233)

About 4 oz (100 g) of very good seedless raspberry jam

Half the recipe for Boston Cream pie filling (above)

Icing sugar

Yet another one of those confusing American cake recipes that calls itself a pie! Like Boston Cream Pie, it is a plain cake filled with a rich sweet mixture; always made in a round tin, never a square or loaf shape, and served cut in pie-shape wedges.

Bake the One-Egg Cake batter in three 7 in. (18 cm) sandwich tins. Cool the cakes on a rack, and spread one layer with the Cream Filling. The second layer is spread with raspberry jam, which for an extra luxurious touch may be slightly thinned with brandy; and the top layer is lightly sprinkled with icing sugar. Sometimes a lacy paper doily is laid on the top layer and the icing sugar sifted through it to make a white-lace pattern.

Individual Danish Pastries

14 fl. oz (400 ml) milk

10 oz (275 g) butter or good margarine

4 tsp dried yeast

2 fl. oz (50 ml) warm water

2 oz (50 g) caster sugar

3 eggs, size 3

½ tsp ground mace or cardamom

1 tsp salt

24–28 oz (675–775 g) plain flour

Why these characteristic American pastries are called 'Danish' is rather a mystery. In Denmark itself they go by the name Wienerbrød, a reference to their Viennese ancestry. Every city in the United States has its own version of Danishes, and its own name. In Chicago and through the Midwest, they will be called 'Sweetrolls' – all one word – with the emphasis on sweet. In New York, you may hear people say 'Dannishes', or call them by the individual name of the pastry such as Bowtie, Bear Claw, Cheese, or Prune Danish.

The dough is really a rich, sweet, rough puff pastry. It is time-consuming to make, but the flaky, buttery result is delightful. Fillings may be almond paste, plum jam, prune purée, sweetened cottage cheese, or apple purée. This recipe will make about two dozen individual Danishes, depending on the size you like. The quantity may be cut in half, of course; or unused dough can be frozen.

1. Heat the milk to blood heat and stir in 2 oz (50 g) of the butter. Mix the yeast with the warm water and let it stand until it froths up. Whisk the yeast liquid into the milk and butter mixture, stir in the sugar, eggs, mace, salt, and about 8 oz (225 g) of the flour. Beat the mixture until it is a smooth batter. Scrape it into a large bowl.

2. Mix in about 1 lb (450 g) of the remaining flour, and beat until you have a smooth, firm dough. You may want to add a little more flour, if the dough is sticky. Cover the bowl with plastic film and let it stand in a warm place until the dough doubles in bulk. Punch it down and turn it out on a floured board, with some extra flour in a bowl at hand. With a floured rolling pin, shape it into an oblong and roll it out to about ½ in. (1·5 cm) thickness.

3. Knead the remaining 8 oz (225 g) of butter until it is smooth and malleable but not oily, and shape it into a flat square cake. Put it in the centre of the dough panel, and fold the two ends over it, pressing the edges together. Give the dough a half turn and roll it out into a rectangle again, fold it in thirds, and repeat the turn-roll-fold operation once more. Wrap it in plastic film and refrigerate for about half an hour, not longer. The butter must not harden to the point where it will break through the dough wrapper.

4. Roll, fold, turn, and chill twice more. After the final session bring back to room temperature. Divide the dough into three parts.

ENVELOPES

Roll out one piece of dough to about ¼ in. (0·75 cm) thickness, cut it in 4 in. (10 cm) square pieces, put a tablespoon of filling in the centre of each. Fold the corners in to the centre, and press the edges firmly together.

COCKSCOMBS

Roll out a piece of dough to a strip about 5 in. (13 cm) wide, ¼ in. (0·75 cm) thick. Put your chosen filling in a line down the right-hand half of the strip, the long way, fold the other half over, and press the edges together to seal. Cut the filled strip in pieces about 4 in. (10 cm) long. With a sharp knife or scissors, slash each piece three times from the folded edge to within about 1 in. (2·5 cm) of the sealed edge. This works best with a fairly firm filling such as almond paste or prune purée, not a soft 'runny' one.

FILLED CRESCENTS

Roll out the dough to ¼ in. (0·75 cm) thickness, cut it in 5 in. (13 cm) squares, and cut each of these in half diagonally. Put a heaped teaspoonful of jam or apple purée on each triangle, and roll them as for croissants, beginning with the long side and slightly stretching the dough. Turn the ends in slightly.

To bake: Put the shaped Danishes on a lightly oiled baking sheet, cover and let them rise until they are about half again the original size. Preheat the oven to 400°F (200°C), Gas 6. Brush the top of the pastries with a mixture of beaten egg and cold water, and bake for about twenty minutes until the tops are golden brown.

Danishes may be glazed with Confectioners' Sugar Icing (see p. 238.

Date and Nut Torte

Serves 4

2 eggs, size 3

2 level tbsp flour

1 tsp baking powder

¼ tsp salt

4 oz (100 g) caster or soft light brown sugar

7 oz (200 g) chopped dates

4 oz (100 g) chopped walnuts

½ tsp vanilla essence

Optional: lightly whipped cream

Preheat oven to 325°F (160°C), Gas 3.

1. Whisk the eggs until very light and pale. Sift the flour with the baking powder, salt, and sugar, then sift again. Add to the eggs and mix well. Stir in the dates, nuts, and vanilla and blend.

2. Grease a shallow baking tin, about 8 × 8 in. (20 × 20 cm), pour in the mixture and bake for forty to fifty minutes. Serve the *torte* warm, not hot, with lightly whipped cream.

Crazy Cake

6 oz (175 g) plain flour

7 oz (200 g) caster sugar

Pinch of salt

3 tbsp cocoa

1 tsp bicarbonate of soda

1 tsp vanilla essence

1 tbsp cider vinegar

3 oz (75 g) margarine or white cooking fat, melted

8 fl. oz (225 ml) cold water

To finish: icing sugar or ice cream

This is a recipe that appears in hand-written 'receipt' books all over the country, from the mid-nineteenth century to the present day. No one seems to know where it originated. It is always given the same name, which has to do with the eccentric method of mixing. It can be mixed from scratch in the baking tin, or – more sensibly – in a bowl as for any ordinary cake. It is a rather puddingy cake, and is usually served scooped straight out of its tin. Children love it topped with vanilla ice cream.

Preheat oven to 375°F (190°C), Gas 5.

1. Sift the flour, then sift it again with the sugar, salt, cocoa, and bicarbonate, into a wide, shallow bowl. Make three wells in the dry mixture with a big cooking spoon. Into the first pour the vanilla, into the second pour the vinegar, and into the third goes the melted margarine. Pour the cold water over the whole thing, and with a hand or electric mixer beat it vigorously until there are no lumps.

2. Pour the batter into an ungreased square or oblong cake tin – the size I use is $10 \times 6\frac{3}{4} \times 2$ in. $(25 \times 18 \times 5$ cm$)$ – and bake for about twenty-five to thirty minutes. Serve warm, with sugar or ice cream.

Colorado Ranch Cake

6 oz (175 g) brown sugar – light or dark

2 oz (50 g) butter or margarine

$\frac{1}{2}$ pt (275 ml) boiling water

10 oz (275 g) raisins or sultanas

$\frac{1}{2}$ tsp salt

9 oz (250 g) 81%–85% light brown flour

1 tsp ground cinnamon

$\frac{1}{4}$ tsp ground cloves

1 tsp bicarbonate of soda

This is an eggless, milkless cake that manages to be rich, spicy, and fruity. It seems to have been invented some time in the early years of the twentieth century, probably on one of those vast ranches where the cattle roamed freely. The ranchhouse could be sixty miles or more from the nearest shop, 'quite a piece to go' as they would have said, on horseback or in a buckboard wagon. Flour was stored in hundred-pound barrels, spices and dried fruit were long-lasting, and there was usually plenty of good butter, churned when the house cow had freshened and milk was plentiful, then stored in stoneware crocks down a deep well or in a turf-covered ice house. So something, even in the snow-covered winter, could always be found to make a truly luscious cake.

Preheat oven to 250°F (130°C), Gas 1.

1. Grease a 2 lb (900 g) bread tin, and line it with greased greaseproof paper. Mix the sugar, margarine or butter, boiling water, and raisins or sultanas in a saucepan, bring to the boil, lower the heat and boil gently for five minutes.

Stand the saucepan in a basin of cold water and cool the mixture to lukewarm.

2. Sift the dry ingredients together, and stir them into the saucepan. Mix well but do not overbeat. Pour into the prepared tin and bake about an hour, until the cake is firm. Depending on the moisture content of the raisins, and on the flour you are using, you may need to bake the cake as much as forty-five minutes longer, so don't try to time its emergence from the oven for the hour when children are arriving home hungry for tea.

Idaho Sunbeam Cake

Serves 4–6

4 oz (100 g) caster sugar, plus 1 tbsp

1 tsp baking powder

3 oz (75 g) potato flour

¼ tsp salt

4 eggs, size 3, at room temperature, separated

½ tbsp lemon juice

Idaho, the great state where the wonderful baking potatoes grow, is the home of many notable cake-baking women – and a good deal of Scandinavian influence in its cooking. This cake is made from potato flour (called potato starch on its home ground), and is a golden version of Angel Food Cake. It is delicate, and dry rather than moist. Frost it if you like, or dust it with icing sugar, or serve it as they do in some places in the American West with richly flavoured home-made jam or preserves. Like all these cakes made without fat, Sunbeam Cake is baked in an ungreased tin, and must be pulled apart with forks and not cut with a knife. It is best eaten a day or two after baking.

Preheat oven to 350°F (180°C), Gas 4.

1. Sift the sugar twice. Sift the baking powder with the potato flour and salt. Whisk the egg whites until they stand in stiff peaks, and gradually beat half the sugar into the whites to make a stiff glossy meringue.

2. Whisk the egg yolks with the lemon juice and beat in the remaining sugar. Scoop the meringue on top of the yolks and gently cut and fold the two mixtures together. Sift the dry ingredients over the eggs, and lightly fold it all together. Gently spoon the batter into an ungreased, very clean tube or funnel tin, as used for an Angel Food Cake, or into a 2 lb (900 g) cake tin. Rap the tin firmly on the table, to settle the batter.

3. Bake about thirty to forty minutes, until well risen and golden – the top will crack open to reveal the pale gold interior. Invert the tin and suspend the funnel on the neck of a bottle, or support the loaf tin with jam jars under its edge. Let the cake hang until it is completely cold, then gently loosen the edges with a palette knife and let it drop (gently!) on to a plate.

Red Devil's Food Cake

Makes two 8 in. (20 cm) layers

8 oz (225 g) caster sugar

7 oz (200 g) plain flour

4 tbsp cocoa powder

1½ tsp bicarbonate of soda

1 tsp salt

4 oz (100 g) good margarine, or white
  cooking fat, softened

8 fl. oz (225 ml) soured milk, or fresh
  milk soured with 1 tsp lemon juice

2 eggs, size 3

1 tsp vanilla essence

*Every American housewife, before the days of cake mixes,
had her own pet recipe for Red Devil's Food. Some tasted so
strongly of bicarbonate of soda (called baking soda in the
US), that they were almost unpleasant – but the red colour
always called forth compliments no matter how the cake
tasted. It's a rather spectacular cake, with a slightly crumbly
texture – not at all rich or fudgy. The traditional finish
is Cocoa Icing (see p. 240), or Butter Cream (see p. 239)
flavoured with cocoa powder to your taste.*

Preheat oven to 350°F (180°C), Gas 4.

1. Sift the sugar, flour, cocoa powder, bicarbonate, and salt
together twice. Stir the margarine into about ¼ pt (125 ml) of
the milk and mix it into the dry ingredients, beating well,
either with a wooden spoon for three or four minutes, or on
the medium speed of an electric mixer. Add the remaining
milk, eggs, and vanilla essence and beat for another two
minutes.

2. Grease two 8 in. (20 cm) cake tins, and line the sides and
base with greased greaseproof paper. Pour in the batter and
bake just below the centre of the oven for about thirty-five
minutes, until the centre of the cake feels springy to the
touch of your finger. If you put a skewer into the centre of the
cake, it will come out with a few crumbs clinging to it, not
completely dry. Let the cakes stand in their tins for five
minutes, then turn out on a cake rack and peel off the
greaseproof paper. Cool completely before sandwiching
together and frosting with Mocha Cream Icing or Butter
Cream.

Silver Cake

Serves 4–6

4 egg whites, size 3

Generous 2 oz (50–60 g) butter or good
  margarine

6 oz (175 g) caster sugar

7 oz (200 g) plain flour

3 tsp baking powder

¼ tsp salt

4 fl. oz (100 ml) milk

½ tsp almond essence

*This is a rich but delicate white cake, which should be
frosted with a thick caramel, butter cream, or mocha icing. It
keeps well, and probably would freeze perfectly – although I
haven't tried it.*

Preheat oven to 350°F (180°C), Gas 4.

1. Whisk the egg whites to stiff peaks, cover with plastic
film and set aside. Cream the butter with the sugar until it is
light and fluffy. Sift the flour with the baking powder and
salt, and sift about one-quarter of this mixture over the
butter and sugar. Mix lightly.

2. Mix the milk and the almond essence and add about two
tablespoonfuls of this to the batter. Continue to sift in the

dry ingredients alternately with the milk, mixing lightly after each addition. Scoop up one heaped tablespoon of the egg whites and lightly whisk it into the batter.

3. Scrape the batter on top of the remaining egg whites, and gently cut and fold everything together. Grease two 7 in. (18 cm) cake tins and line the bases with greased greaseproof paper. Pour in the mixture and bake for forty-five minutes until the top of the cake springs back lightly when pressed. Sandwich the layers together with your favourite rich icing, and frost the top if you like – although it is often left plain and simply sprinkled with icing sugar.

One-Egg Cake *and* Marble Cake

Serves 4–6

2 oz (50 g) butter or good margarine

3 oz (75 g) caster sugar

1 egg, size 2 or 3

6 oz (175 g) plain flour

2½ tsp baking powder

¼ tsp salt

4 fl. oz (100 ml) milk

½ tsp vanilla *or* ¼ tsp almond essence

This is one of the simplest of American 'plain' cakes, not very rich and not over-sweet. It can be made elegant with a thick layer of some luscious mocha, chocolate, or caramel frosting; or finished with the crunchy Broiled Frosting (see p. 239) done under the grill. Its variation, Marble Cake, is pretty to look at when a wedge is cut from it – and has just enough chocolate flavour to make it interesting. Either one makes an excellent birthday cake for children, lending itself to elaborate icing flourishes, candles, and frills which disguise the essential wholesome plainness.

Preheat oven to 350°F (180°C), Gas 4.

1. Grease a 7 in. (18 cm) or 8 in. (20 cm) round cake tin. Cream the butter or margarine well, add half the sugar and cream it again. Whisk the egg with the remaining sugar and beat well. Carefully combine the two mixtures, stirring well. Sift the flour with the baking powder, and salt, and add it by teaspoonfuls, alternately with the milk, to the first mixture. Stir in the vanilla or almond essence.

2. Pour the batter into the prepared tin and bake for about half an hour, until the cake springs back when you press the surface with your finger. A cocktail stick or skewer put into the centre should come out clean and dry. Let it stand in the tin for five minutes, then loosen the edges with a palette knife and turn it out on a rack. Finish with whatever frosting, plain or fancy, that pleases you.

Marble Cake. Make the cake batter as above, but divide it in half in two bowls. Add 1 oz (25 g) melted plain dark chocolate to one half. Drop heaped tablespoonfuls, alternating plain and chocolate, into the prepared tin. Give the batter a quick swirl with a knife-blade, to create the 'marble' effect. A cocoa frosting looks best on Marble Cake.

Gold Cake

4 oz (100 g) butter or good margarine

7 oz (200 g) caster sugar

1 egg, size 3

4 egg yolks, size 3

7 oz (200 g) plain flour

$2\frac{1}{2}$ tsp baking powder

$\frac{1}{4}$ tsp salt

4 fl. oz (100 ml) milk

$\frac{1}{2}$ tsp vanilla essence

This rich, golden cake will use up the egg yolks you will have left after making Silver Cake (see p. 232). A mocha or chocolate frosting is the traditional finish for Gold Cake; but it is very pleasant simply left plain, and sliced to serve with tea or coffee.

Preheat oven to 350°F (180°C), Gas 4.
1. Cream the butter and gradually beat in the sugar until the mixture is pale and fluffy. Whisk the egg and the egg yolks together, and gradually beat them into the butter mixture. Grease and flour two 7 in. (18 cm) cake tins.
2. Sift the flour, baking powder, and salt together, and add alternately with the milk to the cake batter. Add the vanilla, and stir well but do not overbeat. Pour the batter into the prepared tins and bake for about forty-five minutes, until the centre of the cake springs back when pressed with your finger. Let the cakes stand in their tins five minutes, then turn them out on a rack to cool completely before frosting.

Lady Baltimore Cake

6 egg whites, size 3

6 oz (175 g) butter or good margarine, at room temperature

9 oz (250 g) caster sugar

12 oz (350 g) plain flour

3 tsp baking powder

$\frac{1}{4}$ tsp salt

8 fl. oz (225 ml) milk

1 tsp vanilla essence

$\frac{1}{2}$ tsp almond essence or rum

This fine-textured cake is said to have been made first in nineteenth-century Baltimore, Maryland. In those lavish days the quantities in this recipe would have been doubled, and the cake made in five towering layers. In these more modest times, this recipe is calculated to make a big, beautiful, three-layer cake. For smaller families, you may want to cut the quantities in half and bake the cake in two, not three, tins.

Preheat oven to 350°F (180°C), Gas 4.
1. Whisk the egg whites stiff, cover the bowl with plastic film and set them aside. Grease three 8 in. (20 cm) sandwich tins, and line the bases with greased greaseproof paper. Cream the butter until it is pale and fluffy, and gradually beat in the sugar until you have a light-coloured, light-textured mixture.
2. Sift the flour, baking powder, and salt together. Sift about one-quarter of it over the butter and sugar mixture. Stir the milk with the vanilla essence and almond essence or rum. Add a few tablespoons of the milk mixture to the bowl, and stir lightly; then alternately sift in more milk, mixing gently with every addition.

3. Scoop one heaped tbsp of the whisked eggs into the batter, and beat for about thirty seconds, so that the cake batter is made lighter. Then scrape the batter into the bowl of egg whites, and gently cut and fold the two mixtures together. Lightly scoop the batter into the prepared tins and bake for about twenty-five minutes, until the centre of the cake springs back when touched gently with your finger. Let the cakes cool in their tins about five minutes, then if necessary loosen the edges with a palette knife, and turn out on a rack to cool before frosting.

LADY BALTIMORE FILLING AND FROSTING

7-minute frosting (see p. 239)

4 oz (100 g) walnuts or almonds, chopped fairly finely

6 soft figs, finely chopped. (If you like, soak them for half an hour in brandy.)

Set aside one-third of the amount of frosting. Mix the fruit and nuts with the remainder and spread between the layers of the cake. Ice the top layer with the plain frosting.

Hershey, Pennsylvania, Black Magic Cake

Serves 6

7 oz (200 g) plain flour

12 oz (350 g) caster sugar

3 oz (75 g) cocoa powder

2 tsp bicarbonate of soda

1 tsp baking powder

1 tsp salt

2 eggs, size 3

8 fl. oz (225 ml) strong black coffee (2 heaped tsp instant coffee in boiling water)

8 fl. oz (225 ml) buttermilk, *or* fresh milk soured with 1 tsp lemon juice

4 fl. oz (100 ml) vegetable oil

$\frac{1}{2}$ tsp vanilla essence or rum

Hershey's is almost a generic name for chocolate confections in America. They created the all-American Hershey Bar – rich milk chocolate, plain or stuffed with nuts or raisins. In Hershey, Pennsylvania, if my memory serves, one can stand at the junction of Chocolate Avenue and Cocoa Street, inhaling the rich scent of cocoa and vanilla. Here is a recipe lent me by a Pennsylvania friend; I think it may have originally been set down in a cookbook produced by the Hershey people themselves.

Preheat oven to 350°F (180°C), Gas 4.
1. Sift all the dry ingredients together into a large mixing bowl. Whisk together the eggs, coffee, buttermilk, oil, and vanilla, pour the mixture into the bowl and beat well. The batter will be thin.
2. Grease two 9 in. (23 cm) cake tins, and line the bases and sides with greased greaseproof paper. (Or use three smaller tins.) Pour in the batter and bake for about thirty-five minutes. The cake will feel rather damp when you remove it from its tins, but that is as it should be. This cake needs no frosting, but of course you can add richness to richness by the use of a caramel or fudge icing.

Fudge Cake

Serves 6–8

3 eggs, size 3

8 oz (225 g) caster sugar

3 oz (75 g) plain dark chocolate

7 fl. oz (200 ml) milk

1 oz (25 g) butter

2 oz (50 g) white cooking fat

1 tsp vanilla essence

¼ tsp red food colouring

¾ tsp bicarbonate of soda

¼ tsp salt

6 oz (175 g) plain flour

A very rich cake that is almost like a confection: if the batter is baked in small fluted foil cases, this dark-chocolate cake makes a most delicious sweet to hand round with after-dinner coffee. It looks prettiest when frosted with a white icing, and most dramatic finished off with a thin chocolate glacé icing.

Preheat oven to 350°F (180°C), Gas 4.

1. Whisk one egg and mix it with half the sugar. Break up the chocolate in small pieces, or grate it. Put the egg mixture and the chocolate in a small heavy saucepan, stir in 3 fl. oz (75 ml) of the milk, and cook it over low heat, stirring constantly, until the sauce is smooth and slightly thickened. Set the saucepan in a bowl of cold water and cool the sauce to room temperature.

2. Cream the butter and white fat together, and gradually beat in the remaining sugar until it is a pale fluffy mass. Stir in the vanilla and the food colouring. Beat in the remaining two eggs, one at a time.

3. Sift the bicarbonate, salt, and flour twice, and sift about one-quarter of this into the batter. Stir in a few tablespoonfuls of the remaining milk, and continue to add the dry ingredients and the milk alternately, beating well after each addition. Then beat in the lukewarm chocolate sauce.

4. Grease two 8 in. (20 cm) cake tins, and line the bottoms with greased greaseproof paper. Pour in the batter and bake for about thirty minutes, until the top of the cake springs back when lightly pressed. A thin skewer put in the centre will come out with some rather damp crumbs clinging to it. Let the cakes cool in the tins for five minutes, then turn them out on a rack. Cool completely before frosting.

Lemon Chiffon Cake

Serves about 6

5 oz (125 g) plain flour

4 oz (100 g) caster sugar

1½ tsp baking powder

½ tsp salt

2 fl. oz (50 ml) vegetable oil –
   groundnut, soya, in fact anything
   except olive oil or corn oil

2 egg yolks, size 2

This light, close-textured cake is made with oil instead of butter or margarine. It's somewhat like an Angel Food Cake but not so dry, or like a Pound Cake but less rich. It can be frosted, but usually is served simply with a dusting of icing sugar.

Preheat oven to 325°F (165°C), Gas 3

1. Sift the flour, sugar, baking powder, and salt together twice, into a large bowl. Add the oil, egg yolks, water, vanilla essence, and the lemon rind and beat the mixture until it is

3 fl. oz (75 ml) cold water

1 tsp vanilla essence

Grated rind of half a large lemon

3 egg whites, size 2

Pinch of cream of tartar

very smooth. Whisk the egg whites with the cream of tartar until they stand in stiff peaks. Scoop two heaped table-spoonfuls of egg white into the batter and beat it together lightly.

2. Scrape the batter on top of the remaining egg whites and gently cut and fold the mixtures together. Gently spoon the batter into an ungreased 8 in. (20 cm) tube or funnel tin, or a round cake tin with a removable base. Bake for about fifty-five minutes, then raise the heat to 350°F (180°C), Gas 4, and bake another fifteen minutes until the centre of the cake springs back when lightly pressed.

3. Invert the tin and hang it upside down, with the funnel suspended on the neck of a bottle. If you have used a round cake tin, support it on three cups or jam jars under the rim. Let the cake stand until completely cold, then gently loosen the edges with a palette knife and remove it.

Orange Chiffon Cake. Instead of the vanilla essence and lemon rind, flavour the batter with three tbsp of grated orange rind, or more (this depends on the season of the year, as some oranges have more flavour in the rind than others.)

Husband's Cake

Serves 6

6 oz (175 g) butter or margarine, softened

6 oz (175 g) light brown sugar

12 oz (350 g) plain flour, or 81%–85% light brown flour

3 tsp baking powder

2 tsp mixed spice

$\frac{1}{2}$ tsp freshly grated nutmeg

1 tsp bicarbonate of soda

$\frac{1}{2}$ tsp salt

10$\frac{1}{2}$ oz (280 g) tin of condensed tomato soup

6 fl. oz (175 ml) water

4 oz (100 g) sultanas or raisins

4 oz (100 g) walnuts, coarsely chopped

I have been unable to trace the origin of the name of this fruity, spicy, red-brown cake – which may also be called Mystery Cake or Unbelievable Cake. It has a secret ingredient which makes people laugh when it is revealed. Very moist, thick with sultanas and nuts, it keeps superbly, and travels well which makes it a 'natural' for picnics and car journeys.

Preheat oven to 350°F (180°C), Gas 4.

1. Cream the butter and sugar together until as fluffy as possible. Sift the flour with the baking powder, mixed spice, nutmeg, bicarbonate, and salt. Toss the sultanas in this mixture, remove them with a slotted spoon and put in a bowl. Stir the dry ingredients into the butter and sugar mixture, and beat well. Beat in the tomato soup and the water and mix again.

2. Carefully stir the floured sultanas and the nuts into the batter. Grease and flour an 8 in. (20 cm) or 9 in. (23 cm) cake tin, and pour in the batter. Bake for about an hour, until a thin skewer thrust in the centre comes out clean. Cool the cake in the tin for ten minutes before turning out on a rack. Cut in slices or wedges. Ice it, if you like, with a plain white cake frosting – nothing rich.

Boiled Frosting

1 lb (450 g) caster sugar

8 tbsp cold water

Good pinch of cream of tartar

2 egg whites, size 3

½ tsp vanilla or almond essence

This characteristic American frosting is sometimes called White Mountain Cream, or simply American Icing. If you are clever at gauging the temperature of a boiling sugar mixture by making it spin a long thread from a lifted spoon, you will have no trouble with Boiled Frosting. Less dramatic, but safer: cook it to 240 °F (118°C), on a sugar thermometer.

1. Dissolve the sugar in the water in a saucepan set on a very low heat, without stirring. Mix the cream of tartar with a few drops of water and stir it in. Put a lid on the pan and bring it to the boil – watch it carefully, as it rises suddenly and volcanically. Take off the lid and cook it until it reaches 240°F (118°C), and remove it from the heat at once. Plunge the pan into a basin of cold water.
2. Whisk the egg whites stiff. Pour the syrup on to the egg whites, whisking steadily – you may need a helper here. The icing will suddenly lose its glossy look, and the whisk will begin to pick it up in small peaks. Stir in the vanilla or almond essence.
3. Spread the icing quickly over the cake with a wide palette knife – it will harden and crack if not used at once.

Confectioners' Sugar Glaze

5 level tbsp icing sugar

2 tbsp hot milk

¼ tsp almond essence, *or* vanilla essence

The American equivalent of English icing sugar goes by many names, varying from one part of the country to another. It is called confectioners' sugar, powdered sugar, sometimes XXX or 10-X sugar. This simple glaze makes a glistening, very sweet, slightly crackly topping for such sweet yeast breads as Bohemian Braid (p. 221), Tea Ring (p. 220), Individual Danish pastries (p. 228–229), or for cinnamon buns or doughnuts.

Mix everything smooth, and 'paint' the icing onto the bread or pastry surface at once. It may be diluted with more hot milk, or hot water, to make an even thinner glaze.

Seven-minute Frosting

For an 8 in. (20 cm) cake

1 egg white, size 3

5 oz (125 g) caster sugar

3 tbsp cold water

Good pinch of cream of tartar

Pinch of salt

A few drops of almond or vanilla
  essence

Mix all the ingredients in the top of a double boiler over boiling water. Whisk as it cooks with a hand or electric mixer, until it stands in soft peaks – this will take about seven minutes. Flavour to your taste, and beat again until it is of a thick spreading consistency, scraping down the sides of the pan as you whisk it.

Broiled Icing

For an 8 in. (20 cm) cake

3 tbsp butter or good margarine, melted

4 oz (100 g) light brown sugar

1 tbsp single cream or top of milk

Pinch of salt

2 oz (50 g) desiccated coconut *or*
  roughly chopped walnuts

An American 'broiler' is an English grill: this sweet topping for a plain cake is quickly and easily made and browned under the grill. Make sure you have enough headroom under your grill, however, as it burns very easily. Alternatively, it can be brought to brown and bubbling perfection in a very hot oven, 475°F (245°C), Gas 9.

Mix all the ingredients and spread on the warm cake (the kind baked in a sandwich tin is best.) Light the grill and turn the heat to low. Put the cake so that its top is about three inches below the flame and grill until it is caramel-coloured and bubbly.

Butter Cream Frosting

To cover the top and sides of a three-layer 8 in. (20 cm) cake

7 oz (200 g) caster sugar

Good pinch of cream of tartar

5 tbsp cold water

6 egg yolks, size 3

8 oz (225 g) butter or good margarine,
  at room temperature

1 tsp vanilla essence

1. Sift the sugar and the cream of tartar together. In a small saucepan, bring the water to the boil, add the sugar, and stir until it is fully dissolved. Boil the mixture to 240°F (118°C) on a sugar thermometer, or until a small spoonful dropped into very cold water makes a firm ball.
2. Set the saucepan in a basin of cold water and cool until the sugar syrup is lukewarm. In a large bowl, whisk the egg yolks until they are thick and pale, and slowly add the sugar syrup, whisking constantly. Add the butter, one tablespoon at a time, and beat well after each addition until the frosting mixture is thick and velvety. Beat in the vanilla.
3. Chill the frosting until it is firm enough to spread. After you have frosted your cake or cakes, keep them in a cool place, as this rich butter cream melts easily.

Fudge Frosting

Enough for the top and sides of two 9 in. (23 cm) cakes

20 oz (550 g) caster sugar

3 tbsp golden syrup

8 fl. oz (225 ml) milk

8 heaped tbsp cocoa powder

6 oz (175 g) butter or good margarine

1 tsp vanilla essence or rum

1. In a small heavy saucepan, mix the sugar, the golden syrup, milk, and cocoa powder. Bring it to the simmering point, stirring, until it is well mixed. Cook until the mixture reaches 240°F (118°C) on a sugar thermometer, stirring often, as the cocoa syrup catches very easily.
2. Take the pan from the heat and beat in the butter very thoroughly. Cool the pan without stirring, until you can put your palm on the bottom of the pan and hold it there without burning your hand. Beat in the vanilla, and continue to beat with a hand or electric whisk until the mixture will stand in very lofty peaks when you lift the beater blades.
3. Frost your cake or cakes at once, as the fudge mixture does that mysterious thing called 'setting up' – hardening and becoming unworkable. If there is any left, you might set the pan in a bowl of hot water to soften the mixture slightly, then roll it into small balls and dredge it in cocoa powder, to make something like Chocolate Truffles.

Cocoa Frosting

For a 7 in. (18 cm) cake

2 oz (50 g) icing sugar

2 tbsp cocoa powder

2 tbsp butter or good margarine, melted

1 tsp vanilla essence

About 3 tsp of hot coffee, or slightly more

This is a rich but not cloying finish for a plain cake, such as the One-Egg Cake and Marble Cake variation (p. 233) – or as an alternative to the traditional filling for the Lady Baltimore Cake (p. 234).

1. Beat the sugar, cocoa powder, and butter together until the mixture is very smooth. Stir in the vanilla essence, and gradually beat in the hot coffee, adding more until you have a spreading consistency.
2. Dip a knife in hot coffee and use it to spread the frosting in a pretty swirl pattern on the cooled cake.

Bitter Chocolate Sauce

Makes about 12 oz (350 g)

4 oz (100 g) white cooking fat

1 oz (25 g) butter or good margarine

2 tbsp golden syrup

6 fl. oz (175 ml) milk

12 heaped tbsp cocoa powder

4 tbsp caster sugar

Pinch of salt

A rich dark sauce for vanilla ice cream: it is based on unsweetened cocoa powder, can be made in ten minutes, and is as delicious cold as it is warm. If you prefer a sweeter taste, use plain dark dessert chocolate instead of cocoa. The proportions for that variation are given at the end of the recipe. It can be made with all butter, all margarine, or the combination as given of butter with white fat, which of course is less costly.

1. Mix the white fat, butter, golden syrup, and milk in the top portion of a double boiler, over boiling water. Stir until the fats are melted. Set the top part of the double boiler on low direct heat.

2. Sift the cocoa powder and sugar and salt together, and stir into the milk mixture. Cook, stirring often, until the sauce begins to thicken smoothly. It burns easily, so stir all around the bottom of the pan. As soon as it thickens, take it quickly off the heat and beat it with a wooden spoon or whisk until it is thick and velvety. If, as it cooks, it begins to separate and look oily, lift it off the heat at once, pour into a small bowl and whisk it vigorously, which will restore the rich velvety texture. Serve it warm or hot, not cold.

Bittersweet Chocolate Sauce. Instead of the cocoa powder and the 4 oz (100 g) of white fat, substitute 4 oz (100 g) of plain dark chocolate. Melt the chocolate with the butter, in the top of the double boiler, add the golden syrup, the sugar, salt and milk, and mix well. Then finish cooking and stirring on low direct heat as set out in item 2 above.

Bitter chocolate sauces solidify into a sort of fudge-like mass when cold. They can be stored, tightly covered, in the refrigerator, but should be reheated in the top of the double boiler, over simmering water, stirring constantly, to restore the smooth sauce to perfection.

Brandy Sauce

Makes about 1 pt (550 ml)

8 fl. oz (225 ml) double cream

4 oz (100 g) butter (*not* margarine)

4 egg yolks, size 3

6 oz (175 g) caster sugar

2 fl. oz (50 ml) brandy, or more

This luxurious sauce makes even the plainest of bread puddings something memorable. On a Christmas pudding, it's the ultimate taste of richness. The recipe is adapted from the one created by the great American cook and writer James Beard.

1. Half-fill the bottom portion of a double boiler with boiling water and set the top part in it. Bring the cream to the boil, slowly, in the top portion – the water should not touch the base of the pan containing the hot cream. Stir in the butter and let it melt. Whisk the egg yolks until they are thick and pale, and beat in the sugar.

2. Stir a tablespoon or two of the hot cream into the egg yolk and sugar mixture, and blend well, then stir this back into the top of the double boiler. Cook, stirring constantly, until the sauce is thick and smooth. If it begins to curdle, remove the top part instantly and set it on a cool surface and whisk vigorously until it smooths out again. Just before serving, add the brandy. Taste, and add more if you like.

Drinks

Cocktails

There are so many misconceptions about American cocktails that it seems worthwhile putting down here some veritable versions.

MARTINI

This is neither straight vermouth, nor a slapdash mixture of dry vermouth and gin. It began long ago as two-thirds Italian vermouth and one-third gin, but has now evolved into the *Dry Martini,* four to six parts gin and one part dry vermouth (French), with a green olive in it; and the *Very Dry Martini* is about ninety-nine per cent straight gin with the smallest dash of vermouth and a twist of lemon peel. A Martini is always served ice cold, never shaken, but gently stirred. A *Gibson* is a *Very Dry Martini* with a small pickled onion in it.

MANHATTAN

Sweet: one part sweet vermouth, two parts Bourbon or rye whiskey, a dash of Angostura bitters, and usually a maraschino cherry. Dry: one part dry vermouth, two parts Bourbon or rye whiskey, poured over ice cubes, stirred and strained. It may have an olive or a twist of lemon peel.

OLD-FASHIONED

A lump of sugar in a short, wide glass, with just enough water to dissolve it; a sprinkle of Angostura, a little rye or Bourbon stirred around a bit; then cracked ice and one or two jiggers or 3 tbsp of whiskey.

Cafe Brûlot

Serves 8

Peel of one medium orange

Peel of one lemon

1 stick of cinnamon broken into small pieces

½ tsp allspice berries

8 sugar cubes

4 fl. oz (100 ml) brandy

1 pt (550 ml) hot, strong, continental-type coffee

A rather spectacular finishing touch for a gala dinner – a great New Orleans recipe. You should by rights have a silver bowl, a silver ladle, and an attentive audience at a candle-lit table.

1. Finely shred the orange and lemon peel and put it in a flameproof bowl with the cinnamon sticks, allspice, and sugar cubes. Warm the brandy gently in a heavy saucepan but do not let it catch fire. Pour all but one tablespoon of the brandy over the mixture in the bowl.
2. Light the remaining brandy and ladle it into the bowl – the brandy mixture should catch fire. When it burns out, pour on the very hot coffee, stir well, and ladle it into warmed small coffee cups.

Mint Julep

For each person:

1 tsp caster sugar

A little cold water

Sprigs of fresh mint

Crushed ice

1½ fl. oz (35 ml) Bourbon whiskey

Who would guess that the word 'julep' is actually of Arab origin? The Mint Julep is the drink that one associates with the American South, Kentucky Colonels, parties held in white portico'ed mansions, the bluegrass country where blood horses are raised, and a few more Gone with the Wind clichés. At the risk of starting another Civil War – which my unreconstructed Southern cousins are still calling The War Between the States – I give a recipe, one of dozens, for Mint Julep. You can take your choice about crushing the mint in a crystal or silver goblet, and about the important matter of whether a julep is sipped through a straw or straight from the glass. Note that Americans spell their whisky with an e.

Chill silver or crystal mugs or julep glasses in the freezing compartment of the refrigerator. Dissolve the sugar in a little water and set it aside. Here comes the debatable part: either crush a few sprigs of mint in the bottom of the glass, or leave it out. Fill up with crushed ice, pour on the Bourbon, stir in the dissolved sugar. Tuck four or five sprigs of mint down into the ice, and serve with or without a straw.

Georgia Julep. An heretical version which I have only read about, never tried. Instead of Bourbon, use equal parts of brandy and peach brandy.

Punches

FISH HOUSE PUNCH

Serves about 25 people

12 oz (350 g) caster sugar

3 pts (1·675 litres) cold water

1½ pts (900 ml) lemon juice

3 pts (1·675 litres) Jamaica rum

1½ pts (900 ml) brandy

1 wineglass of peach brandy

This wonderful drink originated at 'The State in Schuylkill' – pronounced 'Schoolkill' – the oldest American club, founded in Philadelphia forty years before the Declaration of Independence. It has only thirty members, all expert cooks. After dinner, a rising toast is drunk in Madeira to George Washington. There's a story that in one of Washington's diaries a note appears that he was engaged to dine, on his way to Philadelphia, at The State in Schuylkill; after which there are three blank pages!

Dissolve the sugar in 1 pt (550 ml) water. Add the lemon juice and stir it well, then add all the other ingredients. Put a large lump of ice in a punch bowl and pour on the punch, let it chill two hours, and serve in stemmed glasses.

KNOCKOUT PUNCH

Serves about 25 people

3 bright-skinned oranges

4 oz (100 g) lump sugar

2 pts (1·125 litres) strong strained tea

¾ pt (425 ml) strained lemon juice

¾ pt (425 ml) Jamaica rum

2 pts (1·125 litres) gin

1 tsp Angostura bitters

2 pts (1·125 litres) ginger ale

1. Rub the sugar lumps over the oranges to absorb the flavoured oil. Put the sugar in a big crystal or silver punchbowl, add the tea and stir until the sugar dissolves. Stir in lemon juice, rum, gin, and bitters.
2. Just before serving, put a big lump of ice in the bowl and add the ginger ale.

MAIBOWLE

Serves about 12 people

1 oz (25 g) dried woodruff

1½ tbsp caster sugar

4 fl. oz (100 ml) brandy

2 bottles (26 fl oz, 725 ml each) Rhine or Moselle wine

1 bottle champagne

8 oz (225 g) fine whole strawberries

This is a speciality of the famous old German restaurant, Luchow's, in New York.

1. Tie the woodruff in a piece of muslin, and marinate it in a mixture of the brandy, half a bottle of white wine, and sugar, at least twelve hours.
2. Strain off the liquid in a punchbowl, add two ice-cube trays of ice, and stir in the remaining white wine, champagne, and strawberries.

Chocolate Syrup

Makes about ¾ pt (425 ml)

6 oz (175 g) plain dark dessert chocolate, melted

9 oz (250 g) caster sugar

Good pinch of salt

8 fl. oz (225 ml) boiling water

1 tsp vanilla essence

Mix the melted chocolate with the sugar and salt in a heavy saucepan. Stir in the boiling water and cook, stirring, for five minutes. Remove the pan from the heat and let the mixture cool to lukewarm, then stir in the vanilla essence. Keep in the refrigerator in a tightly covered jar, and use it by the spoonful for chocolate drinks. To make quick hot chocolate, stir one or two tablespoonfuls into 6–8 fl. oz (175–225 ml) of hot milk.

Thick Chocolate Milkshake

Serves 1

8 fl. oz (225 ml) milk

1–2 tbsp chocolate syrup (see p. 245)

2–3 oz (50–75 g) chocolate ice cream

In some parts of the United States, this rich mixture of milk and ice cream would be called a 'frosted'. Although it is so thick, it's usually sipped through a straw.

1. In a blender or with a hand or electric whisk, mix the milk and the chocolate syrup thoroughly.
2. Beat or blend in the chocolate ice cream until the mixture is thick and frothy. Serve at once, in a tall glass.

American Malted Milk

This creamy, rich drink is variously called a 'Malt', a 'Malted', or a 'Malt Frosted'. It is a milk shake, chocolate or vanilla, which has been enriched with about 2 tbsp of malted milk powder and a scoop – about 2 oz (50 g) – of vanilla or chocolate ice cream. It should be blended quickly with well-chilled ingredients. 'Malteds' are a good, convenient way of taking in quite a lot of nourishment (and calories) in a quick easy way – preferably sitting at a drugstore counter!

Fraps, Floats, and Eggnog

FRAPPÉ

6 fl. oz (175 ml) milk

2 tbsp crushed ice

2½ tbsp chocolate syrup (see p. 245)

A frappé (pronounced 'frap') is really a milkshake with ice cream: you begin with the basic milkshake which is very simple.

Beat all the ingredients together in a blender and strain into a glass. Add a scoop of chocolate or vanilla or coffee ice cream and you've made a frap.

FLOATS

A 'float' in one part of the country is something else somewhere else. Rootbeer Float is rootbeer with vanilla ice cream in it, served in a tall glass – in the Midwest it is called (or used to be called), a Black Cow.

EGGNOG

1 egg

½ pt (275 ml) milk

Sugar to taste

Freshly grated nutmeg

Whisk the egg, milk, and sugar together until light and foamy, pour into a glass, and freckle the top of the glass with nutmeg. Very strengthening for anyone recovering from 'flu. Add about a tablespoon of brandy or rum for the grown-ups.

Wines from the New World

As yet, the only American wines available in the United Kingdom come from California, although other states – New York, Ohio, and Oregon among them – have long produced wines of their own. These last, however, are usually pressed from the native 'fox' grapes and taste strange to European palates. California is classic wine country, with its gentle climate, long growing seasons, and a variety of soils that range from stony to richly fertile. It has a 200-year history of winemaking. Vines were brought from France, Italy, and Spain, and often tended by monks who, in their European homelands, had been cellarmasters and vintners. Today, an area of California about the size of Bordeaux and Burgundy combined, is planted with wine grapes.

A great deal of California wine is sold in 'jugs' or carafes, good, sound, every-day drinking wine, bought by the double litre – about a half-gallon in American terms. But increasingly, wine of an astonishingly high quality is being made. In blind tastings against fine French wines in 1979, certain California wines outranked all but the great classics.

The better wines of California bear the names of their parent grape variety. Cabernet Sauvignons, grown on stocks from Bordeaux, make a wine actually heavier and fuller than its Médoc counterpart. The grapes are not heavy croppers, and the wine takes years to mature, therefore a good California Cabernet is apt to be pricey indeed – but satisfyingly big, rich, and full of fruit. Zinfandel, made from California's native grape, is lighter, fresh and fruity, delicious with pasta and cheese. A good Pinot Noir from California is velvety and perfect with game, steak, and roast beef.

California's white wines range from the flinty Crystal Dry, which has Chenin Blanc and Colambard grapes from the Loire in its pedigree, to the rich, naturally sweet wines from the Moscato grape. The Pinot Chardonnays, from the same grape that produces the classic white Burgundies, are dry but with a certain soft mellowness. Wines from Johannisberger Riesling grapes are lighter, flowery, and delicate – lovely with shellfish or chicken. An extraordinary wine

well worth trying – if you can afford it – is the Sauvignon Blanc Fumé from the Napa Valley, which experts say is much like a French Pouilly Fumé but with perhaps even more body and bouquet.

There are vineyards all over California, from the Oregon border down to the Mexican border, but they cluster most thickly around San Francisco. Some produce hundreds of thousands of gallons of wine a year – using some new techniques, such as great glass-lined tanks for storing and ageing wines. The smaller vineyards – some over a hundred years old, some planted as recently as the nineteen-fifties with European stocks – often make very limited quantities of superb wine, with traditional methods of cooperage in aged wooden casks and vats. The names are vivid and poetic: Stag's Leap, Mount Eden, Glen Oaks, Dry Creek Vineyard, and Valley of the Moon.

It's interesting to note that when the feared vine louse, the *phylloxera*, devastated France's vineyards in the nineteenth century, sturdy disease-free stocks were sent from America to be grafted on to the remaining vines. Actually, the *phylloxera* had accidentally been introduced into Europe on some American vine cuttings. But it was found that wines from the American Eastern seaboard were immune to the vine louse: so from them, healthy and immune, came the saviours of the precious vines of Europe.

American wines at all prices are beginning to make themselves known in the United Kingdom. Look for the Paul Masson reds and whites, in attractive litre carafes, from such wine merchants as Oddbins and Gough Brothers. Their Emerald Riesling is light, crisp, and fresh. Some good-value wines from Gallo, one of the largest Californian wineries, are available from Cullens' Stores. Christian Brothers wines are made under the supervision of a Brother Cellarmaster of their order, founded in France in 1680; Peter Dominic stores stock their Crystal Dry and Cabernet Sauvignon. Tesco is introducing California Cellars' red, white, and rosé wines – at the moment of writing only in larger shops in London, but with wider distribution in view. Augustus Barnett shops will also be stocking California wines.

In the more rarefied ranges, one finds Robert Mondavi wines – their Blanc Fumé and Chardonnay reach world class – from Geoffrey Roberts Associates and from Corney and Barrow in London, as well as in other good shops across the country. The Wine Society have Mondavi's impressive Pinot Noir, and a good Christian Brothers Cabernet Sauvignon. Avery's of Bristol sell the fine Beaulieu Vineyard wines – among them the remarkable Beaufort Pinot Chardonnay – and a really legendary Cabernet Sauvignon from the very small Fays Vineyard. Corney and Barrow are agents for the tiny, and very fine, Simi Vineyard: their Special Reserve Zinfandel is of great quality but in extremely limited quantity.

Expect to pay from about £2.25 to £3 at the moment for a very drinkable bottle from, say, Christian Brothers or Paul Masson. But prices can go as high as a staggering £220 a case, plus VAT, for Mount Eden Cabernet Sauvignon. Many of the wine merchants mentioned above have some fine wines in the range from £4 to £6 a bottle. In supermarkets, you can expect to find an increasing variety of California wines of good quality, at prices that can stand comparison with any European wines.

The explosion of cheap flights to the United States has brought the California wine-growing region well within the reach of many a holidaying family. For wine lovers, this can turn into a sort of endless picnic in Paradise, for there are nearly one hundred wineries within a few hours' drive from San Francisco. Many offer wine tastings, and often it is possible to buy a bottle or two of one's choice at the vineyard. Dozens of these wineries have picnic places, and some even offer barbecue facilities.

One of the most interesting of the vineyards in the Napa Valley, about an hour and a half from San Francisco, is Conn Creek Winery. It is actually partly owned by an English family, the Ropners of London and Yorkshire. Their co-owners, the Collins family, live in the vineyard and supervise both the growing and the vintaging. Their Conn Creek Cabernet Sauvignon, and a superb Chardonnay, have won gold medals in blind tastings against some highly-favoured French wines. In London, they are listed by the Tate Gallery Restaurant whose wine-list is one of the most distinguished in England; Windrush Wines of Cirencester have Conn Creek wines in their small but very good list.

About a dozen other vineyards in the Napa Valley are open to the public, including the very highly fancied Heitz Wine Cellars at St Helena, and the popular Christian Brothers' Mont La Salle Vineyard. In Santa Clara county, the superb small Ridge Vineyards offer wine tastings (as their 'York Creek' Cabernet is fetching about £100 a case now in London, this is something not to be missed!) At Paul Masson's Champagne and Wine Cellars near Saratoga there are jazz and classical music concerts in the open air during the summer. Everything you want to know about the California wines, or about visiting the vineyards, can be learned at the California Wine Institute, 165 Post Street, San Francisco, California 94108.

Appendix of Sources

In preparing this book, I have been delighted to find that many American foods, under familiar brand names, are appearing in shops all over Britain. More important, however, was the discovery that there are dozens of food products sold in supermarkets and delicatessens everywhere – such as various types of cornmeal, lentils, and dried beans of all kinds – which work perfectly in many of my originally American recipes. At the end of this section there is a brief list of importers and distributors whose foods I have found useful. All are willing and eager to supply your local stockist with their foods upon request.

With regard to the American brands now being sold here, it seemed to me that a few notes on what they are, and how they are used, might help the reader who has occasion to use American or Canadian cookbooks and who may have been baffled by some of the foods specified.

So here is a rather random set of notes about types of foods, brand names, some reflections on baking tins, and so forth.

Chili Powder
American chili powder is a blend of ground hot chilis, garlic, and other spices. I have used Gebhardt's, made in San Antonio, Texas, all my life, and happy was the day when it turned up in my local London supermarket. McCormick's and Schwarz are the other good brands: they sensibly label their product 'chili seasoning' to distinguish it from the red-hot 'chili powder' sold in packets and tins, usually in Indian shops. This is made only from dried, ground red chilis and cannot be used in recipes for American foods that mention chili powder.

Corn syrup
Americans, including cookery writers, use the term 'Karo' almost as a generic name for the light, sweet corn syrup that goes into many recipes. I have recently found in and around London the Canadian 'Crown' brand, identical to American corn syrup, for use in recipes and for pouring on waffles, pancakes, French Toast or cereal. The nearest English equivalent would be golden syrup, but as this is heavier, darker and sweeter, it

is suitable for table use but cannot be substituted for Karo in recipes.

Molasses
American molasses comes in several types: light, dark, and the crude 'blackstrap' which is often featured in health-food recipes. English black treacle is sweeter, and I think heavier, than American molasses. In baking cookies and cakes I have found that blending it half and half with golden syrup makes a perfectly acceptable end product. 'Blackstrap' molasses, available in English healthfood stores, cannot be used in American recipes that specify 'molasses'. But if you like its strong earthy taste, and want to experiment with it in cooking or baking, I would suggest mixing it half and half with golden syrup. I haven't tried it myself.

Hot pepper sauce
The one I like best and use most often is a thickish orange-red sauce from the Caribbean which has not only tropical heat but a definite chili flavour as well. Its brand name is 'Encona'. However, in any recipe that mentions hot chili pepper sauce, Tabasco can be used.

Dried beans and other pulses
Any city or town with an African, Caribbean, Indian or Italian population, will also have many varieties of the endlessly-useful dried beans. Many of these are identical in appearance, if not by name, with their American counterparts. In place of the pinto or speckled beans which are often called for in Southwestern cookery, I use rose coco (West Indian) or borlotti (Italian) beans. What Americans call 'navy beans' are almost identical with the small white haricots or cannelini beans. Large dried haricot beans can be used, as I have often done, in any recipe that calls for dried white lima beans (or 'limas'). The tinned butter beans available in every supermarket do very well for any recipe that originally called for cooked or tinned 'limas'.

Blueberries
Fresh American-type blueberries – which are

related to the English and continental bilberries and whortleberries – are supplied to Covent Garden and to various markets in the Midlands and the North by their growers, James Trehane & Sons, of Dorset. The season is from about mid-July to late September. They will supply bushes as well to any gardener who has the wish (and the correct soil) to grow his own. Write to the Trehanes at Camellia Nursery, Stapehill Road, Hampreston, Wimborne, Dorset BH21 7NE.

Tomato sauce

American-Italian recipes often list tomato sauce as an ingredient. This is a smooth, mildly spiced sauce widely available in tins or jars in America, and quite unlike anything marketed under that name in Britain. The nearest I have found is Buitoni's 'Napolitan', which has the right texture and flavour, and I have used it in several recipes in this book. Do not try to substitute tomato purée or tomato paste where these recipes specify tomato sauce, they simply won't work.

A note about American muffin tins

The type of quick, sweet bread called 'muffin' in America is baked in flat-bottomed, small tins which are not to be found here. These muffin tins are used for Cloverleaf and FanTan rolls (see p. 152) as well. In practice, I have found that deep bun tins, patty tins, fairycake tins or the like are perfectly all right for making muffins. The shape isn't the same, but the baking time and texture of the muffins is identical. A set of six individual bun tins, silicone lined, made by Progressus, makes muffins or rolls somewhat larger than an American tin would produce, but exactly the right shape.

Sources of American, or American-type foods

Cornmeal (medium and very fine), rose coco, and other dried beans: Sea Isle Brand, distributed by Sea Isle Foods Ltd, Lyon Industrial Estate, Watford Bypass, Watford, Herts. Tel: Watford 40255.

Polenta, various types of cornmeal from coarse to fine, dried beans, split peas, lentils, etc: Encona Brand, from Enco Products (London) Ltd, 71/75 Fortess Road, London NW5. Tel: 01-485-2217-8-9.

American foods including such household names as Skippy Peanut Butter, Old El Paso southwestern foods, Hershey's Chocolate Syrup, Aunt Jemima pancake mixes, Duffy Mott fruits, and so forth: importers and distributors are W & P Food Importers, Ltd, 15–19 Circus Road, London NW8. Tel: 01-722-1496.

Sour Cherry Jam

There is a very expensive German brand of this tart, sweet jam which is used as a filling for certain kinds of cakes, such as the Chocolate Torte (see p. 218). However, it is not widely distributed, and I have found recently that certain morello cherry jams from the Comecon countries (Poland, Czechoslovakia, and Hungary) are deliciously tart and about half the price. Look for them under the brand names of Nova and Krakus.

Index

THE UNITE
OF AM

ALASKA

WASHINGTON
Seattle

OREGON

IDAHO

MONTANA

NORTH DAKOTA

SOUTH DAKOTA

MINNES

Miss

WYOMING

NEBRASKA

ROCKY MOUNTAINS

GREAT

WEST PLA

FAR WEST

NEVADA

Denver

KANSAS

UTAH

COLORADO

San Francisco

Mojave Desert

CALIFORNIA

Grand Canyon

ARIZONA

Phoenix

NEW MEXICO

OKL

TE

San

Los Angeles

HAWAII